pleasure packing

HOW TO BACKPACK IN COMFORT

ACKNOWLEDGEMENTS

I want to express my thanks for invaluable help to Shelby Chapel, Kathleen Cox, Warren Dayton, Jim Edmondson, Mark Erickson, Don Evers, Jack Gilbert, Mike Harding, Dr. Andrew Mirov and Holly Schenck.

—Bob Wood

FUTURE EDITIONS

To keep this book current and up-to-date, revised editions will be issued whenever they are needed. Readers are invited to contribute, comment and correct.

Coyright© 1972 by Condor Books
P.O. Box 7141, Berkeley, California 94707
Library of Congress Catalog Card Number 79-188894
ISBN 0-913238-01-5

Published March 1972
Second Printing June 1972
Third Printing May 1973
Fourth Printing June 1974
Fifth Printing February 1976

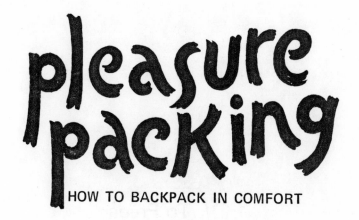

pleasure packing

HOW TO BACKPACK IN COMFORT

by

ROBERT S. WOOD

Illustrations by

WARREN DAYTON

cover photos by TED STRESHINSKY

 To Freda

STARTING OFF

Awakened in the dark
by the purling of Robins
I set myself deeper
in the frost stiff bag
and sink into sleep
as the day takes hold.

With new melted ice
from a rock bound pool
we wash back the night
from our cobwebbed faces
and breakfast on apples
from my father's farm.

As the sun breaks free
from the shadowed trees
and the stillness gives way
to the clamor of day
we gather our gear
and make ready to go.

Then with tentative steps
under unaccustomed loads
we set forth out the trail
in the growing light
through the warming air
on the first long trip
of the new found summer.

PLEASURE PACKING???

Anyone can backpack in comparative misery—and many people regularly do. Every summer I shudder at the number of people struggling through the wilds, plagued by poor equipment and a lack of experience, unable to enjoy the country around them. Backpacking becomes ridiculous when the misery clearly outweighs the pleasure. But when a trip can be made in relative comfort, all the joys of living and traveling in the wilds will unfold. My hope is to help the reader achieve the level of comfort that turns backpacking into *PLEASURE PACKING*.

PLEASURE PACKING is anything but simple, especially for the highly civilized, city oriented individual. The first problem is weight. Comfort means equipment and equipment means weight. Comfort in camp (ample equipment) often means sacrificing comfort and mobility on the trail. And comfort on the trail (a light pack) often comes at the expense of comfort in camp. The backpacker seemingly must choose between the freedom and mobility of a small pack and the shelter and comfort of a happy camp.

But weight is not the only problem. All the gear in the world will not ensure comfort for the hiker who knows nothing about conditioning, trip planning, efficient walking, choosing a campsite, wilderness cookery—in short, technique.

So comfort in the wilds comes from carrying just the right gear and knowing precisely how to use it. And that is exactly what *PLEASURE PACKING* is all about: taking some of the work out of wilderness backpacking so the beauty and happiness are free to shine through.

— *Robert S. Wood, Berkeley, January 1972*

TABLE OF CONTENTS

¹ PACKS

Every summer on the well-traveled trail that passes near my cabin, I see backpackers staggering toward the wilderness loaded down with suitcases, duffel bags, gunny sacks, satchels, baskets, boxes, laundry bags, ice chests and hampers. I have seen Boy Scouts carrying stretchers heaped with gear, families pushing wheelbarrows, even ladies dragging shopping carts.

Finding a decent pack at a reasonable price is not as difficult as these bizarrely burdened travelers suggest. In recent years there have been spectacular advances in pack design, and exceptionally good packs are now widely available. For backpacking on trails and for most cross-country travel, there is general agreement that the tubular metal pack frame, equipped with packsack and hipbelt, is probably superior to all other packs.

Metal framed rucksacks, designed principally for ski mountaineering, are an abomination on the summer trail. Large knapsacks made for climbers are useful for cross-country backpacking where continual climbing and scrambling is involved. But neither of these packs approach the pack frame for capacity and comfort.

The first consideration in choosing a frame is shape. All good pack makers contour their frames so that in profile they form a shallow 'S' that keeps the weight close to the body. When properly fitted, the top of the frame leans forward over the shoulders; the middle bows out around the shoulder blades and tucks in at the waist; and the bottom prongs angle outward to avoid the hips.

A flat profile (straight side rails) means the frame is cheaply made or distinctly out of date. Most frames are built with two to four crossbars joining the rails. Vertical internal members meant to fend off sharp objects in the load may or may not be structurally important. All crossbars below shoulder level should arc away from the body; bars above can and should be straight.

Steel frames are sufficiently strong, but tend to be heavy. They most often are found on very inexpensive frames. Magnesium frames have been produced off and on by various manufacturers for many years, but so far they have proved liable to breakage, difficult to weld properly and subject to wear. Magnesium's allure is its lightness. The weight saving over aluminum is usually about seven ounces per frame. But the last magnesium frame I owned—admittedly some years back—bent out of shape the first time I wore it and was broken before the end of the season. Aluminum alloys, on the other hand, have proved entirely satisfactory when the members are fastened securely. A frame's stiffness and strength can usually be tested by setting the bottom ends of the rails on the floor, then holding them immovable with the feet while vigorously attempting to twist the tops of the rails. Of course, a few frames (like those from North Face and Jansport) are meant to flex safely without sacrificing strength.

Joints have always been the weakest, most vulnerable parts of aluminum frames. Some makers have chosen to bolt or clamp their frames together, but most represent their frames as 'welded.' It can make a big difference whether they are eutectic welded (also known as soldering or brazing) or heliarc gas welded. Brazing is quicker and easier and cheaper, but brazed joints will break under stress. Heliarc welding is slower and more difficult, but the bond is as strong or stronger than the members it joins. Retailers report brazed frames returned for joint failure, whereas heliarc frames seldom break unless run over by an automobile. Denali Corp. (Mountain Master) claims to have tested its heliarc welds at 600 pounds per square inch breaking strength while a competitor's brazed frame broke at 350 p.s.i. Fortunately, the buyer can usually tell the difference: brazed joints have a small, uniform, machine-made-look; heliarc joints have a large, irregular, hand-make-looking bead.

On shoulder strap design there is general agreement; on their rigging and extent there are two schools of thought. The straps themselves, where they bear on the shoulder, are usually padded with two and three eights inch strips of ensolite or dense foam encased in heavy coated nylon duck. From the vicinity of the armpit to the fastening at the bottom of the pack, they are nylon or cotton strapping, with buckles to adjust strap length.

The vast majority of manufacturers fasten the upper end of the nylon-encased pads to the frame's upper crossbar, usually by means of clevis pins with keeper rings. Some offer as many as half a dozen holes in the crossbar so the spread between pads can be changed. Straps can also be raised three quarters of an inch by fastening them above the bar rather than below it. With this strap arrangement, the load is borne entirely by the front of the shoulder. This is the standard means of rigging shoulder straps.

A few manufacturers, however, offer a harness arrangement wherein the padded portion of the straps, instead of fastening to the

Pack-frame joints:

Brazed is o.k.

welded is better.

crossbar, continues over the top of the shoulder and angles down behind the neck to cross, or meet in a yoke, at a point above the middle of the back. A short adjustable strap joins the padded strap to a clevis pin set in the upper crossbar. From the juncture of the pads in the middle of the back, unpadded straps, usually adjustable, lead to the frame's bottom crossbar.

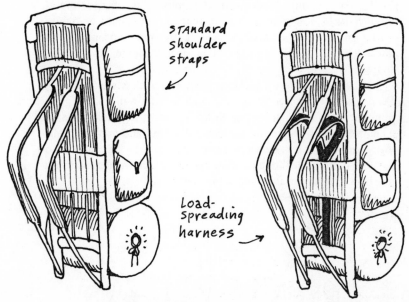

STANdard
shoulder
straps

Load-
Spreading
harness

The effect of this harness is to spread the pack weight over the top and back of the shoulders and neck, instead of concentrating it on a small area on the front of the shoulders. Since each strap has three adjustments, the harness can be finely tuned to support the pack. The three way adjustment also makes it easier to regulate or change the proportion of the load being borne by the hips and the shoulders. With the weight distributed to a longer area of the body, large loads can be carried in surprising comfort.

The harness is slightly complicated in appearance and costs more than the traditional arrangement, and this has caused some experienced backpackers to be skeptical of its virtues. It has also been claimed that a harness permits the pack to ride farther from the back, where it tends to swing from side to side. But I have been using a harness continually since 1963 and consider it a peerless arrangement, especially when combined with a padded hipbelt.

The traditional means of cushioning the back and holding it away from the metal frame is to stretch two bands of heavy fabric around the frame—one at the shoulders, the other at the waist—and lace them drum tight. As frames have improved, most manufacturers have changed their back bands from canvas to nylon, and some have traded the traditional laces for miniature turnbuckles or straps. But only a few have made the big jump to a full back of nylon mesh, an extremely strong open weave netting that looks like cheese cloth and promotes free air circulation instead of sodden shirts. I have been using nylon mesh since 1963 and have found it dry and comfortable, both with and without a shirt.

The hipbelt (not a waist strap) represents the biggest breakthrough in load support in recent time, and it should be only a matter of time before a complete belt becomes recognized as an integral part of the suspension system—as indispensable as shoulder straps.

In the early days of packing, gigantic frameless sacks like the Deluth were supported partly by shoulder straps and partly by a tumpline running around the forehead. The waist strap in those days merely served to secure the bottom of the load and prevent swinging. When rigid pack frames appeared, for the first time it became possible to support all of a pack's weight on the convenient platform provided by the outward swell of the hips.

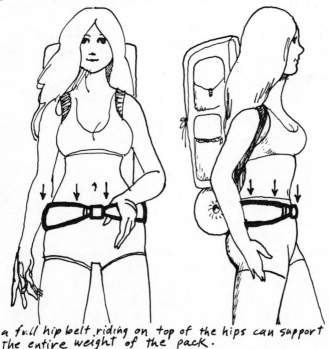

a full hip belt riding on top of the hips can support the entire weight of the pack.

When the hipbelt is cinched in place and the shoulder straps loosened the pack frame settles naturally onto the strongest part of the human body, the buttocks, pelvis and legs. On a first rate belted frame it is possible to allocate weight to the shoulders and the hips in whatever proportion desired, by simply adjusting the tension on shoulder straps and hipbelt. The buckles on my frame allow me to make the necessary adjustments without breaking stride.

Even on the finest frames the best hipbelts are rarely included as standard equipment. And a considerable number of pack makers equip their frames with half belts, which in some ways are worse than no belt at all. The case for the half belt is based on the mistaken belief that the lower backband can double as the back half of the belt. But the backband is generally mounted too high, cannot be drawn tight, and simply is not designed to bear weight from above.

Even when the half belt is drawn painfully tight across the stomach, the lower back band accepts weight in a half-hearted, sagging, uncomfortable manner. A full belt of unpadded webbing is superior to the best half belt made. I have rejuvinated several old packframes by equipping them with full webbed hipbelts that cost less than two dollars apiece.

Since a hipbelt has to be tight to be effective, the broad padded varieties are more comfortable than the webbed, and the small increase in cost ($3-4) is well worthwhile. Padded belts, like padded shoulder straps, usually involve ensolite encased in nylon duck, but they vary in width from two to almost six inches. Hipbelts are generally fastened to the frame by two short reinforced nylon tabs inset with grommets which fit over the clevis pins that secure the bottom of the shoulder straps. They, therefore, can be attached to nearly all frames with little or no trouble. Most belts offer two sets of grommets and this flexibility makes for easier fitting.

A friend of mine, tired of dragging his hipbelt when his pack was on the ground, now suspends it opposite the bottom of the rails by two lengths of shock cord hung from the crossbar above.

All good frames come equipped with tight fitting, hard plastic buttons (or caps) to plug the dirt-catching ends of the tubular rails. Many frames are fitted with a nylon strap attached to the upper crossbar to function as a carrying or hauling strap. Several manufacturers offer an optional shelf for the bottom of the pack, but these are only needed by packers obliged to carry heavy boxes.

The optional extension bar for the top of the frame has considerable utility, especially for family backpackers who need something solid for lashing on extra sleeping bags, mattresses and tents. Some of the more expensive packs come with slotted leather patches or nylon loops at convenient locations for tying on ice axes, climbing ropes, crampons, fishing rods and the like.

It can scarcely be over-emphasized that a pack frame, to be comfortable, must fit. When a hipbelt is worn the fit becomes even more crucial; fortunately the hipbelt makes fitting easier. The hipbelt must fasten tightly across the outward sloping tops of the hip bones—not above them at the waist and not down under the widest part of the hips. When properly cinched, a hipbelt should accept all the weight of a loaded pack when the shoulder straps are loosened; and the tops of the shoulders should still be on a level with the crossbar securing the straps.

To be any good, a frame has to fit.

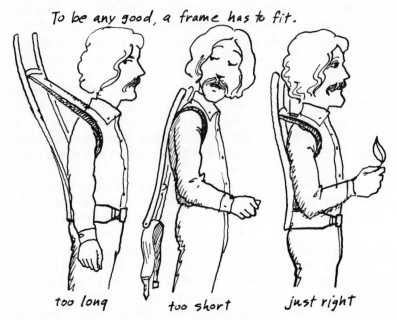

too long   too short   just right

If the frame is too short, it will either be impossible to get all of the weight off the shoulders, or to do so will drop the crossbar well below the shoulders, causing the pack to ride low and away from the back. If the frame is too long it will be impossible to fasten the hipbelt high enough to support weight unless the shoulder straps are abnormally tight. Fortunately, most manufacturers make their frames in three or four sizes and one of them can probably be adjusted to fit.

Compared to pack frame selection, choosing a pack bag is almost inconsequential. The fit, strength and suspension of the frame are vital. The selection of the bag has far less bearing on carrying comfort, even though the best bags cost as much or more than the best frames. Backpackers on a tight budget are advised to put their money in a really good frame and buy a cheap bag or improvise with a tarp.

When I first went backpacking, I owned an excellent frame (for those days) but no pack bag. Keeping weight distribution in mind, I positioned all my gear in a rectangle in the middle of my waterproof nylon ground cloth, folded over the edges to form a neat package, then lashed it to the frame. The resulting pack was as neat and compact and well centered as any that can be loaded in today's pack bags—and better than some. Later I substituted a coated nylon surplus duffel bag, which I lashed on in a way that allowed me to get in to the top without dismantling the entire pack.

Another friend—as accomplished a backpacker as I know—uses a similar packing arrangement today. On top of his sophisticated, up-to-date pack frame he centered a 5 x 7 foot waterproofed tarp of light nylon. Opposite the frame's clevis pins he inserted grommets to fasten the tarp to the frame. Whatever he has to pack—a load of firewood, supplies for an overnight trip, or a mountain of gear for a family safari—he simply lays it on the frame, folds the tarp around it and lashes the load compactly in place. Nobody owns a pack with greater versatility.

Do not imagine from these comments that I scorn modern pack bags. I am as much a slave to their endless convenience as anyone. But I sometimes suspect that packs have grown too large. When I see bulging expedition-type packs being carried for overnight outings in the park, I have the feeling it has become too easy to take along too much. Unfortunately, taking too much results in restricted range or needless discomfort, even with the finest packs.

There are basically two styles of bags: the full frame bag which is meant to hold everything in a single deep cavity and the three-quarter bag which leaves room on the frame at the bottom for the sleeping bag. Advocates of the full bag cite the protection afforded the sleeping bag. Advocates of the more popular three-quarter bag claim a good stuff bag, which must be carried anyway, will provide as much protection as the pack, and the sleeping bag is more conveniently attached and removed when separate. An added argument for the three-quarter bag is that many of them are now horizontally divided to yield a sizeable lower compartment.

The next consideration is fabric. Moving from cheap to expensive, pack bags are made from cotton, canvas, rip-stop nylon (1.9 oz. per 44 inch wide yard), a heavier 3-4 oz. nylon and 6-8 oz. nylon duck. Fabrics rated water repellant are treated with Zelan; waterproof fabrics are double coated with urethane. Water repellent packs need

—how to put on a heavy pack—

rain covers—or the covering of a poncho—in hard or continuous rains. I find a good deal of security, carrying a waterproof pack, in the knowledge that no matter how sopping the outside may get, all of the contents will stay dry.

Of course waterproof material is of little use if the zippers on the pockets will leak in a heavy storm. To keep out moisture, all zippers or other closures need a tightly secured flap that covers them completely. One should be aware of flaps that are stitched on loosely, only cover half the zipper, or tend to roll up under tension, providing little or no protection. Zipper covers are a good place to check quality.

When shopping for a pack bag, one must scrutinize the sewing. Stitches, generally should be close together in heavy dacron thread. Seams, when possible, should be hidden; edges should be double hemmed when the fabric is nylon. Bar tacks (beads of solid stitching at stress points) are an indicator of sewing quality. The points of greatest stress are the corners where the mouth of the bag joins the top of the frame; the structure and sewing at this point are good clues to the quality of the bag.

The best and most expensive zippers are nylon coil made in West Germany. They are light, flexible, strong, hard to jam and easily repaired. Next best are the larger nylon toothed zippers made in Japan. Least desirable are metal. Most modern bags, even cheap and badly made ones, come fitted with hold open bars of aluminum tubing which stretch the mouth of the bag into a rectangle. These are useful enough during the loading process and present no problem when the bag is full. But they are a nuisance on a small load because wind resistance is unnecessarily great and gear has a tendency to bounce around. Some bars are easily collapsed and most can be removed without altering the bag. I remove the bar and thread a cord through the bar pocket to make a drawstring. By cinching down the straps holding the main flap, I keep my gear packed snugly in a minimum of space, which makes a smaller, more compact load for cross-country travel.

When considering pack bags it is important to remember that weight must be kept as close as possible to the back. Bag depth (or thickness) is twice as great in some bags as others. Several leading makers in recent years have redesigned their bags to yield flatter, wider, higher profiles. These bags, by keeping all the weight within eight or nine inches of the back, reduce backward pull and sway, facilitate the support of the load by both the hips and shoulders, and increase pack stability for cross-crountry travel.

Many manufacturers now install a horizontal partition to divide the lower quarter or third of the bag into a separate compartment with access from the outside through a full width zipper. Divided bags make it possible to quickly reach the lunch or extra clothing without undoing the main flap, and unpacking. And they are even more useful in camp for separating gear. I would like to have a bag with two such compartments, either side by side or stacked, comprising the entire lower half of the bag.

Outside zippered pockets seem to grow more numerous every year. On some packs they have become too much of a good thing. The size and number that are desirable depend on the individual. But there is general agreement that pockets are best placed on the sides and top, not on the back where extra weight pulls the center of gravity outward. The exception is a map pocket located in the flap; most of these are disappointingly small. The pocket's purpose is to minimize the number of times a map must be folded, so a large hollow flap is better than a small formal pocket.

My preference in side pockets is for an adjoining pair set high on each side. Top pockets would be only three to four inches deep with zippers placed for easy over-the-shoulder access while walking. Lower pockets would be large enough to conveniently hold one liter bottles or canteens. The flap covering the main cavity should be at least a foot longer and six inches wider than is necessary to cover the opening in order to protect the bulky items (tent, foam mattress, extra sleeping bag) that occasionally get stacked on an already full pack.

Flaps are fastened down in many ways, and modifications are often advisable. Buckles and straps are cumbersome and slow; nylon lines which must be threaded through grommets and tied are not much better. I like to use slide fasteners or rig shock cord lines with clips that snap into grommets in the corners of the flap. Flap size, construction and closure offer another useful index to bag quality.

So does bag mounting. The cheapest bags have a three of four inch sleeve that fits over the top of the frame, with tabs or lines to

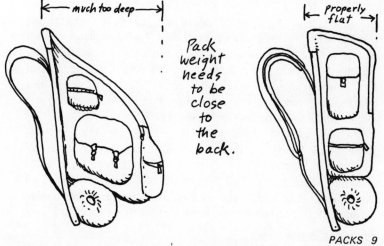

much too deep

properly flat

Pack weight needs to be close to the back.

hold the bottom corners. Better bags have as many as five grommets set in a heavily reinforced flap on either side of the bag. Grommets may be locked in place by rivets, snaps, screws or bolts, but clevis pins are by far the most popular. Pins are secured by either a single wire rod on either side (which rattles and catches on things) or by individual keeper rings. The best bags are side mounted, i.e., the flaps wrap around the tubular rails, to minimize stress on fabric and to maximize bag size.

The final consideration is the fastening of sleeping bags to three-quarter bags. On cheaper packs no provision is made, the job being left to the ingenuity of the buyer. Better packs include a matching nylon stuff bag and a set of buckled straps, laces or shock cord loops.

I generally carry a two or three piece fly rod with the reel attached and the line and leader threaded through the guides to my fly. The best method I have found for attaching this rig to my pack is an aluminum film can taped flush with the bottom of the right hand rail, into which the rod butt and additional section(s) fit snugly. At the top crossbar a piece of nylon line is secured to lash the rod sections flat against the rail. The rod, of course, is somewhat vulnerable in this position, but I have never broken or damaged a section, even during the many years that I carried split bamboo. And the danger, for me at least, is more than offset by the fact that I can be ready to fish within thirty seconds of stopping.

To help the shopper narrow his search, I have tried to evaluate the offerings of half a dozen representative pack makers with whom I am familiar. Included are some of best bargains and the finest packs I know. But since half a dozen new packs reach the market each year, there are doubtless fine packs I never have seen.

Camp Trails, the world's largest pack maker, offers three-crossbar aluminum frames with brazed, not welded, joints that cost $12-18. Four-crossbar frames of heliarc welded magnesium average half a pound lighter at $25.00. Both are more susceptible to breakage than the strong, new heliarc welded aluminum frame. The optional big padded full hipbelt is probably unexcelled. No other maker offers a greater variety of frames and packbags and a wider range of prices.

Only a few years ago a leader in the pack field, Kelty, has slipped back through failure to incorporate recent advances in design. But craftsmanship remains excellent in the rather expensive welded aluminum frame and variety of well-sewn bags.

Anyone paying the $1 membership fee can order from non-profit Recreational Equipment (better known as the Co-op). Prices are excellent, but quality varies. Co-op sells the cheapest Camp Trails aluminum frame with brazed joints and a half hipbelt for $11. Two three-quarter bags (adult and junior) come in coated nine ounce nylon duck (the stoutest fabric available) for $13-18, keeping total

Backpacking — the hard way.

pack price under $30. An even greater bargain is the Co-op Alpine which sells complete for only $18.

Representative of a number of Japanese pack makers, Seaway, principally available in surplus and discount stores, offers cheaply made three-quarter bags on faintly contoured but strongly welded aluminum frames for $20-30. The frame alone is $10. A heavy nylon divided bag with five metal-zippered outside pockets and a draw-stringed top under an oversized flap costs only $10. Another bag with a crudely adjustable shoulder harness and four outside pockets sells for $19.

The newest innovation in packs is the North Face one-piece injection moulded frame of poly-carbonate plastic—the same material used successfully for hard hats and helmets. It is free of joints, slightly lighter and probably stronger than frames of aluminum. This new and promising but untested design offers broad adjustability for easy fitting. Fitted with an excellent harness, a full padded hipbelt, a mesh back and a properly designed bag, it sells for $55-58.

Long one of the leaders, Trailwise (Ski Hut) offers a light, welded aluminum frame with only two crossbars, but two diagonal internal rails provide structural strength. The unexcelled padded harness is fingertip adjustable, so weight can easily be transferred between the full padded hipbelt and shoulder straps The full panel nylon mesh back is likewise unexcelled. Full and three quarter bags are well designed and well sewn. Complete packs run $55.

Other makers doubtless offer equally good products. Although frame-mounted packs offer superior comfort and best serve the needs of the vast majority of backpackers, a case can be made, under certain conditions, for the rucksack or knapsack. Usually made of canvas, rucksacks are simply pack bags, fitted with shoulder straps, which rest directly against the back. Since they rarely extend above the shoulders, the center of gravity is much lower than with framed packs. This low, close distribution of weight is greatly valued by climbers, skiers and cross-country scramblers, who must keep their balance in precarious circumstances.

A few rucksacks are fitted with minimal metal frames or stays so that some of the weight can be borne by a hipbelt. Comfortable carrying weights for frameless knapsacks run 15-20 pounds. In a framed rucksack this may jump to 20-30 pounds. But rucksack comfort does not approach packframe comfort; it often means a lumpy load against a sweaty back, shoulder straps that dig in and a load that tries to pull one over backwards.

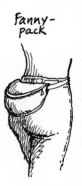

Fanny-pack

Good American framed rucksacks include the Alpine Designs Eiger Pack ($30), the Gerry Vagabond ($27), the North Face Ruthsac ($45) and Rainer ($25). In Europe, where rucksacks are only beginning to be replaced by pack frames, the French La Fuma ($25) and Millet ($18), and Norwegian Bergans ($23-25) and English Atlas ($14) all offer models generally available in this country.

Smaller canvas knapsacks with leather straps and buckles have traditionally been used for day hiking, but in recent years these have largely been replaced by the more streamlined triangular coated nylon day packs, usually divided horizontally. Some have waist belts to secure, not support the pack, leather bottoms, accessory patches and ice axe straps for climbing. Many have padded nylon shoulder straps. Some of the best are made by Alpine Designs, Gerry, North Face, Sierra Design and Trailwise.

Belt-pack

Belt and fanny packs, which wrap around the waist, were first used by skiers, but now are becoming popular with hikers. Many backpackers find them handier than pockets or packs for such often needed items as cameras, compasses, maps, insect repellent, notebooks and pencils, sunburn ointment and lip ice. Usually, they can be adapted to fit on the front of a hipbelt; the smaller variety can even be mounted on a shoulder strap. Day hikers who travel light find them less inhibiting than knapsacks or day packs. Principal manufacturers are Camp Trails, Co-op, La Fuma, Smilie, Trailwise and Universal. These little packs are especially useful for those hikers who cannot seem to get their hands—or anything else—in the pockets of tight jeans.

Load up the dog.

Infant carriers, it must be emphasized, are not designed for men or for extended hikes. Most popular are two models ($11 and $15) made by Gerry and sold everywhere, which take babies from five months to three years. The more expensive Kiddie Pack, of tubular aluminum and canvas, offers a larger, adjustable enclosure with valuable storage beneath. The child faces forward and the center of gravity is as close as possible to the back. Camp Trails also makes a pack ($17) in which the child faces backwards, and the Co-op has three models ranging from a frameless rucksac ($4) to framed seats ($7 and $15).

Dogs like to go backpacking too. But they should be left home unless: (1) the area to be visited permits them; (2) the dog obeys commands and will not attempt to rob the larder or attack wildlife, and (3) the dog has proved a suitable companion on day hikes without developing sore feet. If these conditions are met, there is usually no reason the dog cannot carry his own food. I made my St. Bernard a pair of saddlebags out of coated nylon duck and lashed them to a standard dog harness, adding a second buckled strap around his middle at the back of the bags. An old towel served as a cushioning dogblanket underneath. St. Bernards have very loose skin and consequently the pack needed to be quite tight and perfectly balanced to keep from rolling, but Raff, who loves to walk, never minded carrying a pack—once he got used to it.

An effort should be made not to change a dog's diet on the trip, unless he is used to fresh meat. I once packed two half-gallon bottles full of fresh cooked meat for a ten day trip for Raff, but after five days it began to ripen and after seven it was all I could do to empty the containers in a hole without gagging. The rest of the trip Raff shared our food; he even came to enjoy small overcooked trout. Dry kibbles and canned meat make the easiest combination; and dogs do not mind carrying out the flattened cans. In fact, Raff regularly carried home a good deal of my more indestructable gear.

Much easier than constructing a dog pack, is buying one from Gerry. The Doggie Pack ($15) comes in two sizes: 'Large' for dogs over 40 pounds and 'Small' for lighter dogs. The coated nylon duck matched bags have leather reinforced corners and zippered closures. For most dogs a relatively small load is most likely to prove satisfactory. But well trained working dogs are said to cheerfully carry anywhere from a quarter to a half of their body weight.

So, until packs come equipped with built-in helium balloons, perhaps the best way to guarantee backpacking comfort is to find a large working dog and train him very well.

2 FOOTWEAR

Nothing is more important to the backpacker's comfort than what he decides to put on his feet. Poorly fitting, inappropriate boots can make agony of every step. Without a doubt, the feet are the most abused portion of the backpacker's anatomy, and it is probably no coincidence that boots are the least understood item in his equipment.

The weight of a pack and the roughness of the terrain combine to make any kind of city footwear virtually useless in the wilds. The only exceptions are stout, ankle-high work shoes—and tennis shoes for small children who carry very little. Basketball shoes, even those made of leather, do not begin to provide enough support. Neither do low-cut Oxford walking shoes, which neglect to protect the ankle. Moccasins are too thin, shoepacks and rubber boots are only worthwhile in the wetest country, and high boots constrict the calf muscles without providing additional support.

Back in the days when mountaineering boots were rarities that cost upward of $30, I wore out many pairs of excellent $5 army surplus boots. Nowadays, however, surplus boots are rare and expensive, and decent hiking boots can be bought for as little as $15. Given the importance of proper footwear to backpacking comfort, it seems to me that anyone willing to invest $80 in a sleeping bag and $50 in a pack should be willing to pay $20-25 for genuine mountaineering boots. Still, there are excellent work shoes available at approximately half the cost which are a worthwhile investment, especially for people with growing feet.

A near relative of the hiking boot, the German kletterschuhe, is popular with a good many hikers because of its light weight (1½-2½ lbs. per pair) and low cost ($12-20). For climbing, it is worn painfully tight over thin socks. Heavier kletterschuhes are quite satisfactory on trails where packs are light, although they provide minimal protection and tend to be short lived.

Mountaineering suppliers agree that buying boots by mail is often unsatisfactory for both buyer and seller. The buyer usually needs more help than he can get from a catalog in choosing the right model and getting a good fit. Drawn patterns and shoe sizes are not really reliable; buyers often fail to discover the poor fit until too late, and exchanging boots for 'the next size larger' does not always solve the problem. As a consequence, I strongly urge against buying boots by mail. Most people are better off with the best model and the best fit that a competent salesman can provide than they are ordering a perfect-sounding boot by mail.

Bootmakers, increasingly, are subject to the dictates of fashion. As a consequence, models change from year to year for the same reason that styles in clothes keep changing. Unfortunately, this means that excellent models are often discontinued and replaced by models which are different but possibly inferior—and probably untested. Nevertheless, the variety and design of mountaineering boots are improving, and more and more inexpensive models appear each year.

In selecting a boot, weight, it seems to me, should be the first consideration, since one pound on the feet is equivalent to five on the back. For summer backpacking in the California Sierra, I classify

mail-order boots rarely fit the way they should.

as 'light' those boots weighing less than 3½ pounds. 'Medium' boots will range from 3½ to 4½ pounds and 'heavy' boots start off at 4½ pounds. For pack loads of 30 pounds or less, principally on trails, light boots are sufficient. For heavier loads and rugged, cross country backpacking or climbing, a medium boot is advisable. Heavy boots can only be justified for giant expeditionary loads and extreme conditions.

It used to be said that rough-out (suede) leather was the sign of a cheap boot, but rough-outs have grown in popularity and are now found in all price ranges—partly because smooth leather is easily cut and abraded. Another old myth is that rough-out boots cannot be waterproofed. Actually, a rough surface soaks up more waterproofing and holds it longer than smooth leather.

Better indexes of boot quality are the number and placement of seams and the grain of the leather. Seams can open up, catch on rocks and let in water, so the general rule is 'the fewer the better.' Seams in the toe are especially liable to wear and leakage, and the familiar moccasin toe, not surprisingly, is one of the most vulnerable. The vertical heel seam ought to be capped on the outside and the foot protected from the stitching on the inside.

Leather is either full grain (whole) or split grain (a single layer). Reputable bootmakers do not conceal their use of 'splits.' Split leather is most often found in cheaper boots and kletterschuhes; it does not have the natural water repellency of full grain leather and cannot be effectively waterproofed.

Virtually all mountaineering boots come equipped with heavy lug soles of neoprene (oil resistant synthetic rubber) because it has proven to offer the best combination of wear, grip, spring and rigidity. The brand currently in vogue is Vibram, which includes dozens of different lug styles, thicknesses and compositions. Brown (low carbon) Vibram does not mark floors, but it does not wear well either.

Boot soles and heels are of either one or two piece construction; the latter has the advantage that worn heels can be replaced and the disadvantage that the heels occasionally separate from the soles. Purchasers of mountaineering boots are almost certain to get neoprene soles; it is only the buyers of workshoes who need to pay special attention to sole composition.

Probably a majority of mountaineering boots have steel shanks built into the sole to provide stiffness, support and strength. Most are limited to the middle third of the boot and none run the full length of the sole. In climbing boots, the shank often extends the full width of the boot across the ball of the foot. But the stiffness, weight and the durability of a boot are determined not by the sole or shank, but by the thickness of the leather midsole—the heart of the boot. Midsoles range in thickness from one sixteenth to half an inch. Soles are usually glued (and sometimes screwed and nailed) to the midsole, while the upper is stitched on to it from above.

Nearly all hiking boots are outside fastened, i.e., the leather upper, when it reaches the midsole, turns outward. A narrow strip or cap of leather, called the Storm welt, is laid over the outturned edge of the upper and sewed through in two directions, down through the midsole and diagonally into the innersole. Unfortunately, the stitching is vulnerable and when the edge of the midsole wears through at the toe the boots cannot be resoled. A very common variation, which is still more vulnerable to breakage and leakage, called the Goodyear welt, does not sandwich the upper leather under the welt. Storm welts are found on the better hiking boots; Goodyear welts are common on cheaper boots and work shoes.

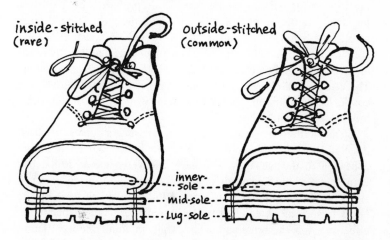

Superior to either of these outside fastened welts is the inside fastening traditional on the Kletterschuhe. Its chief advantage is that the stitches, being concealed within the boot, are protected from abrasion so that badly worn midsoles can readily be repaired and the boots resoled. Soles can be trimmed more closely (of particular interest to climbers) since there is no welt to break, and waterproofing is easier. Since the innersole is stitched down, the edges are not subject to curling when wet. It is ironic that this comparatively little used method of boot construction is less expensive as well as superior. Hopefully it will become more common.

Since the cowhide used in boot uppers is generally flexible and soft, the stiffness necessary to protect the toe and socket the heel must come from such reinforcing materials as stiff leather, plastic, fiberboard, fiberglass and, unfortunately, cardboard. Ideally, stiffeners are sandwiched invisibly between outer leather and lining to form box toes and the socket formed by heel counters. In cheaper boots, stiffening is achieved by stitching on outside leather caps over toe and heel or by stitching inside stiffeners onto the outside leather, rather than cementing them in place.

The construction of the tongue has traditionally been troublesome to manufacturers and hikers alike. Tongues tend to wrinkle, bind, slip, and let in moisture and debris. Manufacturers have tried a variety of designs, some of which solve one problem but create another. There are accordion tongues, stretch tongues, padded tongues, hinged tongues, etc. Padding should be confined to the central portion of the tongue or it will slip over the ankle and cause chafing. Hinges help to prevent foam padding from binding. Hinged, padded tongues have been successful.

The same intent—to reduce binding in the instep—has lead many bootmakers to pad the upper with foam rubber from the middle of the foot to the back of the heel and to deeply notch both sides of the upper at the point in the instep where the greatest bend takes place. There has also been an effort to reduce constriction and abrasion on the Achilles tendon by cutting boots significantly lower in the back, building elasticized sections and adding foam padding. The effect of all these developments has been to make boots more comfortable and more quickly broken-in, without sacrificing necessary protection and support.

Some of the innovation in recent years, one suspects, has been ·directed more to making boots different, better looking and more appealing to the teenagers who have discovered them fashionable, than to satisfying the needs of mountaineers. For instance, speed-lacing, while admittedly fast, reduces the grip of the laces on the boots to such an extent that lacing becomes less, rather than more, effective. And the scree pad collar, while an admirable idea, tends, when it is tight enough to be effective, to pinch the Achilles tendon.

These are some of the considerations one should keep in mind when examining boots and discussing their relative merits with a salesman. Once the appropriate model is tentatively selected (on the buyer's own basis of weight, price, expected use, etc.) the next consideration is a proper fit.

A 'last' is a wooden model of the human foot, around which the shoe or boot is designed. For many years Americans have found European boots (built from European lasts) too narrow in the toe and too broad in the heel, reflecting the differences between American and European feet. Since virtually all mountaineering boots used to come from Europe (and the majority still do), it has long been difficult for Americans to find good boots that fit. Vasque (a division of Redwing, America's largest boot manufacturer) and Fabiano have greatly relieved the problem by producing complete lines of mountaineering boots (many of which are sewn in Italy), made on American lasts. And in the last few years, in recognition of the American market, such manufacturers as Lowa (German), Pivetta (Italian) and Galibier (French) have modified their lasts for export boots.

Boots should be fitted over whatever sock(s) the buyer expects to wear, or, if there is doubt, over a single heavy rag sock. In general, a hiking boot should be a little less roomy than a street shoe—comfortable, but snug. It should be remembered during fitting that the weight of a pack causes feet to flatten out, and vigorous hiking causes the feet to fill with blood and expand. At the same time, it must be remembered that loosely fitting boots will generate painful friction and lessen badly needed support.

Boots being fitted should be firmly laced, especially across the instep. Since leather is certain to stretch, one must be sure that the bands holding the laces remain half an inch apart when the boots are firmly laced or it may be impossible to lace them snugly once they are broken-in. With the boots firmly laced, the toes should have room to wiggle, but neither the ball of the foot nor the heel should move perceptibly when the salesman anchors the boot rigidly and the buyer tries vigorously to twist the foot.

when the boot is firmly anchored the fit is easily checked.

Generally speaking, boots should be snug in width and generous in length. It is vital that the heel be socketed down within the cup formed by the heel counters so that it lifts no more than an eighth of an inch off the innersole when the heel is raised at the end of a step. A small allowance can be made for the stiffness of new boots, but the buyer should be convinced that the boot will fit snugly enough to keep his heel from lifting. Misery and blisters are the alternative. Foam padding around the ankle helps somewhat to socket down the heel. So does an inward taper of the boot's heel profile, but the principal grip comes from the construction and stiffness of the heel counter.

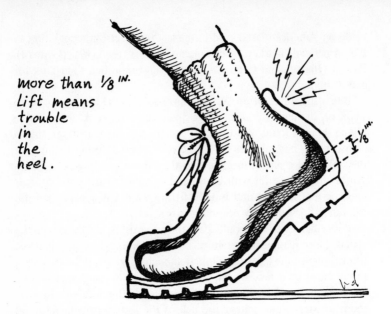

more than 1/8 IN. Lift means trouble In the heel.

Many people buy heavier, stiffer boots than they need in the hope of getting extra wear and protection. Manufacturers are partly responsible in that they offer a number of combination hiking and climbing boots that are often too stiff for the needs of most backpackers. They also fail, in some cases, to distinguish their technical climbing shoes (like kletterschuhes) from light hiking boots.

If the boot passes stationary tests satisfactorily, it is time to take it walking. (Any reputable boot salesman will be agreeable— providing his boots come back promptly, clean and unscuffed.) If the heel remains socketed on the level, one should walk briskly uphill or climb stairs. If the heel lifts more than a little, the boot is too large, at least in the heel. Next, one should walk briskly downhill for at least fifty yards. If the foot slips forward far enough for the toes to hit the front of the boot, it means the boot is too wide or too short, or not laced tightly enough. Patience and thoroughness during the fitting will reward the buyer with many miles of comfortable walking.

There seems to be a good deal of confusion about the proper care and waterproofing of leather boots. Chrome tanned leather is naturally water repellent, but most boots are made of oil tanned cowhide which is not. So most boot uppers and seams need to be dressed to protect the leather (if not the feet) from the wetting and drying that break down, age, wash out oils and dry out leather, causing it to crack, rot and deteriorate.

Since backpackers' feet have been know to sweat, wetting from within can only be prevented if the leather is allowed to breath, i.e., to pass moisture generated by the feet before it can saturate socks. Though not widely recognized, even by veteran backpackers, breatheability in boot leather is vital to the comfort and dryness of the feet. And the better the waterproofing the poorer the breathing.

Frequent applications of boot dressings can be tedious, but it is probably fortunate that all waterproofings wear away and allow the leather to regain its breatheability. The only exceptions are epoxy or lacquer, and these are subject to cracking. Truly waterproof boots are made only of rubber which cannot breathe at all. Waterproofings usually belong to one of three classes: silicones, oils and waxes.

Silicones (liquids applied by brush or spray) protect and increase the water repellency of leather while allowing it to breathe; they are particularly good during dry summer weather when breatheability is important; oils and greases (usually animal) waterproof more efficiently, but soften the leather considerably and cause it to stretch; waxes waterproof as well as oils without softening leather and are important for winter use and wet conditions.

The best known wax, which includes silicone, is Sno-Seal, a thick paste which is smeared on the leather and then melts and soaks in when the boot is lightly warmed by a fire, stove or heater. Raw leather may absorb a dozen coats. Depending upon the conditions encountered, a treatment may last from a week to two months. Shoe Saver is one of several widely available brands of silicone, applied with a swab. I switch to it during the late summer dry months after my Sno-Seal has worn off. During the winter and wet weather, I reinforce my Sno-Seal waterproofing (which is a bother to apply) by giving the seams a quick painting with Leath-R-Seal, an oil which can be quickly applied without heat.

The following five makers offer a variety of boots which are widely available in American mountaineering shops:

Fabiano (American) a wide selection of lighter weight climbing shoes and hiking boots made in Italy on American lasts.

Galibier (French) a selection of footwear ranging from kletter-

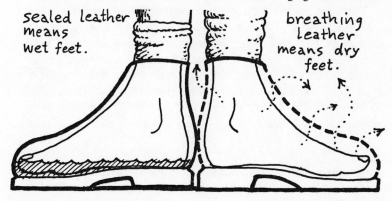

sealed leather means wet feet.

breathing leather means dry feet.

schuhe through light hiking boots to double expeditionary boots, made over an improved last.

Lowa (German) a variety of mountaineering boots (mostly heavy) and climbing shoes built on recently improved lasts.

Pivetta (Italian) A good range of well-made mountaineering boots of varying weights and types.

Vasque a wide selection of footwear from kletterschuhes to heavy climbing boots, some made in Italy, some in the U.S., all with steel shanks and all on American lasts. Street shoe size correlates closely with boot sizes.

To many of us it is a great delight at the end of the day to peel off heavy, damp, hot hiking boots and, after washing our feet, put on heavy, clean socks and featherweight camp boots. The problem, as always, is to find satisfactory footwear at a weight that can be justified. In sharp, shattered rock, it makes no sense to carry soft soled sandals. In dependably damp terrain, quickly-wet canvas shoes are not worthwhile.

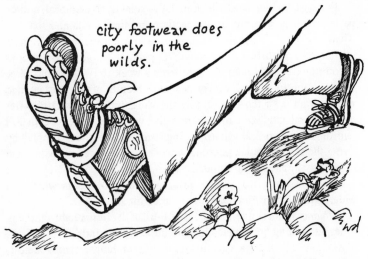

city footwear does poorly in the wilds.

For most country I carry soft leather moccasins with thin crepe soles that weight 13 ounces. They are loose enough to keep my feet cool and I treat them with Sno-seal to keep them dry, but I wish they were lighter. My second choice is a pair of rubber-soled leather sandals, which can be worn with or without socks. Where weight is more critical and the terrain and insects permit, I sometimes carry Zorries (also known as "thongs" or "go-aheads") and wear them without socks. Probably the most popular camp boots are tennis shoes, but I find them hot and too heavy—usually more than a pound.

A great many hikers do not sufficiently concern themselves with socks. People who will spend $100 for an alpine tent and $25 for boots refuse to spend $2-3 for the best in boot socks. There seems to be a tendency to save old socks for camping, or to buy cheap cotton work socks—evidently because they are certain to get dirty. But experienced hikers know that their choice of socks can make the difference between misery and comfort.

Socks serve four vital functions: (1) they cushion the feet against the shock of each step; (2) they absorb perspiration from the feet; (3) they absorb friction between boots and feet; and (4) they insulate the feet from extremes of heat and cold. Socks that can do all four jobs well tend to justify their immodest price tags.

There is no single best sock or sock combination. Too much depends on the fit of the boot, the temperatures expected, the terrain, the tendency of the feet to sweat, skin sensitivity, etc. But it is generally true that too many pairs (too thick a layer) of socks reduces boot support and increases friction, and too thin a layer diminishes all four of the above vital functions. For trail backpacking in the summer Sierra the choice is generally between a single heavy sock by itself and the same sock worn over a light inner sock.

Generally, less sock is needed on easy terrain in well broken-in boots. Two heavy pairs of socks may be advisable for stiff boots or cross-country hiking likely to be hard on the feet. There is considerable variety in heavy socks. The traditional salt and pepper colored rag boot sock originating in Scandanavia is 100% wool, warm, tough, extremely thick, durable and scratchy. They stretch during wear, shrink when machine washed, are warm when wet, and some people find them uncomfortably coarse without inner socks. Stretch rag socks with 15% nylon hold their shape and are therefore more useful. Special allowance must be made when fitting boots if rag and inner socks are to be worn. Rag socks cost $2-3 and weigh 3-5 ounces per pair.

A little more modern and less bulky is the Thermal sock made of elasticized wool (75%) and nylon (25%). Thousands of tiny Terry Cloth loops inside the smooth outer sheath provide excellent cushioning, insulation and moisture absorption. The elasticized top and stretch characteristics, together with a luxurious feel, make this an excellent choice for a single sock. It holds its shape well, does not shrink perceptibly, mates well with light inner socks and can comfortably be worn two at a time. The best and bulkiest versions cost $2.50-4. Lighter weight (medium) stretch socks of the same general type cost about $1.50.

Constructed in the same fashion as the Thermal, Wick-Dry socks are bulkier stretch socks with elasticized tops, made of 50% Orlon, 40% Nylon and 10% cotton. The thick (synthetic) inner pile of Terry Cloth loops wicks moisture away from the feet (or from inner socks) and holds it away from the skin in the somewhat rougher (absorbent cotton) outer shell. Wick-Dry socks live up to their name, but Thermal socks accomplish the same wicking almost as well. Heavy Wick Dry outer socks cost about $3. Mediums, comparable to Thermals, cost $2.25.

Suitable light, thin, inner socks may be made of silk, wool, or an Olefin and nylon combination. Cotton, which is cold, absorbent, and stretchy, or 100% nylon, which is cold and slippery, should be avoided. Wigwam all wool socks are excellent until they find their way into the automatic washer, where they shrink about 40% and must then be discarded. Old fashioned silk dress socks, which can sometimes be found at the back of a bureau drawer, are very comfortable. Mountaineering models cost about $2.25. Wick Dry Liner stretch socks with elasticized tops are 70% Olefin and 30% Nylon and neither shrink nor absorb moisture.

In the summer Sierra, I most often wear medium or heavy Thermal socks over Wick Dry Liners or the Heavy Wick Dry Outer socks alone with my stiffer, heavier boots. With lighter, softer boots I may wear only a medium weight pair of Thermals. Sometimes I take several combinations. I am also fond of stretch rag socks. On an easy trip I carry only one spare set if the country is relatively dry, planning to wash (or at least rinse) a set every day. In damper country I may take two or three extra sets. I never wear socks made of cotton which hold moisture and chill the foot. All the above-described socks, though comparatively expensive, are excellent investments in comfort for even the casual backpacker, who will find them just as comfortable and luxurious when used as ski, work or athletic socks.

Most backpackers will not need gaiters (also called anklets) but there are conditions that elevate them to the rank of necessity; chief of these is the new snow encountered in spring and fall travel. Thick dust or soft dirt that constantly creeps over the boot tops also justifies gaiters, and some people wear them for protection against wet grass, cold, thistles and thorns. These 7-9 inch gauntlets, worn like spats, usually are of waterproof nylon duck with elastic top and bottom, a zipper at the back and a strap or thong for the instep. They weigh three to five ounces a pair and are available from most makers of mountaineering gear for $2-7.

Footwear that meets all the criteria for sound construction, survives all tests for an excellent fit, and is admirably suited to the purchaser's needs is probably a good buy whatever the price. For the buyer of such footwear there is bound to be pleasurable walking ahead.

³CLOTHES

Nothing is so troublesome to equipment producers as the unfortunate fact that the human body—in normal operation—exudes about a quart of water each day through the pores. Were it not for this water—released as vapor—all clothing could be constructed from waterproof fabrics which efficiently seal out all water and wind. Unfortunately, water vapor sealed in by waterproof clothing quickly condenses to turn skin and adjacent clothing sopping wet.

Therefore, all fabrics surrounding the body must "breathe," i.e. be sufficiently porous to allow the gradual escape of the body's moisture. Of course, if moisture can escape through a fabric, so can heat. And if heat and moisture can move out, cold and moisture can move in. The body must conserve the heat it generates in order to remain comfortably warm. But conservation of heat is self defeating if the skin and clothing become uncomfortably damp as a result.

Dry, warm, comfortable clothing, comes from a compromise between insulation and ventilation. Insulation, to be effective, must stop the circulation of air in order to prevent the loss of body heat. Proper ventilation, on the other hand, requires the air next to the skin to circulate to carry off water vapor before it can condense. Insulation and ventilation are in direct opposition, but, because very little ventilation is needed to dissipate the comparatively small volume of water produced, it has been possible to design clothing and equipment in which the two are balanced to yield dry warmth in sub-zero temperatures.

Balance is generally achieved in cold weather clothing by employing several thin layers rather than a few thick ones. The air spaces between layers provide both ventilation and added insulation. It has been proven that several light layers are warmer than a single heavy layer of the same thickness. The all important layer next to the skin must be extremely porous so that water vapor can circulate away from the body. To travel in comfort the backpacker must understand the ventilating and insulating qualities of his clothing. And he must be willing to take off and put on the necessary layers as conditions change to avoid rapid heat loss at one extreme and sweat soaked clothing at the other.

To understand the qualities of clothing, it is necessary to know the properties of various kinds of cloth. Nylon's slipperiness gives it a colder, less agreeable feeling on the skin than cotton; its elasticity makes it hard to sew, it unravels rapidly if edges are not heat sealed, it resists repellents and it soaks through in rain more rapidly than cotton. But nylon offers the greatest strength of any material for a given weight of fabric; and its toughness, light weight, elasticity, breatheability, freedom from mildew and resistance to wind make it a favorite fabric for backpacking gear of all kinds.

Long fibered Egyptian cotton is heavy, tends to tear easily and is subject to rot, but it is pleasant on the skin, sews easily, resists wetting, and, unlike nylon, will readily accept most water repellents. By itself, it is rarely the best available fabric, but combined with nylon it contributes desirable characteristics to yield a superior cloth.

The chief advantage of wool is that, unlike all other fabrics, it retains its springiness and therefore its insulating quality when wet. It is valuable, especially combined with nylon, for socks, mittens, underwear and pants—any garment where wetting is a problem and warmth is important.

Dacron is nearly as strong as nylon and its lack of elasticity makes it ideal as a mildew proof thread for stitching all types of cloth as well as for making very tightly woven fabrics. Orlon has the advantage over nylon and dacron of being resistant to the gradual deterioration caused by sunlight.

Most fabric coatings can be classified as either sealers or repellents. Sealers, such as urethane, polymer or neoprene coatings, form a continuous film over the fabric which (until punctured) makes it largely waterproof. Sealed fabrics, of course, do not breathe, so condensation and wetting can occur from within. Double coated fabric is half again as heavy as single coated, but more waterproof and better protected from abrasion.

Water repellents are altogether different. They clog, but do not seal, the pores of the fabric, allowing it to breathe. Though some moisture may work its way through, wetting from condensation on the inside is negligible. Unfortunately, the best repellents (like Zelan), which are applied at the factory, will only survive two or three washings, and the aerosol silicone base spray-ons (like Rain-Dri or Thompson's Water Seal), which are by far the easiest for renewing repellency, last only a few weeks in heavy weather. Nevertheless, it is well worthwhile to spray all outer clothing before each trip, especially if minimal raingear is being carried.

CLOTHING

Having considered the problems involved in keeping warm and dry—and the fabrics and coatings available—we turn to the consideration of suitable backpacking clothes.

The ideal backpacking trousers, in my view, have yet to be made. The trouble is that trouser manufacturers do not seem to realize that up-to-date backpackers must wear tightly cinched hipbelts a little below the waist. As a consequence, they need beltless trousers free from buckles, belt loops and ridges that will dig into the skin beneath the hipbelt. Despite the widespread popularity of the hip-belt, all trousers come with belt loops—and no other means of support—so the backpacker is obliged to wear a belt beneath his hipbelt.

The closest approach to a backpacking trouser, made by Rough Rider and available in any mountaineering shops, is a tough, light, roomy pair of pants in tan sateen. The front pockets are so deep I can straighten my arms and scarcely reach the bottoms, and each has a patch pocket on top that snugly holds my Spiral notebook and pencil. Two hip pockets have button down flaps. With the inevitable belt loops, they cost about $10. Probably the best trousers for hiking are heavy corduroy or gabardine knee length knickers made for climbers, but neither style nor weight nor considerable warmth appeal much to backpackers.

For many years, like a majority of hikers, I wore blue jeans, usually Levi's. To keep them from getting wet in the rain I used to rub the front of the thigh and the back of the calf with the cake of wax in my fly tying kit—with excellent results: the surfaces that

wax
rubbed on
where
the rain hits
Keeps
legs dry
without
sweating.

were most exposed became waterproof, but the rest of the trousers were free to breathe. I have yet to find a better answer to hiking in a light rain. The trouble with most jeans, blue and otherwise, is that the western styles on which they are modeled are too narrow and tight. Jeans chafe and bind and cause overheating.

Not so fashionably narrow, work trousers are more generously cut and often more durable, and consequently they provide the packpacker with more freedom and comfort. While cotton duck is the usual fabric for trousers, flannels of wool and synthetic blends are popular in some areas, and wool whipcord, gabardine and corduroy have their fans. Probably the best source of a variety of outdoor trousers is the catalog of L.L. Bean. Temperature, terrain and the degree of protection required are the principal considerations in the selection of trousers.

In the summer Sierra, I do most of my hiking in shorts, reserving long trousers (which I always carry) for evening and cold weather wear and protection from insects and thorny brush. Good hiking shorts can be hard to find. Most of those offered, whether in clothing stores or mountaineering shops, are so fashionably slim as to be worthless. Although few people are willing to wear them in this country, Lederhosen (leather shorts) are the zenith of practicality, being unbeatably tough, eventually soft, well-ventilated and roomy, if somewhat heavy. Ideally, they are worn with Ledertrager (suspenders) which allow a loose fit at the waist and enviable ventilation and freedom.

To avoid the inevitable belt loops in shorts, I often substitute canvas boxer-style swimming trunks with a combination drawstring and elasticized waist. Since Americans are allergic to the baggy look, generally the shorter the shorts the greater the likelihood of a comfortable fit. I test shorts by putting one foot on a chair. If this causes the shorts to bind or chafe or even pull tight across the seat or the top of the leg, the shorts are rejected as being insufficiently roomy. Since jeans can never pass this test, cutoff jeans do not make particularly good hiking shorts. Neither do Bermuda shorts.

Sometimes a pair of shorts can be made usable by slitting the outside seam to form a two or three inch vent (which ought to be rehemmed). A good pair of shorts can often be obtained by cutting off below the pockets and hemming a pair of stout, baggy work pants. L.L. Bean makes several cotton-dacron beltless boxer style swim trunks suitable for hiking. The best shorts I have found, though expensive at $15 and designed for a belt, are made by Sportif, with two-ply construction, a double seat and seven pockets. Mine weigh 10 ounces—with the belt loops cut off.

Most summer Sierra backpackers wear city style underwear, thereby missing out on some extremely efficient clothing. Thermal

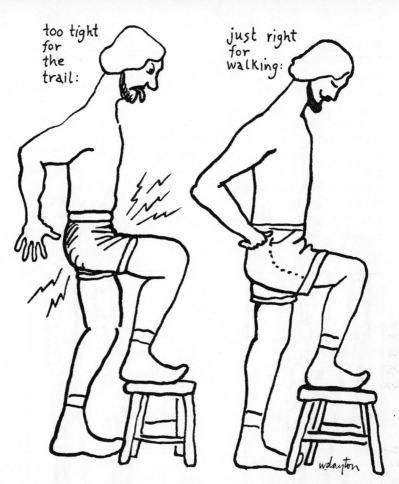

too tight for the trail:

just right for walking:

wdayton

underwear (two-piece with full legs and long arms) are of continuous weave in a waffle pattern designed to form insulating air pockets; they do not wick away moisture or provide for evaporation. Duofold makes a fine mesh fishnet short sleeved shirt, briefs and long johns. They also make continuous weave two layer cold weather long underwear (60% cotton, 40% wool) which wicks moisture from the inner cotton layer to the outer layer of wool where it can evaporate.

Norwegian Net underwear of all-cotton string construction, with large (quarter inch square) holes, comes in long pants and short sleeved shirts. The large air pockets in string shirts allow water vapor to circulate and evaporate, rather than condense. Unfortunately, there are no briefs, and no manufacturer makes boxer style string shorts. Stil Longs of Norway makes a light, stretchy single weight flannel set of two-piece long underwear which is 70% wool and 30% nylon.

Each of these offerings works on a slightly different principle. The Thermal, two-layer Duofold and Stil Longs are designed solely for winter use and are suffocating in Summer temperatures. The Norwegian and Duofold net (or string) underwear is remarkably efficient in both summer and winter. I much prefer the larger mesh of Norwegian net, which greatly reduces the amount of moisture absorbed.

A short sleeved string shirt is superior to the conventional T-shirt in every respect: it is cooler and dryer in summer, warmer and dryer in winter, lighter, and more easily washed and dried en route. I also prefer it to a T-shirt as a pajama top. A clean, dry change of underwear and socks, along with a wool watch cap, traditionally serve the backpacker as sleep wear, except on the coldest of nights. I wear string shirts summer and winter, in the mountains and the city, principally because they stay dry. I only wish I could buy string boxer shorts.

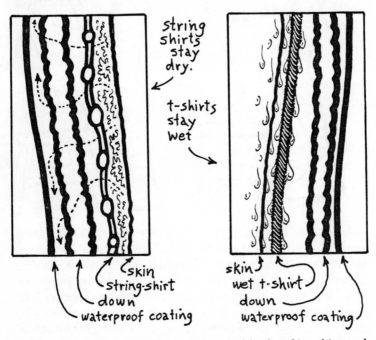

string shirts stay dry.

t-shirts stay wet

skin
string-shirt
down
waterproof coating

skin
wet t-shirt
down
waterproof coating

Since there is no such thing as the ideal backpacking shirt, and since a wide variety are available in clothing stores, shirts are rarely offered in mountaineering shops or catalogs. Several thin layers of clothing do a better job of conserving body heat while permitting ventilation, so I generally choose thin shirts with long tails.

During the warmest weather an inexpensive blue denim cotton work shirt provides excellent protection from sun, wind and bugs. It is light, lacking in bulk and quickly dries after being rinsed out at the end of the day. For slightly brisker weather, I like a long sleeved Hickory pullover with a zippered neck (see cover) or a hard finish khaki work shirt (usually cotton, but sometimes reinforced with synthetics).

A little heavier and bulkier than either of these is a shirt of marvelously comfortable heavy cotton flannel (also known as mole-skin or chamois cloth). Mine comes from L.L. Bean. Warmer and lighter, but less comfortable and more expensive, are flannel shirts of half cotton and half lambswool, and all wool Pendleton shirts. Heavier, bulkier wool shirts and shirt jackets, while often comfortable in cold weather, tend to defeat the purpose of layering by concentrating too much insulation in one garment. Instead of a heavy shirt, I wear a light shirt and a light sweater.

The warmest sweaters are pullovers made of wool or a combination of wool and synthetics. Stylish, bulky ski sweaters are much too thick and heavy for ordinary backpacking, and cotton sweatshirts are heavy and turn cold and clammy when damp. My two favorite' sweaters are a twenty-year-old light pullover of wool and Orlon, and a ten year old Navy surplus wool pullover with a very high turtle-neck. In the sweater classification I include down vests and down sweaters.

As though to make up for the scarcity of shirts and sweaters in their catalogs, mountaineering shops offer an almost endless array of jackets (without hoods) and parkas (hooded jackets). There are parka shells, anoraks, wind shirts, lined but unfilled rain parkas and down filled jackets and parkas. Probably half the offerings are ski or expeditionary parkas designed for sub-zero temperatures, not recreational backpacking. Also inappropriate are sheepskin coats, wool or dacron padded parkas, leather jackets and other heavy or inefficient outdoor clothing.

Parka shells of uncoated nylon are among the most useful and versatile garments a backpacker can carry. Made of a single layer of tightly woven nylon, the shell is generally a pullover with a zippered opening at the neck, elasticized wrists, a pouch pocket, and draw-strings at the bottom and around the hood. Though it weighs only about five ounces, the shell offers a largely windproof, but breathable, covering for half the body, making it an ideal outer layer of clothing. A close cousin to the shell is the hoodless wind shirt, which may contain cotton as well as nylon and can be worn under as well as over other clothing.

On the warmest summer days, I carry a shell or wind shirt, along with an equally ideal string shirt, and leave all conventional shirts at home, confident that I will be amply protected against chill if the day becomes cold or windy. Shells and wind shirts cost as little as $5-8 and have virtually no bulk. Even in cold weather the shell and string shirt constitute my basic upper clothing, but in between I sandwich additional layers of insulation: shirts, sweaters and down jackets. Since uncoated nylon soaks up water readily and does not hold repellents well, if the day promises to be wet, I substitute a coated nylon shell with a zippered front for my uncoated pullover. Rain protection is also provided by ponchos, raincoats, cagoules and storm suits.

Ponchos measure anywhere from 4 x 8 to 5 x 10 feet, depending on whether the pack is to be covered. Cheap vinyl plastic ponchos start at about $3 while urethane coated nylon may cost nearly $20. Weights run 16-24 ounces for either material. Raincoats are less flapable, give better arm and leg protection and average half the weight, but are not so useful or well ventilated as ponchos. The cagoule is a knee length coated nylon pullover with a hood, originally designed for the bivouacing climber. My favorite 2-piece storm suit weighs 20 ounces, folds into an 8 x 9 inch plastic pouch and cost exactly $1.87. It has more than once kept me dry in wind-driven rain while my poncho and parka clad companions were getting wet.

The mountain parka is a heavier, sturdier, longer garment than the shell parka and is designed for maximum water repellency consistent with breatheability. Intended for wear over considerable insulation, it is extremely roomy, lined but not filled, made of tightly woven factory treated 60-40 cloth (60% cotton, 40% nylon) and usually of finger tip length. It has a covered front zipper, big pockets, and a drawstring at the waist. Although the mountain parka offers more protection, durability, water repellency and wind resistance than the shell, backpackers have to measure its utility against its considerable bulk, weight (20-40 ounces) and $30-50 cost.

The mountain parka is ideal for rugged cross-country trips, traveling in brush, climbing, and spring and fall travel. For less demanding use there are even more versatile parkas that make a compromise between the shell and the mountain parka. The Anorak is a single layer pullover like the shell, but has the skirt, drawstring, pockets and water repellent cotton fabric of the mountaineering parka. Cost of the low bulk Anorak is $12-30 and weight is generally under two pounds. Other useful garments include skirted nylon shells, and zipper-front, single layer shells of 60-40 cloth.

When exceptionally efficient insulation is required for below freezing temperatures—found in the California Sierra even in mid-summer—down-filled clothing is the logical choice. Down's only real rival is polyeurethane foam, which lags far behind in bulk and compressability. (Dacron and wool batting are far too heavy for consideration.) The prime quality of a good insulator is its ability to prevent the air circulation that, by means of convection, permits the escape of heat. Very little heat is lost by conduction or radiation.

Given the backpacker's need for light weight, low bulk, efficiency and breathability, down offers an unbeatable combination of characteristics. It yields by far the lowest weight for the largest volume and the greatest compressability. An ounce of good goose down will expand to fill a volume of more than five hundred cubic inches, yet compress to less than two cubic inches. Its fuzzy radiating filaments effectively restrict the passage of air to prevent loss of heat but because it breathes, allowing moisture to escape, it offers twice the comfort range of other insulating materials. A two pound down jacket provides more warmth and comfort than ten pounds of wool shirts, sweaters and sheepskin coats.

The lightest down garments are sweaters and vests. The sweater is simply a short (waist length) hoodless jacket with sewn through seams. A good sweater should have a covered zipper, fully padded front pockets that completely envelop the hands and adjustable wrist closure for control of ventilation. Unlike most parkas and jackets, the down sweater should be snugly fitted for greatest efficiency, and a nylon shell or mountain parka should be carried for protection against wind. Sweaters and vests, in combination with other clothing, are good at temperatures ranging from freezing to −10 degrees F.

People who chill easily and suffer from the cold tend to be fond of down vests and wear them whenever it is cool. Some of us who are less bothered by cold see little sense in insulating the torso, but ignoring the arms. At Sierra Designs, a down vest costs $22 and weighs ten ounces. But for another $10 and six ounces, one can own a down sweater that insulates the entire upper body. A down sweater offers as much insulation as four heavy wool shirts or two thick

expeditionary parkas are rarely needed.

wd

wool sweaters, and much better wind resistance. During the summer, I only carry one when sub-freezing temperatures or constant cold wind are likely.

Those backpackers who feel the need of greater insulation—for climbing, severe climates, skiing or snow camping—will require a skirted down parka or jacket of hip or finger tip length. There are two general categories: (1) sewn through garments with an inch or less of loft (effective thickness of insulation) which weigh less than two pounds, cost $35-55 and are rated for temperatures down to −20 degrees F. (2) Double quilted semi-expedition parkas with lofts of up to two and a half inches weigh two to three pounds, cost $50 to well over $100, and are rated to as low as −60 degrees F. Few backpackers are likely to need the insulation these bulky, expensive, clumsy garments provide.

Experienced wilderness travelers know that on nearly every trip a hat provides valuable protection against sunburn, insects, rain, glare and brilliant light, and for warmth at night. Of course, no single hat both keeps off the rain and is comfortable in bed, so sometimes two hats are needed. Although I forget about rain protection in the summer Sierra, I often carry a pair that together weigh only four ounces. The preferred sleeping hats are two ounce knitted wool Navy watch caps, and the more versatile three ounce Eski Cap which doubles as a balaclava for partial protection of the face. For winter use, a four to six ounce balaclava helmet of felted wool is needed to extend protection to the neck and shoulders. Stocking caps offer the same coverage in much lighter material.

Probably the most popular trail hat is the three ounce hobo or rollercrusher with three inch brim. The back of the brim needs to be turned up sharply or trimmed off to avoid constant rubbing against the pack—a problem with all broad brimmed hats. I like a white two ounce tennis hat with a two inch brim because half the crown is

felt hats
become cooler
after a little
judicious snipping.

nylon netting and my greatest complaint against hats is that they tend to be hot. For the same reason, I like L.L. Bean's two ounce English Kangol Tropic Cap made of washable, open-weave synthetic.

Leather caps and wool berets are popular where sun protection is not vital, and some hikers like a version of the baseball or hunter's cap, some of which have fold-down ear flaps. Most hats, especially those of felt, can be made cooler by judicious use of sicissors on the crown. And all but the snugest hats should be fitted with a cord or thong which can be slipped under the chin on windy days.

Gloves and mittens remain on my checklist, although I rarely carry either on casual summer trips. Mittens are warmer, but dexterity is poor. Leather gloves offer finger control, but warmth is minimal and when gloves become wet they cease to insulate. Silk liners or foam lining helps somewhat, but even repellent leather wets readily. Down or foam filled mittens are warm and comfortable, but must be taken off when the fingers are needed. The best compromise I have found is a medium thickness, heavily oiled, wool glove or an army surplus wool glove. My second choice is rag wool mittens over silk liners, with a nylon mitten shell over the combination for winter mountaineering.

Since the well-equipped backpacker wears a tightly cinched hip-belt, a second belt to hold up the trousers is both uncomfortable and redundant. Suspenders, which tangle readily with pack straps and are unpopular, are no better. Since trousers need to be loose enough at the waist to allow several layers of clothing to be tucked in without producing discomfort, a lightweight belt is usually necessary, though a length of nylon lines works just as well.

Bandana handkerchiefs, available in most mountaineering shops at three for a dollar, are so endlessly useful that I sometimes take two. Extremes of temperature, wind and cold, cause noses to run, and Kleenex is extremely impractical on the trail. Besides their usefulness as handkerchiefs, bandanas often serve as hot pads, dish towels, neckerchiefs for protection against sunburn and insects, compresses, hand towels, large bandages, napkins, slings, wash cloths, etc. Since they dry very quickly, I often include them in the afternoon wash along with my string and denim shirts and socks.

These are the clothes that have proven themselves best adapted to backpacking. Some are found only in mountaineering shops, but many (sweaters, trousers, shirts and hats) are best hunted for at the back of the closet, in surplus and discount houses and at the workingman's store, where discovery of the perfect garment at a reasonable price can bring considerable satisfaction.

⁴BEDS

"Take everything else, but leave me my bed," pleads the old prospector with whom I sometimes travel. "A man's no good for anything if he can't get his rest." The veteran backpacker is likely to agree. After a day of exposure and exertion in the wilds the body demands the restoration of sleep. With adequate rest every night, a backpacker can survive bad weather, heavy packs and hard trails and remain cheerful. Without it, his trip cannot succeed.

The seasoned backpacker is always prepared to make himself comfortable wherever he happens to spend the night. And he usually manages to get a good night's sleep. Sleeping well in the mountains takes a little practice. The beginner should not be discouraged if he is restless or uncomfortable at first. Sleeping well is more than just carrying good equipment. The veteran knows how to pick a site and how to improve it. His body is conditioned both to the exertions of the trail and sleeping on the ground. The slippery, crinkly, confining mummy bag is familiar; so is the night wind, the growing cold and the early sunrise.

Although a good bed is only rivaled in importance by boots and packs, the backpacker, unlike the prospector, is limited to what he can carry on his back. The necessary warmth, protection and comfort must be produced with a minimum of weight—usually a total of four to seven pounds. Requirements, of course, vary tremendously. Generally speaking, young people sleep warmer and need less cushioning than their parents, and women sleep colder than men. As a teenager, I slept on a bed of rocks in a surplus bag with nothing beneath it but a ground cloth, in below freezing weather with no great discomfort. Nowadays, I am happy to carry a foam mattress to insure that I spend a comfortable night.

Because of the differences between people and the variety of wilderness conditions, it is impossible to describe the ideal backpacker's bed. There are a number of considerations. Principal among these are temperature range, cushioning required, cost and weight. Bed components will be discussed in terms of their suitability for conditions commonly found in the California High Sierra during the spring, summer and fall, i.e., a nighttime temperature range of 20-60 F (usually 30-40 F minimums), earth to sleep on that is often damp, probable wind, occasional thunderstorms and the possibility of heavy rain or snow, even in midsummer.

Working from the ground up, a good bed consists of (1) a properly located and carefully contoured site; (2) a waterproof ground cover; (3) a layer of cushioning insulation or matress; (4) a sleeping bag; (5) an optional sleeping bag cover or tarp; and (6) an optional waterproof stuff bag and pillow.

The existence of a suitable bed site is one of the prime considerations in choosing a campsite—along with the availability of water, firewood and shelter. Practiced backpackers will recognize a good place. Beginners will need to consider various criteria, being guided somewhat by where those who preceded them have camped. Of course, blind faith in those who came before can be dangerous. Many an apparently ideal camp turns out to have some disastrous flaw. The chief enemies of a good night's sleep are cold, dampness, wind, insects, running water, flying sparks, falling widowmakers, avalanche (unlikely) and the snoring of one's companions.

The most common mistake is to select a depression, dry ravine, streambank of dried up snowpool because it is sheltered from the afternoon wind. In the summer Sierra brisk winds have a habit of dramatically disappearing around dusk, miraculously turning an unfriendly promontory into an admirable camp. As the evening advances, a gentle but persistent night wind commonly rises to pour cold heavy air down the streambeds and ravines and into those inviting depressions, leaving them as much as ten degrees colder than higher ground only a few feet away.

Breezes during the day flow up the ravines and canyons, on shore from lakes and across meadows. At night the winds move down the streambeds and out onto the lakes and meadows. Dry ravines and snow pools, besides collecting cold air at night, also collect running water quickly in a cloudburst. Meadows tend to be damp and attract heavy dew. Dew results when moist air cools, causing a fallout of condensation. Dew will be heavier near a lake, stream or meadow, and just after a storm. Heavy dew is capable of severely wetting an unprotected sleeping bag in just a few hours. Woe to the weary backpacker who, late on a night of heavy dew, has to climb inside a drenched bag left open or inside out.

There are enough advantages to sleeping beneath a tree to more than compensate for the filtered view of the stars. Trees serve as an umbrella to shield the sleeper from heavy dew and light rain. On a bitterly cold, clear night sheltering branches serve as insulation from solar radiation. The air temperature beneath a tree may be ten degrees warmer than a bedsite exposed to the chill night sky. Since I rarely want to be awakened at dawn, I regularly position my bed to the west of a good sized tree so that it can shade me from the early morning sun. The shade allows me to sleep an hour or so past sunrise without being cooked in my mummy bag. Trees frequently serve as windbreaks, clothes hangers, pack supports, tarp tie-downs, and a source of cushioning pine-needle mattresses. (The cutting of boughs for a mattress can no longer be justifed in America's limited, well populated wilderness.)

this snug sleeper is shaded from the early morning sun and sheltered from the chilly night sky.

It is generally important to know the direction of the prevailing wind in camp and to use this information in locating a bedsite, especially if the weather is unsettled or threatening. Even on a still night it is a bad idea to sleep directly downwind of the campfire. A wind in the night can fan the coals and bombard the bed with glowing sparks, each of which will burn a neat round hole in the nylon fabric. If the fire is utterly dead the sleeper will instead receive a shower of ashes.

A bed should likewise be located a respectable distance from one's companions. Even if (miraculously) nobody snores, it is a good idea to consider in advance the necessity of getting up in the middle of the icy night without disturbing others. Sleeping in the path of a possible avalanche or under a widowmaking snag or dead branch is a poor idea. Beds under cornices or at the mouths of boulder chutes are definitely dangerous.

Badly placed beds are rarely forgotten. One sultry night, making camp after dark, I placed my bed on the crumbled and cushiony remains of a thoroughly decayed log—usually an excellent location. I awoke after an hour, in the rain, crawling with big black ants whose home I had disturbed. Another time I was awakened by cold feet sloshing in a wet bag; a light rain had come up and though I was covered by a tarp a stream had materialized in the shallow gully containing my feet, soaking the bottom of my bag. The wakeful nights that followed both incidents were so grimly memorable that I now scrutinize prospective bedsites for disguised watercourses and concealed inhabitants.

Unusually good beds can be memorable, too. At a windy timberline camp on a rocky exposed mountain, I found a cleft in the rock beneath a prostrate whitebark pine that was just the right size and deeply filled with needles. All night the wind howled a few inches above my head while I lay snug and warm under the fragrant pine. On another windy high country night, I lay on a deep bed of needles in front of the fire in the mouth of a shelter made by roofing the space between two big fallen trees. Though the night outside was freezing, I was snug and warm in my little cabin.

Bedsites need to very nearly level. If there must be a slope, it should run downhill from head to feet. Sleeping on a sidehill is nothing short of torture. One is generally better off with an inferior level site than a sloping bed that is otherwise perfect. It is not uncommon for the sleeper who made his bed on a slope to wake up in the morning ten feet away with the distinct impression of not having slept at all. I believe strongly that a bedsite's most important characteristic is its susceptibility to alteration, and I have yet to encounter one I could not improve.

The finest down bag and the thickest mattress cannot make a lumpy bedsite comfortable. But a bedsite carefully contoured to fit the body is surprisingly comfortable, even without cushioning. As I view potential sites, bare earth is fine, deep pine-needles or duff are perfect, decayed tree trunks are excellent—when not inhabited—sand and gravel are satisfactory, provided I am carrying a cushioning foam mattress. Grass is poor because it cannot be contoured without removing the roots and permanently scarring the ground. Most people looking for a readymade bed mistakenly seek grass for its cushioning and scorn sand or gravel for its unyielding nature.

When I have selected the best available bedsite in all respects and decided where my head is to be, I dig a rectangular hip and shoulder hole. It measures about 18 inches wide, 28 inches long and 2½ inches deep with sloping sides and a slightly concave bottom. All of the excavated earth or sand is heaped into a pillow about three inches thick. From the bottom of the hip hole to the bottom of the foot area, I smooth the ground, removing sticks, rocks, pine-cones and twigs. If the ground is sloping, I often use the earth excavated from the hip hole to build up the area that supports the legs, finding some other way to make a pillow. For maximum comfort, the feet should be a little higher than the hips and I find it well worth the trouble to make sure that they are. In seriously sloping or less than level ground it is sometimes easier to dig the hip hole deeper rather than pad the leg area. Like the highway builder, I try to balance my cut and fill.

Once the preliminary shaping is complete, I lie down on the bedsite on my back to test the contours. If the shoulder section needs widening and the hip hole deepening, I scratch some kind of a pattern with a twig, then get up to make alterations. When I lie down a second time, if everything feels comfortable (nothing pressing or cramped) I roll over on my side. This will generally feel less comfortable and additional excavating will be needed at the point of the hip and thigh. But I dig with restraint, knowing that no hole can fit perfectly both ways. The result must be a compromise which favors the position in which one usually sleeps.

If I am comfortable lying directly on the ground, I am confident of sleeping well with a good bed beneath me. In an attempt to make a perfectly contoured hip hole, the novice will often build up an area to support the small of the back. This is a grave mistake and is guaranteed to produce an aching back before dawn. Women, because of their broader hips, usually are less comfortable on the ground than men; they will want a deeper hiphole that tapers to a shallower shoulder hole.

My contouring operation may seem a waste of time to rubber-boned youth or older stoics who pride themselves on being able to sleep anywhere they happen to drop their bed. But I can think of no better investment of time than the five minutes it takes me to transform a small strip of earth into a comfortable bed that will insure me eight hours of restful sleep.

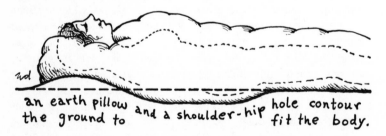

an earth pillow and a shoulder-hip hole contour the ground to fit the body.

No matter how dry the ground may seem, a waterproof ground cloth is probably essential. There is nearly always moisture in the earth and during the course of the night it can dampen an unprotected sleeping bag and chill the sleeper. Even if there were no moisture, a ground cloth would be needed to protect the mattress or sleeping bag. The ground cloth can be dispensed with only when a full length pad of a closed cell material (like Ensolite) or a foam mattress covered with coated nylon is used to protect the sleeping bag.

A good down sleeping bag—the backpacker's most vital, valuable and expensive piece of equipment—should never be put on the ground. Its thin, water absorbent downproof covering must be jealously guarded against dirt, pitch, puncture and moisture. Any one who has attempted to dry out, sleep in, or even lift a sodden down bag will go to great lengths thereafter to keep his bag dry. And the easiest method is to start with a ground cloth.

The ground cloth, unfortunately, must always be a compromise between lightness and durability. The choice is between plastic (polyethylene), which is cheap but easily punctured, and coated nylon which may be four times as expensive but lasts four times as long. Weights are approximately the same. People who are hard on their equipment or disinclined to be fussy are advised to buy plastic and plan to replace it every season (and maybe every trip). Hikers inclined to baby their equipment and carefully clear their bedsites may prefer coated nylon. Thanks to my bedsite preparation, I have nursed plastic ground sheets through several seasons although they certainly were not waterproof after the first few trips. I carry plastic or ripstop tape, which will mend either material.

For the hiker who is carrying a poncho or can share a large tarp to cover his bag, the minimum size practical is 4 x 7 feet. Where the ground cloth is to be shared or must fold over to protect the bag from rain, the minimum size is 6 x 8 feet. Tarps measuring 5 x 8 and 7 x 9 feet will generally be worth the extra ounce or so. Four mil plastic tarps measuring 5 x 8 feet weighs 12 ounces and costs $1.75, while the 7 x 9 foot size weighs 20 ounces and costs $3. Double urethane coated nylon (Nylport) tarps, reinforced, hemmed and grommeted costs $11.50 in the 5 x 7 foot size and weighs 12 ounces, while the 7 x 9 foot size weighs 24 ounces and costs $16.50.

A friend of mine solves the ground cloth problem by simply buying two and a half yards of Nylport off the roll from a mountaineering shop that sells it at $2 per yard. For only $5 he gets a high quality ground cloth without any frills that runs 45 inches wide and weighs only 8 ounces. Some people buy thinner, lighter, cheaper polyethylene and plan to double or triple it beneath them and burn it in the camp fire the last morning out. Paint stores carry 9 x 12 foot drop cloths in varying weights at comparatively low prices. Building supply houses sell various weights and widths by the yard quite reasonably. The Sportsman's Space Blanket (about 5 x 7 feet) makes an adequate ground cloth, but is too easily punctured for the price ($8) and weight (11 ounces).

Several years ago a friend, hearing me complain of sweating in my sleeping bag, suggested I try the North Face Bivouac Cover, a flat envelope seven and a half feet long and 45 inches wide with Nylport on the bottom and light, breathable ripstop on the top. I got one and soon found it indispensible. When the night is sultry and the mosquitos are out, but it is too warm in the bag, even unzipped, I can throw my bag open or lie on top and still be protected from cold, dew and bugs. As the night grows colder I can climb inside my bag, and if the dew is heavy, the cold intense or the wind strong, the cover gives me extra protection.

The cover not only takes the place of ground cloth and tarp, it serves as a tiny tent, keeps clothes, boots and other gear dry and warm at night and secure and clean during the day. As a dressing room, it supplies considerable privacy, and it is unexcelled at keeping a sleeping bag and mattress clean and dry. Although my cover is no less susceptible to puncture and leakage than a Nylport ground cloth, an absorbent foam pad can be used inside it with reasonable safety. Bivouac covers cost $13 and weighs 12 ounces. The Ski Hut sells a Sleeping Bag Cover which is similar in size, weight and price.

The Space Rescue Blanket, a surprisingly tough laminated sheet 5½ x 7 feet that looks like tinfoil and crinkles melodiously, can be used as a sleeping bag cover in an emergency, although its vulnerability to puncture makes it unsuitable as a ground cloth. At only two ounces it has to qualify as the lightest tarp available, but is should be relied upon for emergency, not daily, use. One mild Sierra night I slept wrapped in the blanket—and nothing else. By adjusting the ventilation from time to time I managed a reasonable balance between retaining reflected body heat and minimizing condensation. I slept surprisingly well, but my friends complained that the incessant crinkling kept them awake.

space
rescue
blanket

Unquestionably the simplest insulation, winter or summer, is Ensolite. It comes in 1/8, 1/4, 3/8 and 1/2 inch thicknesses and 56 and 84 inch lengths. The customary 3/8 inch pad measuring 19 x 42 inches weighs 14 ounces and costs $4. Similar and lighter imitations (like half inch O-so-lite) run 22 inches wide and are available in any length at $1.25 to $1.50 a running foot. After several seasons use, the cells in Ensolite begin to collapse and the pads flatten out. Even when new, though they smooth out the bumps, no real cushioning is provided. But in many ways these pads are ideal for backpacking, especially on snow; they absorb no water, need neither a covering nor a ground cloth, and offer reasonable weight, bulk, price and durability.

For a soft, comfortable, well-cushioned sleep, an air mattress or foam pad must be carried. Polyeurethane foam pads have largely replaced air mattresses, despite their greater bulk, because they supply insulation as well as cushioning and never go flat during the night. Foam pads are generally lighter than good quality air mattresses, and most people find them more comfortable. Foam is available in a variety of thicknesses, densities, lengths, types of construction and covering. Unlike Ensolite, foam is more or less water absorbent and must be covered or protected.

A punctured ground cloth can pass enough water during the night to double the weight of an uncovered foam pad. Most foams can be squeezed out, and the remaining water evaporated away. Unless the country is extremely dry or the ground cloth new, urethane foam pads need to be encased in a coated nylon cover or wrapped in plastic.

Foam pads range in thickness from 1-2½ inches. One inch foam offers about twice the cushioning of 3/8 inch Ensolite. Inch and a half solid foam is very comfortable and roughly equivalent in weight and cushioning to two-inch pads with convoluted (also known as egg crate or waffle) bottoms. Thomas Black, an English supplier, offers the ultimate in comfort in its 2½ inch egg crate polyether Kampamat, which is sufficiently resistant to dampness not to require a cover. Most pads measure 18-22 inches in width and from 3-6 feet in length. Probably the most popular lengths are 42, 48 and 54 inches which more than accomodate the shoulders and hips.

Gerry's 36 inch pad of covered, solid 1½ inch foam weighs just over a pound; Sierra design's convolluted, 2-inch covered pads of 42 and 54 inches weigh 1¼ and 1¾ pounds respectively. Its 72-inch pad in 1½ inch stock weighs 2¼ pounds. Black's 2½ inch Kampamat, without cover, weighs 2¼ and 2 and 7/8 pounds for 50 and 75 inch pads. Foam pads range in price from $7 to $14. There is considerable variability in foam stiffness. Very soft foam is not worth carrying, because instead of bearing weight it collapses.

I like the stiffest foam I can get. I have a 48 inch covered 1½ inch thick solid foam pad made by Squires in San Jose, Calif., that weighs 1½ pounds. In terms of stiffness, it is about halfway between Ensolite and the average convoluted foam. It rolls to five inches in diameter, costs $9 and offers many times the comfort of Ensolite. Since nylon bags easily slip off slippery nylon foam covers, several makers (Alpine and Sierra Designs) employ a less slippery cotton nylon mixture on top.

Like Ensolite, foam cells collapse; unlike Ensolite they also deteriorate and crumble with age or prolonged exposure to sunlight. Convoluted pads are notably thinner and less cushioning after a year or two if they are left rolled tight: permanent compression is postponed if pads are stored flat. The boom in backpacking, which is bringing new people into the wilds every year, is also bringing greater demand for comfort, and this is reflected in the trend toward longer, thicker and more comfortable foam pads. Twenty years ago a comparatively inferior sleeping bag and canvas tarpaulin weighed at least eight pounds. Today one can carry a ground cloth, tarp, down bag and full length foam mattress that weigh as little as six pounds. Both beginner and veteran backpackers in increasing numbers are taking advantage of advances in equipment design to increase their comfort by carrying substantial foam pads.

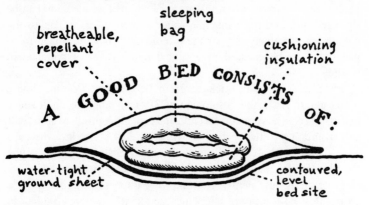

Although air mattresses are declining in popularity, they still have their adherents, most of whom are old hands at the game of keeping them filled and staying on top. Air mattresses take considerable getting used to, even skill, but once the balancing act has been mastered they become quite comfortable. During the years before foam pads became available, I worked my way through quite a selection of air mattresses. The best of these were made by Thomas Black and one of them, surprisingly, is still available.

The Good Companion has a hip length, 4-tube (22 x 45 inch) body with a separately filled large pillow. Made of tough rubberized canvas, it weighs just under two pounds and costs $10. My favorite was a narrow, full length mattress without a pillow, which weighed just over two pounds. Each lasted about half a dozen seasons before the rubber deteriorated and innumerable, unfindable leaks appeared. Until that time, punctures were easily and permanently repaired with an old fashioned Tire Repair kit.

Plastic air mattresses are cheap and light but vulnerable to leaks, subject to faulty manufacture and generally undependable. Even for a single outing they make a poor investment because strangers to air mattresses rarely sleep well the first night or so. The trick is to put in as little air as possible. Ground preparation is important and the hip hole should be made deeper than for foam. Each sleeper must find the point of minimum inflation, but best results come from filling the mattress nearly full, lying in the customary sleeping position and gradually letting out the air until the hips just touch the ground.

Nothing is more uncomfortable, including hard ground, than trying to sleep on a tightly filled air bed.

Stebco is presently the principal supplier of air mattresses. The pillowless hip length model of tightly woven nylon, rubberized on the inside, measures 22 x 48 inches, weighs 1 and 3/4 pounds and costs $10. The full length (22 x 72 inch) model weighs 2 and 2/3 pounds and costs $13. Numerous additional models all weigh more than three pounds.

Aside from the leaks and the difficulty of learning to sleep on them, the main drawback to air mattresses is that they are cold. In the desert, on the beach or in warm country, this can be an advantage. On a windy night above timberline, or on snow, it can be a disaster. The air mattress is a very efficient heat exchanger whose constantly moving air absorbs and dissipates heat through convection. In this respect, sleing on an air mattress is like sleeping on a cot or in a hammock.

Of course, air mattresses have to be inflated. The weight of a pump cannot be justified for backpacking, and inflating them by mouth can be hard work at high altitude. I have seen exhausted backpackers who simply could not do it and others who have nearly passed out. And I have blown myself dizzy on more than one occasion. All things considered, beginning backpackers in the mountains are much better off with foam.

Pillows, as such, are traditionally scorned, but anyone accustomed to one—and that means most of us—must find some way to elevate and cushion his head if he wishes to sleep in any kind of comfort. Half the problem is solved during site preparation by making an earth pillow. Cushioning is generally supplied by a down parka stuffed into one of its own sleeves or the sleeping bag stuff bag filled with spare clothing. Stebco makes a nice little air pillow 13 x 16 inches that weighs 5 ounces and costs about $2.50. A good many of us who carry foam pads simply position them over an earth pillow. Lack of cushioning beneath the head means a pair of sore ears in the morning.

Sleeping bags come in a variety of types and fillings, but only those lightweight models designed to be carried will be considered here. This eliminates wool, kapok and a majority of synthetic fillings designed for car camping. What remains are the down bags, a few polyester (Dacron) bags and two very interesting bags made of foam. Dacron bags are offered for only one reason: they can be sold for $15-30 while good down bags cost $65-95. Compared to down, it takes twice the weight of Dacron—the best of the synthetics—to produce a given thickness of insulation.

Since the warmth of a bag is determined solely by the thickness of its insulation, down, on the basis of weight, is twice as good as

Dacron. Since it is price alone that sells Dacron, most bags are made as cheaply as possible, which further increases the gulf in quality. There are down bags for as little as $34 and Dacron bags for as much as $37 but neither is worth considering in this price range.

Since Dacron does not loft well, cold spots are common and it is necessary to use at least three pounds of fill to provide minimal insulation. Since Dacron does not compress well, bags tend to be heavy and bulky. Most Dacron bags begin to get cold when the temperature drops below 40 F. There are a number of children's bags in Dacron that are very cheap, while children's down bags are both scarce and expensive. For adults, a Dacron bag for backpacking is usually a poor investment unless the climate is dependably warm. Sleeping cold in Dacron is a very poor introduction to backpacking.

Good down bags well cared for have a high resale value, and there are an increasing number of places (like Mountain Traders in Berkeley) where they can be advertised, sold or traded. The resale value of a Dacron bag is nearly nonexistent. Dacron bags are found in sporting goods stores, discount houses and surplus stores, but rarely in mountaineering shops.

As explained in chapter three, when it comes to lightweight, low bulk, breatheable insulation, down offers an unbeatable combination of characteristics. The radiating filaments of the fuzzy little quilless down pods effectively restrict air circulation when allowed to expand. But they compress to one seventh their expanded size with virtually no loss in resiliency. Even after a long period of compression, an ounce of good goose down will expand to stop air flow in a volume of over five hundred square inches.

No sleeping bag made produces its own heat. The most it can do is retain body heat by means of insulation. As long as it prevents air movement internally, one insulation is as good as another. Insulating effectiveness is solely a function of thickness. Down stays thick and effective as long as it is free from pressure. But its great compressibility and lack of bulk cause it to be squashed nearly flat by the weight of the body. Since the resulting quarter of an inch of insulation is virtually useless, a foam or Ensolite pad becomes vital to protect the sleeper from cold and moisture from the ground.

Since down is capable of expanding and compressing enormously, it will tend to move readily if not contained, producing thin or empty places in the insulating layer. Since insulation is only as good as its thinest point, down must be contained in small enclosures that do not inhibit its maximum expansion. The bagmaker's goal is to produce maximum, uniform loft (insulation thickness) with a minimum of down.

The usual procedure is to divide the insulating area between the inner and outer fabrics into a series of tubes by sewing in baffles between them. The first down bags had tubes that ran the length of the bag. Unfortunately, the down had a habit of gravitating to the bottom, leaving the rest of the bag thin, so all makers of good bags switched to a horizontal arrangement of tubes that circle the body. There are three principal tube shapes: box, slant wall box and overlapping (also known as V-tube). An occasional down bag offers sewn-through construction in either one or two layers; both types should be avoided like the plague.

A box tube, offering the cheapest, simplest, highest loft, is formed by parallel baffles placed at right angles to inner and outer fabric. In slant wall box, the baffles are parallel to one another, but slanted at roughly a forty-five degree angle to form a parallelogram. Overlapping tubes are produced by zigzagging a continuous strip of baffling between inner and outer fabric to form a series of overlapping triangles. Which of these is best is a matter of opinion: many of the best bag makers cannot make up their minds. It is argued by some that slant wall box is less likely to create a cold spot than straight box. This is countered by those who say straight box is less likely to constrict loft. A third school claims there is no difference between them if filled with the optimum volume of down.

Overlapping tubes, claim its advocates, prevent down shift (cold spots) better than either and become a necessity for controlling tube cross sectional area in high loft bags, where the distance between inner and outer fabrics is great. Another school points out that overlapping tubes inhibit maximum lofting more than either kind of box, and the increase in baffling results in a significant increase in weight. It seems safe to say that any of these three methods is satisfactory when employed by a first rate manufacturer.

3 types of sleeping-bag tubes:

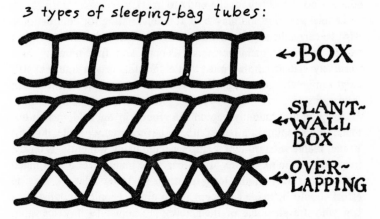

←BOX

SLANT~
←WALL
BOX

OVER~
←LAPPING

When it comes to tube size there is general agreement that six inches is the ideal box width (eight inches for overlapping) on bags of less than six inches loft. For higher loft bags box width may drop to four or even three inches (six inches for overlapping). Significantly wider tubes (8-12 inches) usually signal cheap construction.

A few manufacturers still use cotton netting for baffling and think it entirely satisfactory although cotton is subject to mildew and rot, which can destroy a bag from within. Most makers use half ounce nylon mosquito netting or marquisette, and the best 'hotcut' it (automatically sealing the edges) to prevent the unraveling for which nylon is infamous. Since an average bag might have 25-30 tubes of varying dimensions and require 36 ounces total fill of down, the importance of the right amount of fill for each tube become apparent. A half ounce error in one tube can easily be significant.

Some bag makers meter their down and blow a precisely pre-weighed amount into a given tube. A few of these use a set amount for every tube, varying tube width to keep the volume constant—a second rate technique. Others rely on backpressure on the blower to reveal when a tube is full. But most depend on experienced bag fillers who develop a feel for proper down volume and can turn out bags with remarkably uniform fill. The listed weight of fill for any bag is nothing more than a guaranteed minimum and is often as much as four ounces low.

The number of ounces of fill for a given bag is a meaningless figure, taken by itself. Thirty ounces in a mummy may be good at twenty degrees below freezing while the same weight in a large rectangular bag would be inadequate on a much warmer night. Backpacking bags can be divided into three shapes: mummy, barrel-shaped (or fat mummy) and semi-rectangular. Mummy bags are preferable for two reasons: (1) being minimal in size they make the lightest of beds, (2) because they fit the body they are warmer (there is no excess bag for the body to heat).

People who find mummy bags too constricting for comfort may wish to carry the slightly heavier and less efficient barrel-shaped bag (made by many manufacturers). People who find mummy bags positively claustrophobic must settle for still heavier and less efficient semi-rectangular bags. Very few of these are rated for less than 20 degrees.

Sleeping in a mummy bag on the ground in the wilderness is not much like sleeping in a heated home, but too many people, it seems to me, blame the resultant strangeness and likely wakefulness on the shape or confining nature of the bag. The mummy bag is so much more satisfactory in the long run than its larger relatives that an effort should be made to accept its confines. People shopping for a bag who are skeptical of their ability to adjust to its dimensions would be well advised to rent or borrow one for several trips to give themselves a chance to discover its virtures.

Another area of sleeping bag controversy is 'differential' versus "flat cut." In the first down bags for backpackers, the inside I ad the same circumference as the outside and no one worried about the fact that the inside bunched around the sleeper. Then someone decided to cut the inside on a smaller radius to allow for the thickness of the down. This notion of turning the inner and outer shells into concentric circles became known as the 'differential cut.' The bag looked neater, it no longer bunched around the sleeper; knees and elbows, being unable to press tightly against the outer shell, were supposed to be protected from cold, and the down was supposed to be able to expand evenly to make the bag work like a thermos bottle.

flat-cut sleeping bag:

differentially-cut bag:

Most makers of better bags adopted the differential cut. Now a few are beginning to reconsider. A differentially cut bag tends to stand away from the body resulting in air space that must be heated. Other things being equal, the differentially cut bag will not be as warm as a flat-cut bag in which down pressure causes the liner to gently snuggle in against the sleeper, squeezing out the superfluous air pockets. This consideration seems to me to outweigh the alledged advantages of the differential cut. I own modern bags of both kinds and most of the time I use a differentially cut bag. But I do not assign it any particular superiority, and in anything but a snug mummy bag I would consider it a drawback. Frostline is retreating from the differential cut and Holubar, a major supplier of high quality bags, has never made one.

The weakest part of a bag in terms of heat retention is its zipper. The zipper is therefore one of the best placed to look for bag quality. Cheaper bags often come with half length zippers despite the fact that overheated feet are a principal complaint. Most semi-rectangular bags have zippers that run down the side and clear across the bottom. Mummy bags, unfortunately, and for no urgent reason, do not provide this feature. A good bag should offer at least a 70-inch zipper with double pulls so it can be unzipped from the bottom as well as the top.

Another mark of an inferior bag is a zipper on top instead of on the side. A top zipper reduces bag loft where it is needed most and replaces it with a difficult-to-baffle source of cold. Top zippers are found on cheaper bags because they are substantially cheaper to install than side mounted zippers.

There are three kinds of zippers: metal, nylon tooth and coil. Metal zippers, being cold, heavy and easy to jam or break, have become a sign of a poorly designed bag. Light, strong nylon toothed zippers from Japan are found on most up-to-date bags. Better (and lighter), comparatively expensive coil zippers from West Germany are found on the finest bags. Coil zippers are smooth, flexible, hard to snag, easy to free, strong and self-repairing if separated.

Good quality down bags are made so that a down-filled baffle blocks cold air from the zipper so it cannot reach the sleeper. This can be accomplished by either attaching a draft flap or offsetting the zipper. Most makers back their zippers with a 3-6 inch wide tube that hangs from the top of the bag (on right hand bags). The means by which this draft flap is fastened is a good index to bag quality. On carelessly designed bags the flap is simply stitched on in one place at the edge of the zipper. This produces a sewn-through, uninsulated seam that lets out heat. Carefully designed bags avoid this by fastening the flap to the bag at two points so there are at least two inches of insulation where flap and bag meet.

Skimpy, short, underfilled flaps should be avoided in favor of more generous offerings, especially on bags that are to be zipped together, where zipper baffling becomes critical. Several manufacturers have solved the problem by simply offsetting the zipper about six inches from the edge of the top of the bag so the ends of the tubes serve as a draft flap. This simple solution seems destined to become popular. Draft flaps have a tendency to get caught in toothed zippers, and, as a consequence, several makers have stitched a stiffener into the flaps's most vulnerable surface. Coil zippers make flap stiffeners unnecessary.

Still another indication of bag quality is foot section design. Cheap or poorly designed bags are simply flat envelopes with no more foot room than the conventional bed. But out-thrust feet tend to push sharply through the insulating layer to create cold spots which in turn chill them. To avoid this, the superior bag incorporates an enlarged foot section with a circular flat bottom so the feet can be extended in any direction without pressing against the bag. The foot section should be baffled off from the body of the bag to prevent down shift. Foot sections are so sensible and luxurious—and important to foot warmth—that my bed at home seems uncomfortable without one.

The ease and effectiveness with which a sleeping bag can be drawn closed around the shoulders and head is critical in determining its comfort range and maximum warmth. The old-fashioned hoodless envelope has no real provision for preventing heat loss, but it is still being produced by most bag makers, e.g., the semirectangular down bag. The best closure comes from a semi-circular down-filled pillow flap which, by means of a drawstring, can be turned into a hood that fits around the head.

When buying a bag it is worthwhile getting inside to check length, foot room, snugness and the ease with which the hood can be closed from the inside to a face hole the size of a baseball. Drawstrings should be supplied with some sort of spring loaded clamp that can be operated with one hand. To keep the weight and price of semi-rectangular bags competitive with that of the much leaner mummies, bag makers have left off the hoods, which is a serious disadvantage in any but the mildest climates. The buyer should realize he is sacrificing head protection and overall warmth to obtain extra room. A separate down hood is generally a poor investment.

Sleeping bag fabrics have become largely standardized among the makers of fine bags. Ripstop nylon, which has three times the tear resistance of ordinary weaves yet is extremely light, is generally the choice in weights of either 1.5 or 1.9 ounces per yard. It must have a hard enough finish and high enough thread count to be downproof, but it must be sufficiently porous to breathe. Ripstop or other nylon meeting these requirements will usually be both wind resistant and water repellent. Long staple Egyptian cotton, once the preferred sleeping bag fabric, is now comparatively inferior because of its susceptability to mildew, rot, puncture, wind penetration and the continual loss of down. Some people dislike the slippery parchment-like feel of nylon, but the slipperiness enables the sleeper to roll over without taking the bag with him.

down pod:

Since the term 'down' covers a variety of fillings, with a considerable range in efficiency, it is important that the prospective buyer know something about the quality of the filling. Most desirable is goose down, because the goose produces the largest, highest lofting down pods. A few pin feathers are unavoidable—even the finest goose down is allowed a 7% feather content. Good down may have a 25% feather content and there are fillings represented loosely as goose down that are 50 to 75% feathers. Ducks produce smaller down pods which yield less efficient insulation. Duck down usually produces a 10-20 degree higher minimum comfort temperature than goose down and the resulting bags should be $10-25 lower in price. Duck down's efficiency also drops as the feather content increases.

With goose down, color is unimportant, quality being determined by the degree of refinement (freedom from feathers). In duck down, however, grey is substantially better than white because grey ducks tend to be more mature and their down pods bigger. White duck down has a tendency to smell of fish when wet, because the ducks from which it comes are fishmeal fed. Both goose and duck down are by-products of ducks commercially raised for food and slaughtered when relatively young.

There are two things a prospective purchaser can do to reassure himself as to the type of down used. Through the thin fabric he can feel for lumps and the quills of feathers. In a good grade of down, whether goose or duck, there should be no lumps. And he can check the "bedding label," a tag sewn into the bag by law to accurately indicate the nature of the filling as approved by state inspectors. Furnished for the protection of the buyer, the bedding label accurately, if somewhat generally, labels the filling according to government specifications.

If there is a substantial proportion of feathers the bedding label should reveal it. The buyer needs to be aware of the differences between fillings in order to suspect vague terms like 'waterfowl down,' which probably means a poor grade of feather-rich white duck down. Also to be avoided are additives or treatments used to make poor down loft higher; the effect rarely lasts.

Another index of quality is stitching, which should be in Dacron or nylon thread (possibly sheathed in cotton for abrasion resistance). Eight to ten stitches to the inch is optimum. Shorter stitches tend to cut the fabric. Cheaply made bags usually have long stitches, sometimes only 3-6 to the inch, which makes them extremely susceptible to snagging, besides yielding a comparatively weak fastening.

The best bags have always been designed to minimize down shift in order to prevent cold spots. On the side opposite the zipper this usually means the insertion of a block baffle running the length of the bag to stop down from moving from the tubes on top to those on the bottom. A bag made by Bugaboo and sold by Mountain Traders in Berkeley, however, is designed to allow deliberate down shift. By shifting down to where it is needed the comfort range can be increased and $10-15 is saved by the lack of a block baffle. Making use of the fact that down smashed flat beneath the sleeper offers neither insulation nor warmth, the knowldgeable Bugaboo owner can shake down out of the top and into the bottom for a cooler sleep on a warm summer night. Or for winter use (with full length insulation underneath) he can shake extra down from the bottom to the top for increased loft and warmth.

Bag makers customarily point to the loft of their bags as evidence of their warmth, and if the bags are well made, loft is a reasonable index of insulating capability. Most bag makers likewise—in response to public demand—devise minimum temperature ratings for their bags. A table complied by Eastern Mountain Sports, Inc. shows a good correlation between loft (average thickness after the bag has been fluffed and allowed to stand at least an hour) and the minimum temperature ratings of mummy shaped, goose down bags. For 5-6 inches of loft the minimum rating is 15-25 degrees; 6-7 inches loft yields 5-15 degrees; 7-8 inches provides 5 to −5; and 8-9½ inches offers protection from −10 to −40 degrees.

These figures appear conservative when compared to the findings of the Army Quartermaster Corps whose tests indicate that three inches of insulation (equivalent to six inches of loft) will keep a sleeper warm at twenty degrees below zero in still air with no allowance for ground cold penetration. The EMS ratings assume the sleeper is well insulated from below, in good physical condition and protected from the night sky by a tent or other suitable covering.

Knowing shoppers will prefer right hand bags (lying in the bag the zipper is on the right) to left hand bags because the draft flap hangs from the top of the bag and consequently has gravity's help in blocking off the zipper. Right hand bags outsell left by 2:1. When one of each is purchased to make a double bag it is customary to give the right hand bag to the woman because men tend to sleep warmer than women.

A sleeping bag represents most packpacker's biggest investment in terms of cost, weight and bulk, and the purchase should therefore be made with care. Though the price of a good bag is considerable, probably $75-95, inexpensive bags should be viewed with suspicion, tested, inspected and tried on for size. I would be unwilling to buy a bag by mail on the basis of a catalog description unless the maker's reputation for bags was as good as those of Alpsport, Bugaboo, Holubar, North Face, Sierra Design and Ski Hut.

Before selecting a bag, the buyer needs to ascertain whether he sleeps warmly, cold or just about average. This determination, along with intended use, will largely determine the minimum temperature rating required for comfort. A bag to be used in wind and rain at high altitude by an exhausted, hungry climber will need to be warmer than one used by the same person at the same temperature under milder conditions. It is always a good idea to question backpacking friends about their bags. And when possible, it is advisable to rent or borrow a bag before buying.

Although down has long been accepted as the peerless insulator for lightweight sleeping bags, that claim is now being challenged by Ocaté and Trail Tech, both of which make bags of polyurethane foam, the same material which has replaced air mattresses. The Ocaté bag consists of a mummy-shaped envelope of one inch thick sheet foam lined inside and out with breatheable ripstop nylon. Its comparative rigidity causes it to stand away from the body.

A drawstring converts the entrance of this zipperless bag into a

foam offers a new alternative:

flattened-down down
provides no insulation.

foam bags insulate
under the body.

hood in the same manner as a down bag; another drawstring laces the body of the bag more closely around the sleeper. The adult bag weighs about 5 pounds and costs less than $50, but it is difficult to reduce to twice the bulk of the average down bag. The makers claim an unprecedented seventy degree comfort range (70 F to 0). A down bag comfortable at zero is invariably like a steam bath at merely freezing temperatures. The bottom of a foam bag—unlike any down bag—provides both insulation and cushioning.

Sleeping in the Ocaté is a little like sleeping in a coffin, because the tunnel of foam tends to arch above the sleeper and only touches him occasionally. I found this disconcerting at first, sleeping without clothes, but wearing pajamas helped me to feel more at home. Both the comfort range and the breathability of the bag are greater than on any down bag I have tried. I am accustomed to sweaty feet in most down bags, but I have slept in the Ocaté bag in a heated room without sweating and been almost as comfortable sleeping on snow in the wind. At high temperatures the excellent ventilation, together with foam's great breathability, keeps the sleeper dry and comfortable.

As temperatures grow colder, I gradually close down the size of the Ocaté's hood opening. At freezing, I closed the hood all the way (to an unfortunately large 14-inch diameter) and tightened the body laces slightly. At twenty degrees in the wind I wore thermal underwear and socks, stuffed a shirt into the hood opening and closed the body laces about halfway. A one inch thick foam mattress under the bag provided luxurious cushioning. At one point during the night my foot pressed the bag directly against snow and I awakened with a cold, damp foot, but when I moved the bag back onto the pad my foot dried and warmed up quickly.

The new Trail Tech summer bag uses a more compressable foam which is an inch thick on the bottom, but only half an inch on top; the bag's weight and bulk are more nearly comparable to that of down bags. The foam is fire retardant, the hood is improved, the bag is less rigid and therefore settles around the body, and a full length zipper runs down one side and across the bottom. There is also a winter bag of heavier foam. Trail Tech has improved on the Ocaté design, but Ocaté has also continued to improve.

As the price of down continues to rise, and lighter, more compressable urethane foams are developed, I expect foam to become increasingly more important in the sleeping bag market. In fact, down sleeping bags and jackets, though still superior to their foam counterparts, may well be on the road to eventual obsolescence.

5 COOKING

For a majority of backpackers, wilderness cooking must be classi-fied as work—work which hunger and weariness, darkness and wind, can easily elevate to the level of misery. Comfort in the kitchen often depends on starting dinner while the sun is still high—after a healthy snack to ward off approaching hunger. It certainly depends on the selection of tasty, easy-to-prepare food (discussed in chapter 5). But it also depends to a large extent on carrying good cooking gear and knowing how to use it.

The first decision the cook must face is whether or not to carry a stove. Twenty years ago stoves were eccentric devices used only by serious climbers bivouacked above timberline. Nowadays, they are much less eccentric and commonly used by backpackers. For many years, even when I was climbing, it did not occur to me to carry a stove. Now, I would not think of going off without one. I like a big campfire to sit beside in the evening as much as anyone; I feel deprived if I have to do without one. But the scant wood supply in the high country is fast disappearing and my conscience is easier if I cook on a stove. Firewood has grown so scarce in heavily-traveled areas that wilderness managers may soon ban wood fires altogether and require all parties to carry stoves.

But stoves do more than conserve scarce firewood. They provide dependable, even, controllable heat and a liberation from greasy, soot-blackened pots. (In my pre-stove days I generally re-turned from a weekend trip looking like an overworked chimney-sweep.) The convenience of a stove allows the indulgence of a craving for hot soup at lunch or a cup of tea in mid-afternoon. Instead of digging in the ashes to rebuild a collapsed fireplace, or blackening fresh rocks, one can perch the stove conveniently at waist height on a sheltered ledge or boulder and cook without stooping or squatting. Lastly, there is no fire to feed feverishly, no leaping flames to subdue, no smoke to fight and no fallout of ashes in the tea.

Stoves, of course, have disadvantages too. The small single burner means only one dish at a time can be cooked, and the first course will not stay warm while the next is cooking (except with a cooker). The small concentrated circle of heat makes cooking on large surfaces (frying pancakes or trout) difficult. No stove works well, if at all, if not well sheltered from wind. A shelter must be built if none can be found. Then there is the fiddling with fuel, the assembling priming and preheating, and, of course, the weight of the stove and fuel. But I view the lack of a second burner as a blessing rather than a limitation; it forces me to employ one-dish dinners or eat in courses, which enormously simplifies meal planning and automatically rules out fussy, difficult-to-prepare city-type meals.

A good many backpackers have never purchased a stove because they look so intricate, because they are rumored to explode or simply because the catalogs and shops offer such a bewildering assortment. With as many as two dozen models to choose from, how does one know which is best? The guidelines that follow should reassure the buyer as to intricacy and safety and help him narrow the field to not more than two or three models.

Stoves, first of all, may be divided on the basis of fuels. Kerosene (or coal oil) though slightly less potent, ounce for ounce, than gasoline, is the cheapest, most generally available fuel. It produces more odor and soot than gasoline but it does not explode. Since it is difficult to light without a wick, kerosene stoves normally require a more volatile priming fuel (alcohol, gasoline, etc.) for the necessary pre-heating.

White gasoline or Coleman Fuel, though of maximum potency, is capable of exploding. Unlike kerosene, spilled gasoline lights readily on clothes or hands. Its cost is reasonable, it is generally available, and it tends to be clean smelling, oil-free and produces less soot than kerosene. Preheating is necessary, but since white gas lights readily a separate priming fuel is not required. Though instructions call for 'un-leaded' gas, the modern 'no-lead' and 'low lead' gases contain additives that make them unsuitable for stoves.

Butane and propane are compressed gasses sold in pressurized metal cartridges. The liability of explosion is low providing used cartridges are not thrown in the fire. Both fuels are considerably less potent than kerosene or gasoline, comparatively expensive and the least readily available. But both are clean and soot free. Since butane and propane stoves require no filling, priming or pre-heating, they are unquestionably the easiest and most convenient of backpacking stoves.

Despite a relatively low heat output, alcohol for many years was the traditional stove fuel, due largely to its cheapness and availability in Europe. (Virtually all stoves are of European origin.) But with the development of butane and propane as stove fuels, it has sunk to

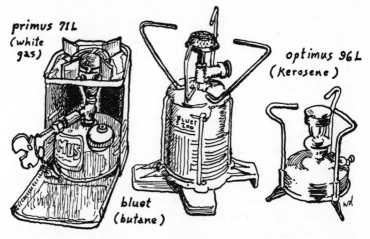

primus 71L
(white
gas)

optimus 96L
(Kerosene)

bluet
(butane)

fourth place and need no longer be considered. Sterno (canned heat), heat tabs, and even candles, can be used to cook food, but these fuels, like alcohol, are too inefficient for serious consideration.

Kerosene and white gasoline stoves work on nearly identical principles; in fact conversion kits are available for some models. Both fuels must reach the burner in a vaporized (gaseous) state before the stove will function properly. Fuel is vaporized as it passes through a heated chamber called a generator located between the fuel tank and the burner. The necessary heating is accomplished by filling a small bowl just beneath the generator (called the spirit cup) with an easily lighted primer fuel (white gas, alcohol, benzene, lighter fluid) and lighting it—with the stove turned off.

Flames envelop the generator for perhaps half a minute to preheat it. Just before the flames die, the operator turns on the gas. If the generator is hot enough, the fuel will vaporize and the vapor will be lighted by the last of the flaming primer. Once the stove is lighted, heat from the burner keeps the generator working.

The process is considerably simpler than it sounds. After an hour's experimentation in the backyard, most purchasers of a new gasoline or kerosene stove will be sufficiently experienced to take it on a trip. Those people unwilling to master the procedure can join the growing thousands who rely on effortlessly-operated butane and propane stoves.

Kerosene expands less than gasoline when heated and therefore all kerosene stoves have small hand pumps to force the fuel to the burner. They do not, however, have valves to control the flow of fuel. Flame height and intensity are controlled solely by pump pressure. Extra pumping keeps the flame at maximum; opening the air vent reduces the pressure and therefore the flame. But a low flame (for simmering or warming) tends to be difficult to maintain.

Kerosene stoves are favored for expeditions because fuel purity is not critical, kerosene is available in almost any country, and the stove will not explode no matter how it is handled. Expeditionary technique circumvents the need for a separate priming fuel by capitalizing on the fact that raw kerosene will light if fed through a wick. A twisted square of toilet paper placed in the kerosene-filled spirit cup provides an easily lighted wick. Kerosene stoves are equipped with either 'silent' or 'roarer' burners; the fiercer flame of the latter is slightly more resistant to wind. In below zero weather, kerosene stoves perform especially well, largely because fuel pressure can be maintained by pumping.

The smaller white gas stoves have no pumps; they depend on the heat transferred from the generator and burner to the fuel tank to expand the highly volatile fuel and force it toward the burner. To provide room for pressure buildup, the tank must never be filled more than three quarters full. With these stoves, pre-heating must accomplish two things: vaporizing the fuel (as in the kerosene stoves) and generating pressure in the fuel tank. Spring-loaded pressure-relief safety valves located in the tank caps protect against explosion, but occasionally are sources of pressure leaks.

Since white gas lights well, neither priming fuel or improvised wicks are required. The manufacturer suggests that, with the vent closed and the valve open, the warmth of one's hands wrapped around the tank will develop enough pressure to force gas out through the burner and down into the spirit cup. Of course, if the stove has been sitting in the sun with the valve open, hand temperature will not warm it and this method fails. Increases in altitude also create pressure which causes the gas to flow; by filling the stove at sea level one is assured of pressure at the first use in the mountains.

The cooling of a stove after use creates a vacuum in the tank. So does a decrease in altitude. The vacuum must be relieved by momentarily loosening the tank cap or the stove cannot function. The surest way to extract gas from the stove to fill the spirit cup under all conditions is with an eye dropper. Plastic droppers from old medicine bottles or the drugstore tuck comfortably in the housing of most stoves. A still quicker method is to put one's mouth to the tank opening and blow.

an eye-
dropper
fills the
spirit cup.

Butane and propane come in pressurized cartridges or tanks. Empties must be carried out, and most butane cartridges must not be disengaged until they are entirely empty. Butane and propane are notoriously poor in exceptional cold, when tank pressure drops to cause sluggish flow and the lower temperature of the flame becomes apparent. Butane is worse than propane, but I have more than once used a Bluet S-200 in the snow, when the temperature was ten degrees below freezing, with perfectly satisfactory results. Lighting butane and propane stoves is no different from lighting a kitchen stove that has no pilot. One simply holds a lighted match to the burner an instant *before* turning on the gas.

For lighting kerosene stoves, the routine goes as follows: (1) open vent in tank cap; (2) fill and light spirit cup to pre-heat stove; (3) just before flames die, close vent in tank cap and, (4) quickly take two or three quick strokes on the pump; (5) if burner fails to ignite from the spirit cup flame, light it with the match set aside for that purpose. If the flame burns blue the stove is ready to use; if it burns yellow—signifying raw fuel rather than vapor—open the vent to shut off the fuel and pre-heat again.

For pumpless gasoline stoves the lighting procedure is slightly different: (1) open, then close, the tank cap to relieve any vacuum in the tank; (2) after closing the shut-off valve, fill the spirit cup and light; (3) just before the flame dies, open the shut-off valve wide— only a quarter turn. (4) If burner fails to ignite from the spirit cup flame, light it with the match held ready for that purpose. If the burner flame is blue the stove is ready to use; if the flame burns yellow, shut off the valve; when flames begin to die, open the valve again and hope for a blue flame. Continue this process until vaporized fuel burns a constant blue.

Stoves may be further divided on the basis of size, weight and heating capacity. Most fall into one of two classifications: 'Backpacker' stoves capable of cooking for one to three people in pots of up to two quarts, and 'Expeditionary' stoves built to handle groups of four or more and heat pots of two to five quarts. Backpacker stoves usually weigh one to two pounds, while Expeditionary models run two to four pounds. Two burner stoves weigh six to twelve pounds.

The number of models to choose from shrinks considerably with the discovery that the Primus, Svea, and Optimus stoves are all made by the same company and are often identical except for name. For instance the Primus (P) 71 is the same, except for label, as the Optimus (O) 80. The dozen stoves listed below are the best, most popular, most readily available I know. There is no 'best' stove. The best choice for any individual depends on the importance he chooses to assign such considerations as weight, convenience, burning time, heating capacity, price, etc. All gasoline stoves listed have safety pressure relief valves to prevent explosion and should be considered safe in the hands of adults familiar with their operation.

BACKPACKER STOVES:

P-71 (O-80). Probably best known and most popular model, this pumpless gasoline stove weighs 20 ounces, burns well over an hour, comes in a rectangular box-stand-windscreen, and costs $9-12.

Bluet S-200. This french butane burner is the easiest, simplest stove to operate, weighing 19 ounces and costing $9-10 (including vital windscreen). Ten ounce cartridges burn 2-3 hours and cost $4-5 per case of six. Not powerful enough for heavy or winter use.

Svea 123. The lightest gasoline stove at 18 ounces, the pumpless Svea comes with tiny pot, gripper and two-piece windscreen for $10-13. Burning time and convenience rate slightly behind the P-71, but wind resistance is better.

P (0) 8R. This newer pumpless gasoline stove offers a self-cleaner, gravity gas feed to the burner and a low center of gravity. Burning time ranks between the P-71 and Svea 123. Comparatively heavy at 27 ounces, the stove costs $12-14.

P (0) 96L. Equipped with a pump, this kerosene stove with silent burner comes in a box and must be assembled for operation. At 32 ounces it is the heaviest, safest, longest burning (2 hours), and the cheapest to operate stove in its class. Cost is $15.

Primus Grasshopper. A 30 ounce propane tank makes the third leg of this easy-to-operate, stable 12 ounce stove. Tanks burn six hours, cost $1.50 each and may be removed when partly full. Stove costs $8-9.

EXPEDITIONARY STOVES:

P (0) 111B. A larger version of the 8R equipped with a pump, this powerful 3½ pound gasoline stove costs $20-22.

P-210L (0-00L). This intermediate-sized kerosene stove with roarer burner is the lightest in its class. Collapsible (meaning assembly is required), it burns two hours, weighs 2¼ pounds and costs $13-15.

P-100 (0-48L). A larger version of the 210L with silent burner, this stove is collapsible, weighs 3¼ pounds, costs $10-14 and burns four hours on a quart filling of kerosene.

Phoebus 625. This powerful Austrian gasoline stove (which can burn leaded as well as white gas) burns 1½ hours, weighs 2¾ pounds and costs $14.

TWO BURNER EXPEDITIONARY STOVES:

O-22B. A two burner version of the 111B with pump and built-in cleaner, this gas burning stove measures 15 inches wide, burns 1½ hours, weighs 6¾ pounds and costs $30.

P-2049 (0-870). There is some variation between the two models of this deluxe, instant lighting propane stove. Both use the same disposable tank as the grasshopper, or any American-made refillable tank. Stoves weigh 9½-11 pounds, cost $34-40.

Gasoline and kerosene stoves require the purchase of either aluminum bottles ($1.50-2.50) or fuel flasks ($2.00-2.50), both of which come in pint and quart sizes. The flat flasks with pouring spouts pack more conveniently, although the mesh screen must be punched out in order to insert a polyethylene funnel which contains its own filter screen (35¢). The bottles are more likely to leak than the flasks. Plastic bottles are not suitable for fuel. Heavy cloth and plastic bags are useful for packing stoves, especially where a box is not included (or has been discarded). Also needed is a rag for cleaning both stove and cook, and the proper stove cleaning needle.

One of the prime disadvantages of stoves—keeping the first course warm while the second is cooking—can be overcome by using one of two cookers made by Sigg. These ingenious five piece combinations, beginning at the bottom and working up, consist of a two piece stand-windscreen, two pans stacked one above the other, and a lid-pan. While a casserole cooks in the bottom pan, the soup, just above it, keeps warm. Or, by filling the lower pan with water, one produces the controlled, even heat of a double boiler above.

The Sigg Tourist, built solely for use with the Svea 123, offers 2½ and 3½ pint pots, nests with the stove inside to measure only 8¼ x 5 inches, weighs 2¼ pounds and costs $18-20. The cooker alone weighs 1½ pounds and costs $10. The Edelweiss Cooker, built for the 71, will also take the Svea and 96L. (The 71 specially made for the cooker is almost an inch shorter than the standard box-mounted model and holds a third less fuel, but I use the standard 71 in both box and cooker without any difficulty.) The Edelweiss comes in three pot sizes: one quart (solo), one and a half quarts (two man) or two quart (expeditionary). In each case, both pots are the same size. With one and a half quart pots and the regular stove, the Cooker weighs two and a half pounds. Cookers are somewhat specialized items and are most valuable in winter (for snow melting), in wind, and for expeditionary use.

The alternative to carrying a stove, of course, is to build one out of native material and gather native fuel to fire it. Ease, efficiency, and effectiveness are generally doubled by carrying a small grill. The

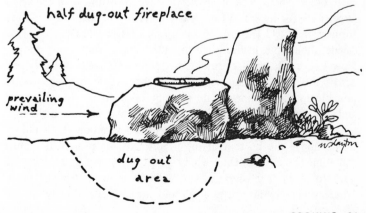

half dug-out fireplace

prevailing wind

dug out area

smallest and lightest, sold by Camp Trails, measures four and a half by fifteen and a half inches, is made of welded tubular steel, weighs only four ounces, cleans easily, comes in a fabric case and costs $6. It is easily mounted on a modest rock fireplace and will accommodate two carefully placed pots.

Still easier to mount on an uneven surface is the Gerry grill, a five by fifteen inch U-shaped stainless steel rod that weighs six ounces and costs $1.75. A conventional nine by thirteen inch steel grill weighs eight ounces, costs $2 and needs a cloth or durable plastic bag for a cover. A Swiss nine by ten inch, one and a quarter pound grill from Co-op, has seven-inch legs, costs only $1.50 and saves blackening rocks.

There are larger grills, some with legs, for expeditionary use, at weights of two pounds and more. The cheapest grills are oven and refrigerator shelves and broiler racks from used appliance and second hand stores. The campcraft books are full of fireplace designs and ingenious ways to suspend pots, most of which are far too much trouble for the backpacker, who is likely to choose a campsite late in the day and move on again in the morning.

My favorite cooking fireplace design is the half-dugout. There are two advantages: smaller, flatter rocks can be used to insure a more stable structure, and the fire is easier to light and easier to protect from wind. If I were faced with rebuilding a heap of blackened rocks into an efficient cookstove—assuming the location is appropriate and safe—I would first clear a circle about four feet across and sort through the rocks in hopes of finding a matched pair about the size and shape of bricks. Such rocks are never to be found, of course, so I settle for the best I can find (concave upper surfaces are better than convex).

Using the direction of the breeze, the lay of the land and the pattern of branches on nearby trees to determine the path of the prevailing wind, I place my rocks parallel to that path and also to each other—about a foot apart. On the downwind end, I place a larger rock (or rocks) to form a chimney, so the resulting structure forms a squat 'U.' Then, using a sharp rock fragment as a trowel, I excavate about four inches of earth and charcoal from inside the pit. Now I am ready to place my lightweight Camp Trails or Gerry grill across the opening, supporting it on the two 'bricks' as close as possible to the chimney. Care must be taken to see that it is solid and will not slide or wobble—or the dinner may end up in the fire!

I like to set my grill about two inches above ground level and six inches above the bottom of the firepit, but the proportions must sometimes be altered. On a windy day, I dig deeper and sometimes have to block the windward end with rocks to control the draft. Where there are no rocks at all and the grill sits directly on the ground, the firepit must be deeper still. Inexperienced stove builders invariably build too large a firebox and set the grill much too high. Increasing grill height from six to ten inches probably triples the volume of wood needed to cook dinner. Small fires are easier on the cook, easier on the wood supply and heat is more easily regulated. Expert backpackers emulate the Indian and try to cook their food with the smallest fire possible.

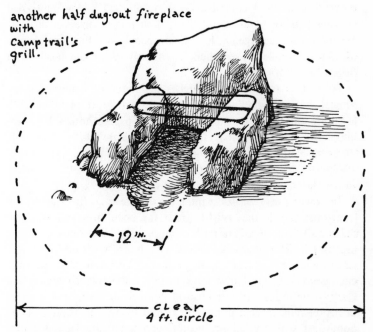

another half dug-out fireplace with Camp trail's grill.

12 IN.

cLear 4 ft. circle

The traditional structures for kindling a camp fire are the lean-to (match-sized twigs leaned against a larger piece) or the tepee (a cone of twigs). The most common mistake among fire builders is not having good quantities of dry twigs, tinder, toilet paper and burnables of all sizes within easy reach before the first match is struck. I usually start with three squares of toilet paper loosely crumpled, cover that with a handful of dry pine needles, then build a tepee of the smallest, lightest twigs by tilting them against the paper from all sides.

After carefully leaning half a dozen finger sized sticks against the pile, I crouch low to block the prevailing breeze (if it is strong, I block the entrance to the fire pit temporarily with rocks) and thrust a lighted kitchen match beneath the paper with one hand while I shelter the match from stray zephyrs with the other. Once the paper is lighted, I add the match to the tepee and use both hands to shelter the embryo blaze until all the wood has caught. Care must be taken not to put the fire out by knocking down the tepee with fresh wood, by skipping the intermediate sized sticks and adding heavy branches, or by letting the tepee burn up before adding fresh wood.

There are differences of opinion, not surprisingly, about matches and lighting fires. Some people carry only paper book matches, others (like myself) take only wooden kitchen matches; wooden safety matches that can only be lighted on the box are a bother in the summer but indispensable in the winter when snow covers the rocks. I have used commercially waterproofed and windproofed matches and found them excellent, though expensive, for difficult conditions and emergency kits. Some people dip their matches in parafin or candle wax; others laboriously paint the heads with fingernail polish.

Still others carry all their matches in waterproof matchboxes. My simpler, but probably less secure strategy is to stuff lots of matches in all the waterproof outside pockets of my pack. Another dozen are inside my watertight first aid kit. The climate of the California summer Sierra does not seem to me to demand a waterproof matchbox, and I have never carried one. A handfull in a securely closed plastic bag makes a decent enough emergency supply.

In wet country or for winter mountaineering, fire starters are sometimes worth the weight (both for open fires and kerosene stoves). I like 'Fire Starter,' made by the Bernzomatic Corp., because the styrofoam-like sheets are almost weightless, crumble into any size and pack easily in plastic bags. A seven ounce package costs sixty cents. I know some people who disdain matches and carry cigarette lighters and a can of fluid, giving their tinder a squirt of lighter fluid to help things along. And I travel the deserts of the Southwest with an old prospector who habitually kicks together some brush and wood, douses it with a cup full of gasoline, and nonchalantly tosses a lighted match over his shoulder as he walks away.

Twenty years ago, a friend and I assembled a backpacking cook kit very simply. From the pots and pans bin at the Goodwill Store, we first selected the smallest practical aluminum pot (about three cups) and found a lid. Then we hunted down two more pots and lids so that the three would nest with the lids on. At home we sawed off the handles, punched holes and added wire bails, then we fitted a drawstring into a flour sack to hold the kit. For frying we bought a twelve inch square of eighth inch sheet aluminum and turned up the edges slightly in a vise to form a lip. Our set was completed with aluminum pliers, aluminum pie tins, aluminum measuring cups (with the handles taped) and Goodwill silverware.

At that time it was impossible to buy a comparable kit in mountaineering shops at any price. Today there are a number of good cook kits on the market for small groups and a variety of good pots, pans and kettles. But thoughtful backpackers will still be well advised to devise combinations suited to the particular requirements of their menus. And the Goodwill stores and supermarkets still offer bargains and a variety not to be found in mountaineering shops.

Ideal pot design depends somewhat on whether a stove or open fire is to be used. For stoves, pots need small, perfectly flat bottoms of small diameter for maximum stability. The thicker the bottom the less likely that the small concentration of heat will cause scorching or burning. Heat is not a problem at the handle, bail or lid. Pots for an open fire can be any shape and uneven on the bottom, but lids should be easily removed and handles or bails must be usable when flames envelop them. All pots should have rounded edges and no grooves or seams or cracks to trap food and dirt.

Tin cans, or billycan, for this reason, are poor except for making tea. The most popular pots, often called Scout Kettles, are made by Sigg of grooveless spun aluminum. They offer three quarter inch wide bails that lock in place for easy pouring, a handle bracket and tight-fitting lids shaped to double as plates or pans. They come in 2½, 3½, 5¼, 7 and 8¾ pint sizes (which nest) and are widely available at prices ranging from $3.50 to $7 each.

Since I rarely use the lids for cooking, but find them impossible to lift with any gripper, I fit mine with a knob by drilling a hole and running a half inch long bolt from the inside to a pair of easily gripped nuts on the outside. Smilie makes an excellent selection of six aluminum pots ranging from 1-14 quarts and $5-10. Other good pots are available in limited sizes and in various combination cook kits.

sigg pot lids lift off easily when fitted with homemade Knobs.

Mixing pans are a luxury that backpackers must forego. Properly planned menus avoid nearly all special mixing of ingredients; and unavoidable mixing should be easily managed in deep plates, large cups, pan lids, plastic bottles and polyethylene bags.

Frying pans or griddles are a nuisance for the backpacker because they require a wood fire which blackens them and thus require a heavy cloth or plastic case. Decent frying pans and griddles are not light because heavy guage metal is needed to evenly spread the heat and prevent burning. Steel is better than aluminum, which in turn is better than magnesium; and cast iron, though prohibitively heavy, is best of all. Since flapjacks and even bacon and eggs are fast disappearing from the efficient backpacker's breakfast menu, frying pans are most often taken for trout. The best compromise for the backpacker is a shallow eight or nine inch pan of thin steel or thicker aluminum, with either a ridged or waffled interior to spread heat, or a Teflon coating to prevent sticking. Pans of these three types, with folding or removable wire handles (superior to fixed handles or the use of tongs) weigh 15-25 ounces and cost $2.50-7.00.

After making coffee or tea for many years in whatever pot was available, it dawned on me that I could do a far better job and leave one pot at home (not to mention avoiding a scum of grease from the soup) by carrying a real teapot. Efficient, compact, versatile teapots are not easily found in mountaineering shops and catalogs. Often enough, they cannot be bought separately from large complete cook kits. There are basically two styles: the (American) billycan with lid and creased lip for pouring, or the squat (European) tank type teapot with smaller lid and stubby pouring spout. Although both double as pots and the American design nests and packs better, I prefer the European model. Co-op makes a good one with a seven inch diameter, three inch depth and 1½ quart capacity for $2. Supermarkets and import stores also offer a variety of light aluminum (Japanese) teapots.

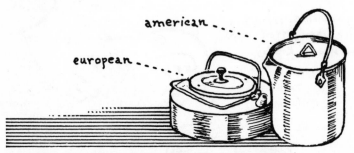

a tea or coffee pot is the ideal 'second pot'.

People who are deeply attached to certain dishes, or who genuinely like to prepare fancy meals, are often obliged to carry additional equipment, like ovens, toasters and pressure cookers. Fresh bread, biscuits, gingerbread and cake are extremely welcome in the wilds, more so after a week of dried foods. A flat-folding reflector oven of sheet aluminum capable of accommodating a ten inch pan weighs 2½

foil .... pie pan oven .... hot coals

office clamps ..... pie pans

pounds and costs $7 at Co-op. Though its use requires more experimentation and fiddling, an oven made from two aluminum pie pans fastened together with two spring stationary clamps and suspended over a bed of coals is far lighter and cheaper and nearly as effective. Coals must also be spread on the top pan and covered with a piece of aluminum foil.

Bread tends to dry out and squash and is therefore not taken in great quantity by most backpackers, but for those who carry it and are addicted to toast, a toaster may be rationalized as necessary. The somewhat crude boy scout or hobo method of toasting is simply to bend a slice of bread and skewer it with a sharpened stick of green willow. A grill or grate works well over coals, and a frying pan or skillet produces fried toast readily. So does aluminum foil. But the connoiseur of toast will demand a five ounce folding wire and aluminum toaster that works on stove or fire and costs around 50¢.

For backpackers determined to cook beans or a good many other raw foods at high altitude, a pressure cooker becomes a necessity. Though the trend is toward pre-cooked and freeze-dried foods, there are situations and places when it is not available. Cooking time can be cut in half with English-made four and five quart 3-4 pound aluminum cookers from Co-op which cost $14 and $18.

Eating and cooking utensil requirements range all the way from the couple who carry a single large spoon and jacknife between them to parties in which each person has his own knife, fork and spoon, wears a sheathknife, and carries additional utensils for the cook. Obviously, the larger the party, the more cooking gear required. Knife, fork and spoon sets of stainless steel and aluminum are widely available for from 50¢ to $2.50. Old kitchen silverware or Goodwill or dimestore offerings weigh slightly more but are easier to handle.

Most experienced backpackers using easily prepared dishes forget about table knives and forks and carry only an extra-large spoon apiece and a good-sized simple pocketknife. In addition, the cook needs an aluminum soup ladle with detachable insulated handle (Co-op, 50¢) for cleanliness and to insure an equitable division of the stew. I sometimes carry a large extremely useful hinged aluminum fork-spoon combination; other times I combine ladle and spoon in one huge (11 inch) solid nylon spoon that weighs one ounce and costs 50¢.

A knife is an absolute necessity in the wilds. Some hikers are not secure without a sheath knife, and though these commonly weigh a heavy half pound, one per party is often useful. The smallest sizes are well worthwhile. Swiss army knives with their endless assortment of gadgety blades also have their adherents. But thoughtful, weight conscious backpackers usually prefer a good-sized, good quality pocketknife with one or two blades. The knife I like best has a big, comparatively blunt tipped blade suitable for spreading crackers and cutting salami—and a shorter, slimmer sharply pointed blade for cleaning trout. Brightly colored handles help prevent loss. If I am traveling alone, I put a tiny single bladed jacknife in the outside pack pocket containing the first aid kit.

my best knife

Pot grippers or tongs or pliers may be needed to lift lids and serve as pot handles. Aluminum pot grippers weigh little more than an ounce and cost about 50¢, but the handle is too short for an open fire and the lack of a spring makes operation awkward. Longer, stronger spring-loaded steel grippers of similar design weigh a quarter of a pound. Neither fits all pots. I prefer cast aluminum hot pot tongs (3 ounces, $1.25) which, being a large pair of pliers, is a more versatile tool. Many people find an old padded cloth pot holder indispensable.

Can openers should not be needed if canned food is left at home, but a good many of us, after many weight-saving economies, like to take along some canned luxury like sliced apricots in heavy syrup. Besides, the army can opener (now being replaced by a slightly heavier, more expensive and breakable commercial model) costs only a dime and weighs an eighth of an ounce. The remaining principal kitchen tools are spatulas, forks, mixing and stirring spoons, and water dippers. Nylon spatulas though subject to fire damage are light, cheap and needed for teflon pans.

Every backpacker needs a cup, and the more experienced choose large ones and dispense with plates. The traditional pie pan, whether of steel, aluminum or foil, cools too quickly, is hard to hold and a nuisance to clean. Pan lids offer the same disadvantages and paper plates, though cleaning is eliminated, are more difficult to hold and do not retain heat. Of course a big cup cannot satisfactorily replace a plate for a city-style meal, and strangers to backpacking may view the lack of a plate as uncivilized and crude, but eating from a cup happens to be eminently practical and efficient for a dinner which proceeds by courses from two cups of soup to two cups of stew to a cup of applesauce or pudding and finally to many cups of tea, coffee, lemonade or water. The cup needs only to be wiped and rinsed clean between courses. I always carry a one ounce aluminum measuring cup as a spare and for mixing.

Using a cup for a plate is especially appropriate when cooking on a stove, because dinner (or any other meal) is only ready one course at a time. Since food cooked at high altitude never reaches temperatures common at sea level, and since it cools with amazing speed in even the warmest breeze, this arrangement is the most effective for getting hot food to the stomach before it can cool. Cup-style eating may be difficult to appreciate until one has labored long and hard to prepare three dishes simultaneously on a wood fire, then discovered with the first bite that the plate and all its contents were stone cold.

In the west, where the influence of the Sierra Club is strongest, the Sierra (or Sierra Club) cup has become an object of worship to some, and consequently an object of scorn to others. This wide-mouthed, nesting, stainless steel cup holds 12 ounces and weighs 3 ounces. The wire handle which hooks to the belt, stays cool enough to hold when the cup is filled with boiling tea. Cost is $1. Though the Sierra Club cup's virtues are undeniable, I prefer a 12 ounce capacity plastic cup which costs 20¢, weighs only 1½ ounces, retains food heat better, cleans more easily and, when the bottom of the handle is cut, snaps more securely to a belt or nylon line.

For backpackers not yet ready to eat from their cups—or who cannot abide an oily film from the stew in their tea—a small, deep, unbreakable, boilable polyethylene bowl (25¢, 1½ ounces) is a greatly superior alternative to metal or paper plates.

When it comes to food storage, plastic bottles, bags, boxes, canisters and jars have all but replaced containers of all other materials. Many containers are so commonly available in markets that some mountaineering shops no longer bother to stock them. I make a habit of cruising the kitchenware sections of supermarkets to hunt for merchandise adaptable to backpacking.

In choosing plastic containers, I shun all but screw-on caps likely to form a watertight seal and avoid corners and recessed seams that will trap food and be hard to clean. And I buy wide-mouthed containers whenever there is a choice. Most big mountaineering suppliers offer small and wide mouth pint and quart bottles as well as a variety of small ones. The same is true of wide-mouthed jars, although markets tend to be a more dependable source. Some of my best containers are recycled. When I spot an unusual bottle around the house, I wait until it is empty and then boil it out and add it to my collection.

Refillable squeeze tubes, made by Gerry (3 for $1.25) are invaluable for leakproof, easy dispensing of jam, jelly, catsup, butter, peanut butter—anything of similar consistency. I regularly half-fill two with about a quarter pound each of jelly and jam for use on crackers at lunch. The tubes boil out easily between trips and have yet to leak when properly assembled.

I use a squat, wide-mouth screw-top icebox jar of appropriate capacity (they come in half a dozen sizes) for sugar because it fills easily, is hard to overturn, and because I spoon rather than pour my sugar. Many people who like to pour their sugar and do not object to filling with a funnel, prefer a small-mouthed bottle. Powdered milk presents a more difficult problem. When the wind is blowing the only way to avoid considerable spillage is to squirt the powder from a plastic catsup squirter bottle (available at large supermarkets) directly into the cup.

My squirter holds enough to make a quart; the only positive cap I have found for the spout—to withstand the pressures inside a cinched down pack—is a plug made from a wooden match inserted from the inside. Milkman and other brands come in flat, foil-lined quart packages which are themselves so handy that I carry them as refills for the squirter; in fact I often use them as dispensers by tearing off a small corner and keeping the opened package in a plastic bag.

tube & clip for carrying jam or honey

Salt and pepper shakers come in half a dozen clever designs that weigh ½ to 1½ ounces and cost 25¢ to $2 at mountain shops. The most popular are an aluminum divided cylinder with screw-on caps at each end, and a more easily operated transparent plastic model with flip-top caps that has side-by-side compartments that both dispense at the top. Unfortunately, all shakers hold enough for only 2-3 days for 2-3 persons. Salt companies now offer a variety of pre-filled plastic and cardboard shakers which are handy and safe if carried in plastic bags. For many years, I carried an old tin spice can filled with a mixture of three parts salt and one each of pepper, onion, garlic and celery salts. It is still my favorite shaker.

For carrying butter and cheese—an important part of my food supply—I still, out of habit, use aluminum provision cans: squat cylinders containing plastic inserts and gasketed, hermetically sealing inner lids. Available at many mountain shops in four sizes weighing 2-7 ounces and costing $1.50-2.50, they offer greater protection than squeeze tubes and many plastic jars.

For backpackers who insist on carrying individual fresh eggs, 2, 4, 6 and 12 egg plastic containers weighing 1-6 ounces are available at most shops for from 50¢ to $1.50. Fresh eggs are more compactly carried, where measuring is not a problem, by breaking them into a doubled plastic bag which is sealed to exclude air and packed into a suitably sized, wide-mouthed jar.

For larger parties or where water is scarce, collapsible jugs and bags are extremely convenient. They range in capacity from 1-5 gallons and weigh as little as 7 ounces for a 2½ gallon bag. Five quart jugs weigh 4 ounces and cost about $1.50. They roll up or press flat, and eventually they spring leaks, but if I am planning a dry camp on a ridge I carry a collapsible jug to fill at the highest water.

Though the quart bottle I carry for making lemonade doubles as a canteen in wet country, where water is scarce and must continually be carried, the one quart, rigid plastic Oasis canteen with belt clip and attached metal cap, is excellent, although the $2.50 price is more than double that of my poly bottle. Flat plastic flasks for 'sportsmen' come in various sizes, but I often use a reclaimed vitamin pill bottle to carry 4 ounces of brandy.

To keep containerless stoves and fire blackened pots from spreading soot in one's pack means storing them in bags. Even very heavy plastic does not do nearly as well as cloth. The best are of closely woven and paraffined cotton or urethane coated nylon, with drawstrings and square bottoms. Cost runs from 50¢ to $2.50 for sturdy washable bags that will last. Standards of cleanliness vary in the woods, but are dependably lower than at home. Kitchenware must be washed daily to prevent the formation of bacteria that can cause debilitating stomach illness. A few people scrupulously boil everything in soapy water after every meal; many only scrape out pots and pans and rinse in cold water—and cross their fingers.

My procedure lies somewhere in between. For a short 2-3 man trip, I carry a 4-inch square abrasive scouring cloth and a 3-inch square sponge backed with emery cloth. Both are soapless. Completing my kit are a vial of liquid bio-degradable soap—which is incredibly effective at cleaning skin as well as pots—and a clean diaper or small absorbent hand towel. Old threadbare towels are inefficient. I also carry large, heavy duty garbage bags, which I double for carrying out trash.

After scraping the food from a dirty stew pot with my big spoon, I rinse and throw the food scraps into the bushes well back from lake or stream to avoid unsightly pollution. Then I pour half a cup of hot water from the teapot and add 2-3 drops of bio-degradable soap. After scrubbing with the scouring cloth and/or sponge, I rinse with cold water and set the pot upside down to dry in the sun and breeze. Fire blackened pots are best wiped with wet paper towels, rinsed and allowed to dry before being packed away in individual plastic or cloth bags. Pots rubbed with soap before being put on the fire are comparatively easy to clean.

Cooking, for the majority, may never rival good eating as a source of pleasure, but proper gear, good technique and considerable planning can keep it from becoming a miserable chore.

6 FOOD

Backpackers, like armies, travel on their stomachs. Food can make or break a trip. Most seasoned backpackers can recall trying to read complicated recipes by flashlight while nursing a smoky fire after an exhausting day; or endlessly chewing cold and tasteless food in the dark. Even with the marvelous foods now available, mealtime for many people means tepid, unappetizing dishes that yield neither energy nor satisfaction. One of the principal causes of this grief is the impulsive but mistaken attempt to reproduce meals in the wilds that look, taste and nourish like those we are accustomed to enjoying in the city. Manufacturers of mountaineering foods are partly to blame.

To eat well and happily in the wilds, one must set aside the rigid and ritualized habits of urban eating (like the stricture to eat three square meals and not to snack between them) and adopt, instead, an entirely different set of rules. For instance, the principal purpose of wilderness eating is to keep the body fueled and fortified and capable of sustained effort. Energy production, ease of preparation and lightness of weight must all take precedence over flavor. Actually, a thick hot dehydrated stew at the end of a strenuous day often tastes better than a juicy steak in the city.

A backpacker's tastes usually change in the wilds. The body's needs are altered by heavy exertion and prolonged exposure to the elements, and these needs frequently are reflected in cravings for carbohydrates and liquids and a disinterest in other foods (like fats, meat and vegetables).

Individual meals lose much of their significance. To keep the body continuously fueled, the backpacker should eat, or at least nibble, almost constantly. Many snacks and small meals provide better food digestion, which means better utilization and energy production, than several large meals. A backpacker who makes it a rule not to let an hour pass without eating a little something will enjoy more energy and less weariness and hunger.

I start nibbling soon after breakfast if I am hiking, and on a long day I eat two lunches, one before noon and another in mid-afternoon. Some hikers I know go one step farther: to avoid the bother of fixing meals, they dispense with them altogether, eating every hour and fixing a larger snack (or a hot one) when they feel the need.

A hiker living outdoors in a dry climate should drink at least as often as he eats. Since his body may easily lose a gallon of fluid in a day, and since the dehydrated food he eats will absorb additional moisture, a backpacker can scarcely drink too much—provided he takes only a little at a time. Severe dehydration results if most of the lost fluids are not replaced every day. Although I sip from every brook I pass, and drink with every meal, I often consume another quart of water, tea or lemonade between dinner and bedtime. Since water loss means salt loss, backpackers benefit by salting their foods liberally and taking salt tablets if water loss is extreme or if nausea, aches or cramps signal a salt deficiency.

Every experienced backpacker knows that hot food must be cooked, served and eaten one course at a time, if it is going to reach the stomach before turning cold. Nevertheless, it is a common sight to see frantic cooks trying desperately to serve two hot dishes simultaneously and equally frantic eaters trying to finish them before they get cold. Where exertion is great or the climate cold, hot—really hot—food is psycologically important.

Veteran backpackers usually rely on a pot of steaming soup for dinner, followed after an interval by an equally hot one-pot dinner that can best be described as stew. In warm weather, food preparation can be reduced by curtailing cooking. More than a few backpackers avoid cooking altogether, especially on short trips. They find the saving in time, labor and weight (stove, grill, pots) more than makes up for the absence of hot food.

A truly varied diet in the wilds is usually a luxury. But the ingenious backpacker can increase his variety by the clever use of spices. The latest pre-cooked freeze-dried dinners by Oregon Freeze Dry and others make it possible to dine differently each night with a reduction rather than an increase in preparation.

The importance of easy preparation can scarcely be over-emphasized. After a long hard day the weary, starving backpacker cooking over an open fire on the ground, perhaps in the cold and wind and dark, needs all the help he can get. Steps that seem trivial in the city kitchen become difficult operations under wilderness conditions. In the wind, cooked food may be five times as hard to prepare as uncooked food. A recipe that calls for milk may be twice the work of one that requires water. At high altitude, raw dehydrated food might take ten times as long to cook as a pre-cooked, freeze-dried dish.

Many of the dishes offered specifically for backpacking in mountaineering shops, while perfectly good to eat, are patterned after city meals and require an unreasonable amount of preparation. If the directions run more than a sentence, or if more than one pot is required, I quickly lose interest. Two dishes designed to be eaten at the same time I pass over quickly. Dinners with low calorie yield are also rejected. Packages that contain three or four separate containers do not interest me.

simple directions on the package mean easy preparation in camp.

Despite my disappointment in some of them, backpacking foods form the nucleus of my diet. But the shopper who knows what he is looking for can find a growing number of ideal foods in supermarkets, health food stores and Oriental markets. And the return of interest in organic foods is a boon to backpackers. It is possible (at least in Berkeley), to completely provision a backpacking larder without recourse to mountaineering shops, at no great sacrifice in quality and at significant saving in cost per meal.

Since backpacking is one of the more strenuous activities and since it is sustained for days and weeks at a time (usually without shelter, often in the cold) it is hardly surprising that the body's fuel intake must increase significantly in order to keep up with the increased energy output. The body's energy requirements and the energy production of food are both measured in calories. It takes twice as many calories to walk on a smooth level surface at sea level at 3 mph as it does to walk at 2 mph. And it takes more than twice as many calories to walk at 2 mph as it does to sit quietly in an office. Walking at 4 mph takes nearly twice the calories of a 3 mph pace. And it takes 2½ times as many calories to gain a thousand feet of elevation as it does to walk at 2 mph on the level for an hour. Rough terrain, cross-country travel and the weight of a pack increase the caloric requirements considerably.

A variety of studies have shown that—depending on innumerable factors involving distance covered, terrain and the weight of the individual—it takes somewhere from 3000 to 4500 calories a day to keep a backpacker properly fueled. Long distance hauling of heavy loads, or climbing, may require 5000 calories, or more. Leisurely family trips may burn only 3000. For those who wish to compute the energy content of their menus, 4000 calories a day should be adequate. By comparison, the U.S. Army allows 3500 a day for semi-sedentary garrison duty and 4500 for strenuous work.

Backpackers who take in fewer calories than their systems need will find that the body compensates by burning fat to produce energy. Stored fat is efficiently converted to fuel at the rate of 4100 calories per pound. The backpacker who burns 4000 calories, but takes in only 3590 (410 fewer), will theoretically make up the difference by burning a tenth of a pound of body fat, although individuals vary widely where fat conversion is concerned.

Backpackers unused to strenuous exercise will usually lose weight, but probably not from lack of caloric energy. Exposure to the elements results in water loss, and the change from the high bulk diet of civilization to low bulk dehydrated foods tends to shrink the stomach. For most people, a little hunger and a loss of weight is beneficial to health and need not be construed as the first signs of malnutrition—as long as energy levels remain ample.

An understanding of the caloric yield of various food is necessary, if only to avoid overeating. There is a tendency, even among experienced backpackers, to eat until they feel full, forgetting that concentrated low-bulk foods yield far more power than a high bulk city diet. It is common to see a hungry hiker eat up two days' supply of the community lunch at one sitting, because he knows he needs fuel and because he is accustomed (in the city) to eating until he is full.

To avoid depleting the larder, it is often a good idea to separately package each day's lunch. Eating concentrated food until the stomach is full often causes nausea and cramps. If the food is dehydrated and insufficient liquid is supplied, bloating and dehydration will result as the food absorbs moisture from the body. The backpacker must exercise restraint, have confidence in the caloric production of his food and remember that the semi-empty feeling in the stomach. after eating reflects a healthy lack of bulk, not a dangerous lack of fuel.

It goes without saying that food must be light and resistant to spoilage in any kind of weather. Weight and bulk can usually be saved by repackaging food into plastic bags and jars. Menus can be devised that provide the needed 3500-4500 calories per day at weights of anywhere from 1½ to 2½ pounds per day per person. Averages are only reliable for parties of four for a minimum of a week. Two people on a three day trip can (and usually will) carry half again as much.

The most desirable foods on the basis of low water content are freeze-dried and dehydrated (usually 3-5% water) and air or sulphur dried (as much as 25% water). Food packed in glass or tin cans—quite apart from the weight and liability of the containers—is seldom worth carrying, even if repackaged, due to its high water content and vulnerability to spoilage.

Food is divided into three major components: fats, proteins and carbohydrates, all of which are essential to the backpacker's diet. The ideal proportions are essentially unknown and vary according to the temperature, individual, environment and type of activity—but a rule of thumb suggests that caloric intake be roughly 50% carbohydrates, 25-30% protein and 20-25% fats. There is a myth that the more strenuous the activity the greater the protein need, and many backpackers go to great lengths to load their diets with the common proteins: meat, cheese, milk and eggs.

Actually, protein requirements are unaffected by activity. Excess protein can be a liability in that it is comparatively difficult and slow to digest. Large intakes are poorly assimilated and provide no immediate energy. Furthermore, protein at 1800 calories per pound provides less than half the energy per pound of fat (4100). Most protein-happy hikers would do better to switch their enthusiasm to fat, in which they probably are deficient.

Fats are no easier to digest than proteins, but they supply more than twice the energy and release it gradually over a long period of time. The principal fat sources for backpackers are oil, butter, margarine, nuts, meat fat and cheese. The digestion of protein and fat demands the full attention of the body's resources for a considerable period of time. Consumption should be limited to small amounts at any one time, i.e., intake should be spread through breakfast, lunch and snacks rather than being concentrated in a heavy dinner. Even relatively small amounts should not be eaten before or during strenuous exercise. The blood cannot be expected to circulate rapidly through exercising muscles and digest complex food in the stomach at the same time without failing at one function or the other.

Carbohydrates may conveniently be thought of as pure energy. Digestion is rapid, undemanding and efficient and the energy is released within minutes of consumption. But fast energy release means that carbohydrates are completely exhausted of their power in as little as an hour, and more must be ingested if the energy level is to be maintained. The backpacker who lives on carbohydrates must eat almost continuously to avoid running out of fuel.

Since trail snacks and lunches tend to be chiefly carbohydrates, it is not a sign of gluttony to eat all day long. Or as *Freedom of the*

Hills aptly puts it "As soon as breakfast is completed the climber commences lunch, which he continues to eat as long as he is awake, stopping briefly for supper." The nature of carbohydrate digestion makes clear why fats (for slow efficient energy release) and proteins (for constant body repair and rebuilding) are necessary to balance the backpacker's diet. The common sources of carbohydrate are cereals, fruits, sugar, starches and candy.

With the exception of victamin C (which is a natural antibiotic and prevents infection and is best taken in pill form), vitamins and minerals can usually be forgotten since they are provided in adequate quantity by any reasonably balanced diet. Even though storage is comparatively small, there would be virtually no effect on the body for at least a month if vitamins and minerals were absent.

In recent years, there has been considerable study and experimentation in an effort to produce maximum work capacity in climbers, backpackers and cross-country skiiers. Dr. Per-Olof Astrand (*Nutrition Today,* June 1968) suggests that work capacity can be increased as much as 300% by careful dietary preparation. His studies show that a carbohydrate-rich diet several days in advance of heavy prolonged exercise greatly improves the body's respiratory quotient (oxygen supply) and thereby improves capacity for prolonged hard work. (Utilization of carbohydrate depends on the rate at which oxygen is supplied to working muscles.)

The most startling increase in work capacity, however, comes from emptying the body's store of glycogen about a week in advance, then building up a fresh store just a few days before the trip. Glycogen is a starch normally stored in the body in small quantities. It can be quickly converted into glucose to answer sudden energy demands upon the body.

The higher the body's glycogen content, the greater its work capacity. By flushing the glycogen from the system a week ahead of time by heavy prolonged exercise, and keeping it low with rest and a carbohydrate-free diet for four days before building it up again with a heavy dose of carbohydrates, a substantially higher level of gly-

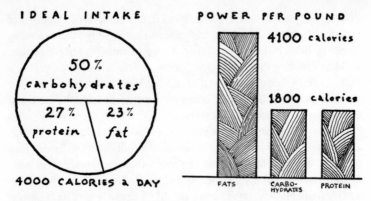

IDEAL INTAKE

50%
carbohydrates
27%
protein
23%
fat

4000 CALORIES a DAY

POWER PER POUND

4100 calories

1800 calories

FATS   CARBO-   PROTEIN
         HYDRATES

cogen storage is achieved and work capacity is therefore greatly increased.

Dr. Astrand found that a man who could do one hour of heavy work on a fat-protein diet could do two and a half hours of the same work after that diet had been heavily supplemented with carbohydrates for three days. When the man flushed the glycogen from his system a week in advance and followed the same diet, he was able to produce up to four hours of work.

So the backpacker who wishes to start a trip on Sunday with the greatest possible capacity for prolonged exertion should, the Sunday before, load up a pack and take a practice hike that thoroughly tires him out. Then on Sunday, Monday and Tuesday he should eat fat and protein exclusively to keep his glycogen down—avoiding carbohydrates—get plenty of sleep and limit his exercise to a walk around the block. On Wednesday, Thursday, Friday and Saturday he should gorge on carbohydrates while continuing to consume ample protein and fat. On Sunday he should be admirably prepared for the most strenuous hike.

To prepare menus—both before and during a trip—the backpacker obviously needs to be able to evaluate any given food in terms of water content, caloric yield, and relative proportions of protein, fat and carbohydrate. The figures in this chapter—as well as those found in *Freedom of the Hills* and most other books—are compiled from Agriculture Handbook No. 8, entitled *Composition of Foods* (available from the U.S. Government Printing Office, Washington, D.C. 20402 for $1.50).

For each of the thousands of foods that are listed the number of calories per pound or per 100 grams (equal to 3½ ounces) is given, as well as a precentage breakdown into water, protein, fat, carbohydrates, vitamins and minerals. Food combinations like Birchermuesli are not listed and cannot be computed accurately, and brand names have been excluded, but it is possible to estimate the quantity and types of fuel contained in most backpacking foods with reasonable accuracy. I like to browse the book in hopes of finding unconventional foods that might be appropriate for the trail and to check out favorite dishes. Any calorie counter or backpacker interested in getting more power per ounce will find it a good investment.

Even for the veteran backpacker, food planning must be taken seriously if the menu is to provide plenty of calories, light weight, a good balance between fat, protein and carbohydrate, maximum ease of preparation, and no waste, spoilage or surplus. Beginning backpackers will find it easy to spend many hours in menu planning, shopping and packaging for the simplest trip. But the alternatives—unappetizing meals, complicated preparation, insufficient fuel, hunger, heavy loads, etc.—make all the preparation worthwhile. And gradually, as proficiency grows, the task becomes easier.

In order to profit from each trip, before I leave I list all the foods I am taking and their weights or amounts. Then, immediately after I return, I note on the list after each entry: (1) how much I brought home, (2) how much more I should have taken, (3) foods to be forgotten, and (4) unfilled cravings or needs. Such a list becomes invaluable in planning food for the next trip.

Food planners should be able to make distinctions between food requirements for different types of trips. There is no satisfactory all-purpose menu. For instance, when I go on an easy, leisurely trip with my wife, daughter and St. Bernard, we take a greater variety of foods and worry less about preparation: we are likely, for instance, to carry lemons and a frying pan for trout, more and softer bread, popcorn, avocados, and so on.

If I am going on a cross-country ridge walk with a friend, foods are chosen for the energy they provide and ease of preparation. Variety is forgotten. The food list that follows lies somewhere in between. Weight is not as criticial for four days as it is for two weeks, but must still be watched carefully where, as in this case, the hikers expect to cover about thirty miles, move every day and travel cross-country as well as by trail at relatively high elevation in the California Sierra. Four days should lie close to the length of the average recreational backpacking trip.

It has been the habit of a good many writers on backpacking to dismiss or scarcely mention freeze-dried foods because of their expense. In my view, backpacking is so inexpensive as vacations go, and freeze-dried food so cheap when compared with restaurant meals, that its slightly greater expense is hardly worth considering. Backpackers spend such a relatively short time in the wilds (during which they would have to eat anyway) that to skimp on quality seems foolish. I have spared no expense in the food list that follows, yet the cost per man per day is $3.83—less than the price of dinner in a modest city restaurant.

PLEASURE PACKING FOOD LIST
(2 men for 4 days)

Brand	Quantity–Item–Packaging–Serving	Wt. (in ounces) Packaged for carrying	Total Cost
Tea Kettle	(1)Beef Almondine–foil pan–serves 2	4.1	$1.25
Tea Kettle	(1)Tuna a la Neptune–foil pan–serves 2	4.4	1.50
Tea Kettle	(1)Turkey Tetrazzini-foil pan–serves 2	4.0	1.25
Tea Kettle	(1)Chunk Chicken–foil pan–serves 2	4.5	1.50
Co-op	(2)Sliced Mushrooms–poly bag–serves 2	0.6	1.10
Maggi	(1)Oxtail Soupmix–foil bag–serves 2	3.0	.30
Maggi	(1)Mushroom Soupmix–foil bag–serves 2	2.7	.30
Knorr	(1)Leek Soupmix–poly bag–serves 2	3.5	.40
Knorr	(1)Green Pea Soupmix–poly bag–serves 2	3.6	.40
Richmoor	(1)Cottage Cheese–poly bag–serves 4	3.1	.95
Richmoor	(2)Applesauce–poly bag–serves 4	9.2	1.20
Richmoor	(2)Fruit Cocktail–poly bag–serves 4	12.2	1.80
Mtn. House	(1)Strawberries–foil bag–serves 4	1.2	1.00
Mtn. House	(1)Ice Cream–foil bag–serves 4	2.1	1.10
–	1 lb. Butter–alum. can	18.0	.85
Familia	¾ of 2 lb. box–Birchermeusli–poly bags	24.3	1.50
Wilsons	(2)Bacon Bar–foil bag	6.4	2.20
–	2 lb. loaf Pumpernickle bread–poly bags	32.3	.85
–	Gorp–poly bags: 1/3 dry raisins 1/3 salted almonds 1/3 M & M's	32.3	1.50
Atkinsons	1½ bars–Mint Bar–poly bag	9.1	.75
Atkinsons	1½ bars–Rum Butter Candy–poly bag	9.1	.75
–	Cheese–alum. can–Gouda ¾ lb. –Cheddar ¾ lb.	26.0	1.25
–	Salt & pepper mix–metal shaker	2.0	.50
	Spice mix–metal shaker	2.0	.40
Milkman	1 qt. pkg.–Instant Low-fat Dry Milk– poly squeeze bottle	4.5	.25
–	Sugar-poly bottle	9.0	.25
Wylers	(6)Lemonade Mix–foil bags	19.8	.90
–	(12)Tea bags–English & Oriental– alum. can	1.5	.50
Richmoor	(1)Toasted Coconut Pudding–poly bag– serves 4	5.7	.50
–	Trout mix–poly bag	2.0	.25
–	Strawberry jam-squeeze bottle	8.4	.40
–	8 sticks Beef jerky–poly bag	4.2	2.15
–	8 dried pineapple rings–poly bag	8.0	.85
		282.8 *	$30.65

*Total food weight includes 17 ounces of packaging.

Although I cannot make an accurate assessment of the combinations of foods that make up the bulk of my dinners and breakfasts, I am confident that the energy produced by this menu is comfortably in excess of 4000 calories per man per day, with a balance of

approximately 25% fat, 25% protein and 50% carbohydrate. The weight is barely over two pounds per day per man, nearly 60% of which is lunch and trail food. As backpacking menus go, variety is great but not at the expense of ease of preparation. We get along nicely with one (1) 1½ quart lidded Sigg pot, a teapot, 10 ounce cups and a few stout plastic bags.

DINNER: Maggi and Knorr soups yield 1½-2 cups per man, the first step in replacing liquid lost during the day. Half of the remainder of the day's allotment of butter and bacon bar (originally 4 and 1½ ounces respectively) goes into the pot. So does any leftover milk or jerky. There is nothing to do but boil soup in a quart of water, then simmer until ready. The four Oregon Freeze Dry dinners, each of which comes packed in a foil pan, are even easier to fix. Each produces at least a pound of casserole.

At sea level I peel back a corner of the foil top, pour in the prescribed cup and a half of boiling water, reclose the top and keep the pan close to the fire or at least out of the wind. Since I am fond of mushrooms, I add a quarter ounce packet of freeze-dried slices to the dinner every other night when I add the hot water. At 6000 feet and above, since the soaking-cooking time is more than twice the five minutes suggested, I forget the pan and empty its contents directly into the remains of the soup for easier reheating. Just before serving, I stir in a pinch of spice mix and a tablespoon of butter.

I am fond of cottage cheese served cold with salt and pepper, but I only take it when I am sure of a snowbank or icy rill in which to chill it. The package makes an easy side dish in a plastic bag for one or two meals. The applesauce, strawberries and fruit cocktail (each of which serves four) are half for dinner and half for breakfast. The choice of the evening is cooked in the tea pot.

After half of it is eaten the remainder goes in a heavy plastic bag so the pot can be rinsed and water put on for tea. The pudding (for dessert every other night) requires no cooking and is made in a plastic bag. The ice cream is for the other two nights. All courses are eaten successively from plastic cups. On cold, late nights, the casserole and soup are cooked together in the big pot. We often finish off the day's allotment of a quart and a half of lemonade in the evening, perhaps with a slice of buttered bread and jam, or a succulent dried pineapple ring.

BREAKFAST: In the city, I rarely eat breakfast at all. In the mountains, I have very little interest in the traditional cooked breakfast foods (bacon, eggs, oatmeal, etc.). But I get off to a good start, nevertheless, with a cup of cold fruit, a cup of Birchermuesli with milk and sugar, and a cup or two of Sherpa tea.

Birchermuseli, based on the formulas of Swiss dietician Dr. Bircher-Benner, is an ideal dry cereal from the backpacker's point of view. I have tried half a dozen different brands and found little variation. Familia, the best known, is composed of oat flakes, apple flakes, wheat and rye, millet flakes, dried raisins, unrefined sugar, honey, crushed almonds and wheat germ.

Three quarters of a measuring cup provides the three ounce allotment for breakfast. To this, we add at least a tablespoon of dry milk powder from the plastic squirter bottle, along with about half a teaspoon of sugar (Birchermuesli is quite sweet and sugar is not needed, except for its energy value). After stirring in enough water to produce the desired consistency, and adding as much of the cold, stewed fruit as the cup will hold, breakfast is ready. Birchermuesli has been computed to yield about 1600 calories per pound, a quarter of which probably comes from protein and fat. I like it best with freeze dried strawberries mixed in.

To assure an ample supply of fat to last me through the day, I rely on Sherpa tea, the drink that is a staple in the diet of Sherpa porters who carry enormous loads at extremely high altitudes in the Himalayas. Sherpa tea is simply strong, milk-rich, sweet tea with anywhere from a teaspoon to a heaping tablespoon of butter (or margarine) stirred into the boiling water in the cup. The result is hot buttered rum with tea instead of rum. I know of no easier, more palatable way to ingest fat in the wilds—especially early in the morning.

LUNCH: Lunch usually begins about an hour after breakfast—if I am carrying a pack—with a square of rum fudge or mint bar followed by half a stick of jerky. By sucking first one then the other, I manage to make the snack last half an hour. If the day is strenuous, we may stop twice for lunch to thickly spread slices of pumpernickle with butter, jam, cheese and crumpled bacon bar, and to make up a pint of lemonade in a wide-mouthed plastic bottle. Our four ounce daily allotment of pumpernickle means three generous slices each,

lunchtime..

and we share a cube—four ounces—of butter each day. The pound and a half of cheese is divided into four six-ounce chunks to prevent overeating. Dessert is mint or fudge bar, or a piece of dried pineapple.

Gorp is likewise eaten during lunches, but it is also extremely handy in the afternoon, along with fudge bar, as the body begins to slow down. By late afternoon, I am interested solely in the quick energy of carbohydrate and I rely entirely on squares of mint bar slowly melting in my mouth to keep me going until dinner can revive me. On layover days or when activity is light, I generally reduce my intake of snacks and settle for a single lunch, saving the excess for climbing or carrying days.

There are too many foods available for backpacking for anyone to list, much less try, them all. The notes that follow are limited to common items and those with which I have had some experience. Listings are alphabetical.

APRICOTS, DRIED (also peaches, dates, figs, prunes and other sun-dried fruit): The trouble with this otherwise excellent source of carbohydrates is that the 25% water content makes it too heavy where power per ounce is concerned. Handbook No. 8 rates dried apricots at 260 calories per 3½ ounces whereas dehydrated apricots offer 332 calories and only 3.5% water content.

APRICOTS, DEHYDRATED (also any other vacuum or freeze-dried fruit): is excellent raw on the trail, stewed, mixed with cereal, baked in bread, etc. Banana chips, date nuggets, freeze-dried peaches and strawberries are all delicious. The increased cost per pound becomes immaterial when water content is considered.

APPLES, APPLESAUCE, APPLE SLICES: The apple is the most widely available, generally most pleasing, dehydrated fruit, and it has the highest calorie count (353 per 3½ ounces) of the common fruits. Instant applesauce merely requires opening the poly bag, adding water, fastening it shut and shaking. Some brands come with cinnamon, sugar and lemon crystals for added flavor. Applesauce eaters know the daily sugar allotment per person depends on whether or not their sauce comes pre-sweetened. I often add cinnamon and nutmeg to the package beforehand. Vacuum or freeze-dried, not sun-dried, products are recommended.

RAW BACON: Long a delicious backpackers staple, raw bacon yields 665 calories per 3½ ounces—when completely consumed. But when all of the fat, representing more than 500 of those 665 calories, is not eaten, raw bacon becomes an impossibly wasteful, inefficient food (protein being only 8.4% by weight). Most backpackers throw away all or most of their bacon grease. Bacon addicts know that unsliced bacon keeps best, but no bacon keeps forever. Canadian bacon has double the protein, and a quarter the fat of cured bacon, but only a third the calories and a very high (61.7%)

water content. Furthermore, both kinds of raw bacon are (by my standards at least) troublesome and messy to prepare. Hot bacon grease is not easily captured, stored or reused. Being a bacon-lover, I faithfully carried it (pouring the grease—most of which I never used— in a plastic bottle which I had to throw away after every trip), until I gratefully discontinued it in favor of Wilson's Bacon Bar.

BACON BAR (pre-fried bacon): Like Wilson's Meat Bar, Bacon Bar is a nearly ideal product from the backpacker's point of view. Its three ounces of precooked cured bacon is equivalent to 12 ounces of raw bacon, but there is no preparation, waste or spoilage. Bacon bar offers a compressed, conveniently packaged, palatable fat and protein combination with great flavor; I find it useful in all three meals, snacks and emergency rations. It is the closest widely available approximation to the fabled pemmican, which is simply lean dried beef mashed into suet (animal fat).

BAKING: A great many people enjoy baking biscuits, cornbread, gingerbread, bannock, coffee cake and the like, and fresh baked breads are extremely welcome, even craved, after a number of days on the trail. Bakery products can provide considerable power, especially the sweet ones that are cooked with (or eaten with) butter or margarine. Small backpacking parties can seldom justify carrying even the lightest reflecting ovens, but a pair of featherweight pie pans held together with spring stationary clamps makes a durable oven.

Surprisingly good baking products can be produced with foil, frying pan and the leftover pans from Tea Kettle Casseroles. Conventional supermarket packaged mixes need more water and additional flour, and they rise higher at high altitude. Mixes packaged for backpackers are becoming less temperamental, but the chef who has never baked anything should not expect immediate success in the wilderness. Pre-baked products (bread, cake, doughnuts) are seldom practical for backpacking trips, being usually mangled and squashed into an unrecognizable paste.

BEANS: A staple for travelers since the beginning of time, beans provide a fair source of carbohydrate and bulk and a popular starch base for many one-pot dinners. The raw bean is virtually uncookable at high altitude. Only precooked dehydrated beans should be considered. I like Seidel's sweet Boston Baked Bean Mix with half a crumbled Bacon Bar. A packet of freeze dried meat turns it into a fine dinner.

BREAD: The problem with breads is bulk, spoilage, ease of crushing and drying out. Generally speaking, the harder and darker the better. Pumpernickle, Rye, Oatmeal and German Black are all good, yielding about 250 calories per 3½ ounces. A variety of small unsliced exotic loaves are now available at organic and health stores, but one must beware of labels that brag of the absence of preservatives, for mold will quickly grow. Many backpackers, especially the more stoic, find bread too much trouble and substitute crackers.

BOUILLON: Virtually weightless, ageless foil-wrapped cubes are ideal for flavoring soups and casseroles and for impromptu broth when the body is too tired for food or a sudden storm makes a hot drink at lunchtime desirable.

BUTTER (MARGARINE): Only oils and animal fats surpass butter and margarine (about 720 calories per 3½ ounces) as a source of fat. Served in Sherpa tea at breakfast, on bread or crackers at lunch, and in soup or stew at dinner, butter palatably provides an ideal source of high yield, long-lasting energy.

CANDY: Since candy is an always welcome, rich source of calories (about 400 per 3½ ounces) and carbohydrate energy, it becomes an ideal staple of the backpacker's lunch and snack bag. Tastes change slightly in the wilds, but mountaineers are usually fond of lemon drops, toffee, coffee, caramels, butterscotch, sour lemon and bitter orange. Nonmelting hard candies or those wrapped in cellophane are most popular, but I often carry juicy, sugar-coated orange slices for variety.

CANNED FOODS: Many a backpacker still carries canned tuna, corned beef, Spam, sardines, vienna sausage, etc., to serve as the base of his antiquated dinner, and many of the cans unfortunately remain in the wilds. Given the heavy use of wilderness and the availability of a great variety of uncanned foods, it is hard to find a reason why cans still need to be carried. Makers of mountaineering foods have found that lighter, more compact, more easily carried out plastic and foil packages are far more appealing than the lightest aluminum can.

CASSEROLES, PREPARED: Makers of backpacking foods are gradually abandoning complicated city-type meals in favor of easily prepared one-pot casserole dinners. The leading producer, in my

making dinner — the hard way

view, is Oregon Freeze Dried Foods. I have used every one of its foil packed Mountain House dinners and pan-packed Tea Kettle casseroles and found them all exceptional in flavor, weight and ease of preparation. Cost runs a reasonable 60 to 70 cents per portion in one and two man packages, but drops much lower when No. 10 cans are purchased. Other manufacturers offer casseroles I like almost as well, but do not match OFD's overall consistency and excellence. A gob of butter fortifies and flavors any casserole.

CASSEROLES, HOMEMADE: Opportunities for constructing casseroles from scratch have never been greater. Small packets of freeze-dried beef, chicken, pork, turkey or ham are easily combined with pre-cooked dehydrated starches, mixed freeze-dried vegetables, soups or gravy mixes and spices. Cost savings can be significant for larger groups. Heavier, cheaper one-pot meals can also be produced from recipies shown in Appendix 2 of *Freedom of the Hills*, published by The Mountaineers, and the Sierra Club's *Food for Knapsackers* by Hasse Bunnelle.

CEREALS, COLD: Birchermuesli is easily the king of dry cereals on the basis of energy yield (about 350 calories per 3½ ounce average serving) and compactness. And it can easily be fortified by the addition of applesauce powder, banana chips, date nuggets, more raisins, wheat germ and crushed nuts—in addition to sugar and milk powder. Competition like Granola, Smilie's Harmony Grits and organic store concoctions are also excellent and far superior to old staples like Grape Nut Flakes and Raisin Bran. Corn flakes and its cousins are bulky and nutritionally worthless.

CEREAL, HOT: Many hikers feel the need of a hot breakfast, believing that heat somehow adds energy to the food. Actually, cooking reduces the potency of grains. The favorite hot cereals are instant oatmeal, Wheatena, Wheathearts, Farina, Cream of Wheat or Rice, all of which may be fortified in the same way as Birchermuesli, but which also permit the addition of margarine or butter. On frigid mornings, I sometimes make my Birchermuesli with boiling water from the tea pot.

CHEESE: Deservedly a mountaineering staple because of its high energy output (almost 400 calories per 3½ ounces for Cheddar—divided about equally between protein and fat), cheese, nevertheless, produces little more than half the energy per ounce of margarine. And even relatively dry Cheddar and Swiss have a very considerable (34-40%) water content. Soft cheese like Jack, Edam and Blue are often more than 50% water. The driest cheeses are Italian Romano, Parmesan, Provoloni, Kasseri, etc.

CHOCOLATE: Unsweetened chocolate provides more than 50% fat and 10% protein and yields about 40% more calories per ounce than plain sugar or sugar-type candies. Carbohydrate quick enery is proportionally lower, of course. Because of its high fat content, chocolate is far more difficult to digest than other candy and should not be eaten in large amounts during (or just before) strenuous activity. Many people fail to make this distinction between chocolate and other candy, and the result is often a queasy stomach instead of a burst of energy.

COCOA MIX: Though higher in carbohydrate than chocolate, cocoa mix still yields about 20% fat and protein and is therefore a comparatively powerful drink. Mixes like Swiss Miss which contain sugar are handiest. Some cocoa-coffee addicts make their mix at home with the proportions of cream and sugar they like.

COFFEE: The old rituals of settling the swirling grounds with cold water or egg shell have disappeared with the emergence of freeze-dried coffee, and the saving in weight and preparation have been enormous. Maxim and Oregon Freeze Dry produce ideal products, except that sugar and milk powder must still be added by those of us who cannot drink coffee black.

CRACKERS: Hard biscuits and crackers, hard-pan, pilot biscuit, Triscuit and the like, though subject to breakage, are preferred by many to bread, because of the reduced bulk and water content and freedom from slicing and spoilage. Wheat thins, rye saltines, Ryecrisp, Melba toast and Zweibach all have their fans. Fignewtons, though heavy, have always been popular. My current favorite is Lillie's Muesli Fruit Biscuits which combine all the Birchermuesli ingredients into a hard, mildly-sweet all-purpose cookie-cracker.

making lemonade

DRINKS, FRUIT: Wyler's lemonade and other flavors, and similar drinks by a number of imitators, come in foil envelopes weighing 3½ ounces, including sugar, that make a quart of imitation, but refreshing lemonade with a few shakes of the poly bottle. Also popular are fruit juices made from citric powders, orange and grapefruit crystals, Tang, Kool Aid and Fizzies, although the latter two require the addition of sugar. Artificially sweetened drinks are lighter and less bulky, but without sugar's quick energy. Canned fruit juices are popular on deserts or climbs where water is absent and must be carried, but should not be considered for ordinary backpacking.

EGGS, OMELETES: Powdered eggs have come a long way since they gagged the foot soldier in World War II; they now are available from every food manufacturer in a variety of highly edible forms. Omelete fanciers and those for whom breakfast is not breakfast without eggs, can easily find a different featherweight dish for every morning of the week packed in foil or plastic, usually with ham or bacon bits. Calorie content is very substantial (usually upwards of 600 calories per 3½ ounces). Whole eggs, if they must be carried, should be broken into tripled plastic bags, the air squeezed out and the bags packed in wide mouthed bottles. Even so, they must be kept cool and eaten promptly. Hardboiled eggs are 73.7% water, but I like them with salt on day hikes.

HONEY: Although sticky and heavy, honey is only 17.2% water and offers fine flavor and quick energy (300 calories per 3½ ounces). It may be used as a spread, dessert, syrup or frosting; it is most easily carried and squeezed from Gerry tubes.

INSTANT BREAKFAST: On the face of it, Instant breakfast and its relatives like Tiger's Milk should be ideal for backpacking, but my friends and I have reluctantly abandoned them because they dependably produce diarrhea within an hour if we are hiking. I have not tried them on inactive layover days, but I suffer no ill effects in the city where fresh, rather than powdered milk is used.

JAM: Like honey, jam and jelly tend to be messy and should be packed in reusable Gerry tubes. They offer slightly fewer calories and nearly 30% water, but are extremely welcome in the wilds.

JELLO: Many people swear by jello as a drink, hot or cold, but the weight per serving is far higher than for other powdered fruit drinks, even though the calories per ounce of carbohydrate is high. Chopped dehydrated fruit mixes and vegetable mixes are packed in gelatin powder by Dri-Lite and are extremely useful dishes as salads or desserts where there is snow or cold water to assure prompt jelling.

MEAT, FRESH: For years I carried a fresh, juicy steak to broil the first night out. Gradually I discovered that it was my city oriented association with steak, not the steak itself, that seemed appetizing. On that first night in the wilds, steak usually has less appeal for the weary hiker than soup, starchy stew and cold lemonade. Hamburgers or hot dogs are more satisfactory, but I prefer a freeze-dried casserole like OFD's Beef Almondine. In most climates, fresh meat (50% water) should be eaten within two days to prevent spoilage.

MEAT, DRIED: Wilson's Meat Bar, though far less flavorful and fat rich than Bacon Bar, is useful for all meals, snacks and for emergency rations. Beef jerky is a tasty trail food, but cannot be re-constituted and is therefore unavailable for cooking (it will flavor soup, but bouillion is better and cheaper). Dry salami, though 30% water, yields 450 calories of fat and protein per 3½ ounces and keeps very well unsliced inside its skin. Chipped Beef spoils quite quickly as many people have learned to their sorrow.

MILK, ETC.: Like Dried eggs, dehydrated milk has gradually come to taste almost like the real thing—especially when allowed to stand fifteen minutes, and served cold. Most convenient are 4 ounce foil packages of Milkman instant low-fat dry milk product, which make a quart with a few shakes of the poly bottle. The flavor is better than that of whole, skim or non-fat milk products. A few drops of vanilla or a little coffee or cocoa mix help mask the slightly artificial flavor. Malted milk powder and milkshake mixes are favored by some, but the latter, including sugar, seems excessively heavy. Milkman probably yields over 400 calories per 3½ ounces.

molasses –
a
natural
laxative

MOLASSES: This raw, crude liquid cane sugar, though nearly 25% water, quickly converts to energy and is used like honey or jam by those who like the strong sweet flavor. And a teaspoon or two works beautifully as a gentle natural food laxative—often necessary after a change from city fare to a steady diet of low bulk, dehydrated food.

NUTS: Dried, roasted, salted nuts (almonds, walnuts, pecans, peanuts, etc.) contain very little water and yield 525-700 calories per 3½ ounces, divided roughly into two parts fat and one part each of protein and carbohydrate. Nuts are an ideal snack and a perfect complement to high carbohydrate candy, fruit and bread. Peanut butter, though sticky, is a fine source of protein and fat when carried in a Gerry squeeze tube or a can.

OIL: For frying pancakes or fish, oil is sometimes carried in addition to margarine or butter. Salad fanciers also take it, along with vinegar, for dressing. A few drops of Vegalene in frying pans keeps food from sticking. Ultra weight conscious hikers, noting that oil is unexcelled in the production of calories (884 per 3½ ounces), have tried to subsist on periodically ingested oil capsules and little else.

PANCAKES: I shudder when I think how many hours I have spent cooking pancakes in the hot morning sun and then cleaning out the gluey batter pot. Pancakes, in my view, belong to the dark ages of backpacking on the basis of preparation alone. They do, however, provide an adequate source of carbohydrate, especially when sweetened.

PEMMICAN: The legendary wonder food on which the mountain men of the early west lived almost exclusively, takes some getting used to and is therefore not ideal as a steady diet for recreational backpackers on comparatively short trips. A balanced diet, strong on carbohydrates, will produce more energy and contentment. True pemmican is half lean dried meat, half cooked animal fat, with the two mashed together into a paste. Recipes for pemmican and jerky are widely available.

POTATOES: Like beans, potatoes are a favorite base and source of bulk in one-pot dinners. Instant potato powders easily produce genuine-tasting mashed potatoes, and the leftovers can be fried for breakfast. Potato cubes are great in stews, hash and french-fried.

PUDDINGS: Satisfying desserts that contrast well with sweet trail snacks can be a problem in the wilds where sweets are craved. Puddings (like Jello Instant) can be bought cheaply in the markets and shaken with milk powder in a plastic bag (later burned); since they set promptly without regard to temperature, they are a boon to backpackers. Mountaineering Shops offer a number of excellent puddings, as well as strudels, cobblers, pies and cheesecakes.

SPICES: Amateur cooks tend to know very little about spices and would be well advised to experiment at home, not on the trail. Too much of the wrong spice can seriously impair the edibility of dinner. Judicious use of spices, however, can sometimes transform unfortu-, nate concoctions into savory eating. Spice Islands' 'Fines Herbs,' a mixture of thyme, oregano, sage, rosemary, marjoram and basil, is a safe all-purpose seasoning when used at the rate of half a teaspoon for four servings. And, unless I add it at home, I take a mixture of three parts cinammon to one of nutmeg for applesauce and other fruits.

SALTS: Individual shakers for various salts and peppers are a nuisance to open and close in the dark. After struggling with various clever designs, I have returned to a single shaker loaded with two parts salt to one each of pepper and onion, garlic and celery salt. This all-purpose seasoning is just as good on eggs or stew as on trout; my companions have yet to complain. With my salt mix in one shaker and Spice Islands Fines Herbs in another, I am well equipped with flavor.

STARCHES, OTHER: Like beans, potatoes and pancakes, spaghetti, noodles, rice and macaroni form the heart (and provide the bulk) of a backpacker's casserole. Kraft Dinner, which served me in Boy Scout days, is still a good bet, especially when cooked with a packet of freeze-dried chicken, slivered almonds, sliced mushrooms and the above mentioned herb mix. Pre-cooked rice is the quickest of starches to prepare, but pasta has more protein and a shade more calories.

VEGETABLES: Few backpackers will bother with a side dish of hot vegetables; the flavor and calorie output (around 300 per 3½ ounces) fail to justify the extra preparation. As components of the one-pot dinner, however, vegetables are indispensible. In order of preference, I like dehydrated mushrooms (hard to find), onions, celery, carrots and peas and tomato flakes. I also enjoy chopped mixed vegetables in gelatin (Dri Lite's Sierra Salad). Green salad addicts take along oil and vinegar to make rehydrated vegetable salad, hoping they can find wild onion and miner's lettuce.

There are doubtless a good many delectable dishes of which I know nothing. Readers are invited to share their discoveries for possible inclusion in future editions.

7 SHELTER

There is probably no greater misery in the wilds than desperately needing shelter and being utterly without it. Most of us know how it feels to stand dripping in the rain, watching sorrowfully as our beds grow progressively wetter, in a storm that simply can not be. It is remarkably easy if the trip is to be short and the forecast looks optimistic to gamble on fine weather and leave the shelter at home. The weight saved often seems to justify the risk.

Such reasoning is based on the assumption that adequate shelter means significant weight. But this need not be. Adequate shelter can be obtained for as little as a pound and a few dollars per man. There is no longer any need, for the backpacker who plans ahead, to endure the misery of a storm without shelter.

I am willing to gamble to a certain extent on the weather, but I have worked out certain minimum standards of shelter to protect me from real discomfort. These fluctuate with the season, weather prediction, remoteness and friendliness of the area, length of stay and wishes of my companions. If I were taking a family or a girl on a first-ever backpacking trip, I would certainly take along a tent; if I were going cross-country with a hardy companion we would probably take minimal shelter. By devising certain minimum standards I limit my discomfort in camp, while minimizing my discomfort (excess weight) on the trail.

To enforce my minimum standards of shelter, certain items of equipment have 'essential' status on my checklist, along with matches and first aid kits. For instance, I never go off overnight without a waterproof ground cloth and a water repellent cover for my sleeping bag. In a heavy rain I can trench around my bed which allows me to reverse the ground cloth and cover, putting the watertight fabric on top. My foam pad keeps me and my sleeping bag above the damp ground. With time to prepare and a little luck, I can probably survive the night without getting wet.

This minimal shelter, of course, is only sufficient for a one or two night trip in unusually friendly country with a forecast of fine weather. Under progressively more threatening conditions, I raise my standards to include a wrap-around tarp, poncho tent, tube tent, tarp tent, forest tent or alpine tent—whatever the situation seems to call for. Maintaining minimum standards of comfort under widely varying conditions means the risks, and my resulting requirements, must be calculated afresh for each trip.

For inexperienced backpackers this can be difficult. But shelter should not be thought of as a necessary evil. If the weather stays fine and the tent remains unused one can be thankful it did not rain. If the storm materializes, one can be even *more* thankful for having the foresight and wisdom to carry protection. Personally, I like a good storm, providing, of course, that it does not penetrate my shelter, ruin my plans or last too long. Short and spectacular afternoon thunderstorms that end before dark add definite dimension to a trip.

If it only rains at night I rarely complain. There is something tremendously exciting about lying in the dark while only inches away a storm lashes the camp. I remember with joy a long ago night I spent wrapped in a huge, stiff, sulphurous-smelling tarp in a howling rainstorm beside a roaring creek. Again and again I awoke in the dark to luxuriate in my comfort on that wild wet night. This affinity for small shelters goes back, I suppose, to a childhood yearning that we never quite outgrow for the dark, warm, private little nests that we used to construct by draping blankets and bedspreads over tables, chairs and the back of the sofa. For children of any age, tents and other shelters hold an appeal that borders on fascination.

Though usually carried for protection against rain, tents can be even more valuable in snow or high winds for protection against cold and wind chill. A dependable weatherproof enclosure significantly raises the comfort range of a sleeping bag by limiting the possibility of heat loss.

carrying tent

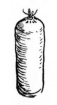

More than ninety percent of the tents that are made are big, heavy, clumsy affairs that would cripple the backpacker who tried to carry them. Built to be carried by cars or mules, these portable houses can easily be recognized by their fabrics (cotton duck, poplin or drill) and by their utter disregard for weight (usually ranging upward from twenty pounds). I still have vivid memories of carrying a 12-foot square canvas umbrella tent for several shadeless miles as a teenager. Without poles and umbrella it weighed nearly forty pounds, and it turned out to be far too hot to sleep in.

Backpacking tents are entirely different, being comparatively small and cunningly designed from the lightest fabrics to weigh an average of two to three pounds per occupant. Backpacking tents can conveniently be divided into five separate categories; starting with the most efficient and complex and working downward to the

bulky car-tent

simplest emergency shelter, namely: alpine tents, forest tents, tarp tents, tube tents and poncho tents.

The alpine, timberline or mountaineering tent (variously labeled by various manufacturers) is designed for use by climbers and mountaineers under the most extreme, dangerous and demanding conditions. It must withstand hundred mile an hour winds, be snowproof in a blizzard, conserve heat, resist snowload and be rainproof while providing ventilation; it must permit cooking, storage of gear and the drying of wet clothing. Its failure to perform even one of these services can, in extreme conditions, mean danger or death for its occupants. At the same time, of course, it has to be light. These are among the finest tents made and, as might be expected, they are heavier and more expensive than other backpacking tents: prices begin at better than $100 and the weight per occupant is usually 3-4 lbs.

Forest tents, as the name implies, are meant to be used below timberline where winds will rarely exceed 20-30 miles per hour. The best of them (alpine-forest hybrids that are dependably snowproof) are suitable for winter camping in sheltered locations where wind and snow load will not be extreme. At the opposite end of the forest tent scale are 'floorless,' 'flyless' or 'endless' models which offer little more protection than tarp tents. For the most part, forest tents are relatively water and bugproof floored tents with reasonable wind resistance and good workmanship.

While alpine tents customarily accommodate 2-3 people, forest tents offer a variety of designs, some of which offer standing room in the larger models. This is the tent for the majority of recreational backpackers; and good ones, offering floors and flies, start at about $75 for 2-man models and weigh 2½-3½ pounds per person.

Tarp tents are variously cut sheets of waterproof fabric designed expressly to be pitched for overhead shelter. As such, they must be distinguished from tarps customarily used on the ground. Pitching tarps are expensive and must never be walked on or the inevitable punctures that accompany ground use will soon render them worthless as rain shelter. (Tarps often get pitched so that puddles develop, and puddles and punctures mean showers not shelter.) Good tarps can be pitched in an amazing variety of ways, depending on the terrain, the availability of trees and other rigging points and the needs of occupants. Flexibility and versatility are their greatest virtues.

Most tarps designed for tenting are ten, twelve or fourteen foot squares with a variety of tie points and grommets; no poles, floors, entrances, mosquito netting or side walls are provided. Some hybrid tarp-forest tents are constructed to form one or two definite tent designs and often have poles and zippered closures. There are a great many excellent tent designs that are never seen in backpacking fabrics, and most are comparatively easy and inexpensive to make from coated nylon yardage available in mountaineering shops. Tarp tents, in addition to their adaptability to the terrain, have the virtue of being inexpensive compared to Forest and Alpine tents—($20-35) and light (½-1½ pounds per occupant).

two tarp tents

Tube tents are a recent and useful addition to the tent family; they offer quickly erected, lightweight, inexpensive shelter; their greatest drawback has nothing whatever to do with their design: it is the ease with which conscienceless backpackers abandon them in the wilds instead of burning them in a hot fire or carrying them home. They furnish perfectly acceptable emergency shelter (perhaps half a dozen uses if treated with care), but their increasing appearance as litter has caused more than one concerned mountaineering shop to discontinue them. Conventional models are nine foot long tubes of 3 or 4 mil colored polyethylene plastic designed to be supported solely by a nylon cord ridgeline tied between two trees. Weighing 1¼-2¼ pounds, these open-ended shelters cost a mere $2-3.

Ground sheet and poncho shelters are essentially emergency versions of the tarp tent. Though comparatively inflexible and inefficient, they yield short notice shelter that often makes the difference between misery and comparative comfort. Sometimes their convertibility to shelter hinges on the presence of a few strategically located grommets or the possession of fifty feet of nylon line. More often it depends on the backpacker's foresight.

For several years I carried a 7 x 9 foot coated fabric poncho. When combined with the 6 x 8 foot plastic ground sheet carried by my partner, it provided us considerable shelter. After carefully preparing the bedsite to reduce the chance of puncture, I used it as a ground sheet, covering my bag on cold or dewy nights. Two corners on one side were fitted with permanent peg loops while the other two were fitted with 20-foot nylon cords.

When it threatened to rain, we tied off the hood, drove pegs to windward, tied the cords to trees to make a lean-to (or used pack frames for poles and pegged them down if it were treeless); we did what we could about controlling the drainage and wrapped our bags in the ground cloth. Many a short thunderstorm was weathered in this manner, and we once endured two days of solid rain on the shores of Lake Shasta without wetting our bags.

Two ponchos that snap together with a waterproof overlap can also be pitched as a sizeable pup tent. Most mountaineering shops offer grommet tabs for polyethylene ground sheets, not to mention snaps, stitchers, visklamps, velcro and various kinds of gadgets that can be used by the ingenious to make gear more adaptable. The choice between durable but expensive coated nylon ground sheets and those of expendable plastic should be influenced by comparative usefulness and adaptability as emergency storm shelter.

The backpacker in search of shelter must first of all determine which kind of shelter suits him. This will not always be easy. One must look into the future and accurately foresee the length and type of trip and the climate and friendliness of the country. Once the ideal is established in terms of need, there are likely to be modifications based on weight, cost, bulk and simplicity.

A tent is often a backpacker's biggest purchase, and to those who have never tried one, evaluation of a given model may be bewilderingly difficult. Whenever feasible, the prospective purchaser should borrow or rent the closest possible approximation of what he wants before buying. Two nights in a tent (one in fair weather, one, ideally, in foul) will reveal far more than any book can tell.

Before individual tents can be evaluated it is necessary to examine the basic problems in tent design and some of the principles employed in combating them. Beside the ever-lurking need to keep down weight, the central problem in tenting is the same as that in sleeping bags and waterproof clothing: namely breathability. Since the chief aim of a tent is to provide a watertight enclosure, it would seem at first glance that the obvious solution would be to construct an entirely enclosed cocoon of completely waterproof fabric. That design, unfortunately, yields a portable steam room, not a tent.

As evening comes and the temperature drops, water vapor in the air begins to condense. Added to this is the fact that the human body exudes during a night's sleep anywhere from a pint to a quart of water. In the city this is easily absorbed by the considerable volume of air in a bedroom. In a small, watertight, sealed-off tent this moisture will condense on the walls and run down onto the the sleepers. In the course of one night, two sleepers can produce enough water to turn their sleeping bags sopping wet.

Finally, there is the need of the tent's occupants for fresh air. In an utterly sealed tent, breathing gradually exhausts the limited supply of oxygen and converts it to carbon dioxide. Though poisonous in large quantities carbon dioxide signals its presence, even to sleeping campers, by headaches, a feeling of nausea, or a heavy closeness to the air; this discomfort wakes sleepers and enables them to let in a fresh supply of air.

Cooking in a sealed tent is extremely dangerous. The carbon monoxide produced by combustion of stove fuel and limited oxygen produces no physical symptoms or sensations and consequently its buildup in a closed tent can pass unnoticed and even unsuspected. A very considerable number of winter mountaineers and polar explorers have died peacefully in tents and ice caves which accidentally became sealed by heavy snowfall in the night.

So, in even the worst weather, tents must provide reliable ventilation. And if the chilling claminess of condensation is to be avoided there must be considerable ventilation, more than many tent buyers (and tent makers) imagine. There is an inescapable inverse relationship between condensation and ventilation. The more there is of one, the less there is of the other. So there is close correlation between ventilation and comfort. The problem, then, in tent design is how to get the water vapor out and the fresh air in without also bringing in bad weather. It is a problem with which tent makers have been wrestling for decades; the ideal solution has not yet appeared and one must consequently choose between several types of compromise.

Most emergency shelters of pitched ground sheets and ponchos avoid the problem of ventilation, but do not keep out the weather. The problem returns when watertight fabrics are wrapped snugly around the sleeping bag rather than pitched; condensation in such cases can produce more wetting from within than would likely be received from without. Tube tents in the largest diameters provide adequate ventilation as long as both ends are kept fully open. One-man tubes and partially closed larger tents tend to produce puddles on the floor. Tarp tents, by virtue of the fact that two or more sides are generally open to the weather, rarely offer a ventilation problem; if they are large enough, most of the rain can be kept out.

A few tent makers, in an effort to produce something that can be advertised as a waterproof tent, offer waterproof tarps shaped to close up completely. An hour zipped into one of these little nightmares is more than most campers can endure. The rule of thumb for pitching any kind of thoroughly watertight tarp is that both ends or one whole side must be open to the outdoors if uncomfortable condensation is to be entirely avoided.

The ventilation problem really becomes acute in floored, totally enclosed forest and alpine tents. The best solution so far is double-walled construction. The tent itself is made (ideally) from a light, uncoated, open weave fabric which readily permits the escape of water vapor from within before it can condense. Suspended three or four inches above this is a second roof called a rainfly made of coated, watertight fabric. The rainfly prevents rain from entering and the space between the two roofs allows moist air from within to be carried away.

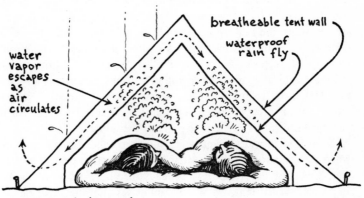

breathing in the rain

Double-walled tents, if properly pitched and well equipped with additional ventilation at both ends, work extremely well. The draw-back from the weight-conscious backpacker's point of view is the bothersome necessity of carrying (and pitching) two roofs instead of one. Rainflys for two-man tents generally weigh 1½-2½ pounds. Not surprisingly, tent makers continue to strive mightily for a better, lighter, single walled solution. The best alternative, at least in theory, has been to greatly increase ventilation in single-walled, coated tents. The resulting designs usually offer large areas of mosquito netting which are sheltered from wind and rain by moveable sections of coated fabric.

Noteworthy examples are the Camp Trails 720, the Co-op Hi-Light and the Ocaté Ventura. The principal drawbacks in this design are that the tents are extremely vulnerable to wind which penetrates to disturb and chill the occupants; and in rainstorms, when coated walls must be battened down to block the netting, ventilation becomes inadequate to present excessive condensation. In a different approach the Camp Trails 727 utilizes a single-walled coated fabric which has been lined on the inside with a thin layer of foam. The foam, besides providing insulation from heat and cold, acts as a sponge to absorb condensing water vapor before it can trickle down to wet the sleeper and his bag.

Unfortunately, the moisture remains in the tent and the atmos-phere tends to be damp and clammy. If the tent is left pitched in the sun all day with the door wide open the moisture will probably be gone before nightfall. But if the tent must be folded and packed away promptly in the morning, its weight will be increased by the volume of water retained in the sponge (conceivably as much as three pounds), and the water will still be there when the tent is pitched again.

The traditional solution, especially in large campground tents, is the use of cotton fabrics for a compromise between water repellency and breathability. Cotton, unlike nylon and other synthetic fabrics, absorbs water and in the process tends to swell. The nature of cotton fiber allows it to be woven into a tighter, more nearly windproof fabric than is possible with synthetics. When the tightly-woven, twisted fibers of long staple Egyptian cotton (pima cloth) are wetted, they swell to form a highly water repellent surface. Furthermore, cotton accepts and holds water repellents (not watertight coatings) which further clog the pores of the fabric.

So cotton provides adequate to good resistance to condensation when dry, and about equally satisfactory protection from rain when wet. Of course the greater its repellency the poorer its breathability. In a single walled tent, when rain cannot get in, water vapor cannot get out, and the result is condensation. Unfortunately, cotton has other disadvantages. Its tear strength is little more than half that of nylon and it is subject to mildew and rot. A cotton tent must never be rolled up wet, or stored until it is bone dry, and cotton dries rather slowly.

Even when coated with repellent it will leak if the inside is touched while the fabric is wet, and in a hard rain water will probably spray through. The problem is not great in a roomy campground wall tent, but in the confined space of a backpacker's tent it is inevitable, even in a brief storm, that heads or shoulders or elbows or sleeping bags will brush the fabric and wick the water through. Perhaps the greatest drawback to cotton is its considerably higher weight. For adequate strength, cotton backpacking tents must be made of 5-6 ounce fabric. A cotton tent will generally weigh twice as much as its nylon counterpart and more than a nylon tent with a fly. Despite the fact that the losses clearly out number the gains for cotton tents, backpackers who shop largely on the basis of price will buy them.

Though it has its own drawbacks, nylon is clearly the superior fabric for tents. It cannot be woven closely enough to be windtight; it has a slippery feel that some people find unpleasant; and it is comparatively expensive. Its lack of permeability keeps water repellents from adhering well, and the smoothness of its fiber and its failure to swell cause fabrics to pass rather than shed water. Although this lack of natural repellency is a drawback in many cases, it becomes an advantage where breathability is needed. An uncoated nylon tent produces much less condensation when closed than a similar model in cotton.

Although nylon will not hold water repellent treatments, it readily accepts the more adhesive neoprene, polyethylene and polymer coatings used to seal a fabric's pores and make it impervious to water. And nylon is exceptionally strong, usefully elastic, light in weight and cannot mildew or rot. Coated nylon (although the coatings eventually wear and crack) is ideal for tent floors and flysheets, while uncoated fabric makes admirably breathable tent walls. Attempts have been made to combine uncoated nylon and long staple cotton in the hope of combining the virtues of each. But fabrics of this sort (like 60-40 cloth) have not yet been widely used for tents.

The backpacker in search of shelter, having determined the type of tent he wants, needs to be able to recognize and evaluate quality. This, in part, can be accomplished by dealing with tent makers known for superior design, materials and workmanship and the willingness to stand behind their products. In part, it means inspecting tents and questioning salesmen—especially when bargain hunting. Since alpine tents are the most sophisticated and expensive of the breed, and since their performance is so critical in winter and ferocious winds, they require unusually careful consideration.

cord-loaded poles spring into shape.

The typical 2-3 man alpine tent is about 4½ feet wide, 8 feet long and is suspended from two sets of 'A' poles. The triangular tent end should be roughly equilateral to provide a pitch that will spill rather than trap the wind and still shed snow readily. 'A' poles are often canted slightly inward to assure wind spillage on flat ends. Double 'A' poles are essential for resistance to high wind; any tent which substitutes an 'I' pole (single upright) at the foot must be classed as a forest tent.

'A' poles (also known as angle poles) must join securely at the top with maximum rigidity. The bottoms of the poles must never depend for support on the ground beneath them. (They could sink out of sight in mud, sand or snow, causing the tent to gradually sink with them.) The foot of the pole on good tents is usually a prong that fits snugly into a grommet in a well-reinforced peg loop in the corner. Telescoping poles have become largely obsolete because of their greater weight and their vulnerability to damage.

Poles loaded with elastic shock cord are heavier and more expensive and the cord will eventually need to be replaced, but the time and difficulty saved in both pitching and packing make them almost a necessity where conditions are likely to be difficult. Shock cord loaded poles virtually spring into shape when released and cannot come apart. Anyone who has fumbled in the snow trying to combine sections correctly and then had a gust of wind separate a pole when the tent was half pitched will find cord-loaded poles a delightful innovation.

Satisfactory poles should be made of 6061 aircraft aluminum tubing in sections of fourteen to twenty-four inches in length. For poles of less than five feet, the tubing can be five-eights of an inch in diameter with a wall thickness of .028 inches. For longer poles the tubing should be three-quarters of an inch with .058 walls. Ordinary soft aluminum should be avoided.

Wrinkled fabric catches the wind and causes a tent to flap. A long confinement in a flapping tent is a maddening and unnerving experience. Wrinkles likewise catch rain and snow and cause strain in the fabric. Improperly designed tents are destined to wrinkle no matter how tightly and well they are pitched. All tent ridges sag and hang in a slight curve no matter how tightly they are drawn. All of the finest alpine tent makers have taken this sag into account with a catenary cut ridgeline that eliminates the extra fabric that causes the wrinkles. The result is a tent that pitches under normal tension with flat unwrinkled sidewalls, despite a normal sag in the ridgeline.

Tent floors are always a compromise between sturdiness and light weight. Floors, like ground sheets, take a good deal of beating from both above and below, and once they are torn or punctured their utility swiftly drops. Tent floors are not easily replaced, or even patched, and the patches tend to leak and sag. But coated fabric tough enough to stay waterproof for the life of the tent would be much too heavy to carry. Ideally, tent floors should be constructed of eight ounce coated fabric, certainly of four ounce, but because of weight and cost considerations two man tents usually come with floors of two and a half ounce fabric. The best four man tents, with room to walk around, are floored with four to eight ounce coated fabric.

Since floors are generally the weakest, most vulnerable part of a tent, they must be treated with great care. The ground should be as carefully prepared for a tent as for a sleeping bag; all sharp rocks and twigs should be removed so that the floor rests on earth, pine needles, duff or the like. A 2.5 ounce floor is not designed to be walked on, which means boots should not be worn in the tent, and care should be taken to keep debris and sharp objects (knives, ice axes, crampons) where they cannot create damage from within. Backpackers determined to keep their floor watertight and safe carry a 4 x 8 foot 4-mil vinyl ground sheet (weighing about 15 ounces) on which to pitch it. This cheap, disposable sub floor can be discarded when it becomes abraded, which is certainly better than discarding the tent.

The vast majority of tent floorings are of nylport, a 2.35 ounce urethane-coated nylon, but a few tent makers (North Face, Co-op) have switched to a new polymer coating which has three times the resistance to puncture and tearing. Polymer coatings, because of their high silicone content and their tendency to bridge rather than sink into the pores, are nearly equivalent in waterproof quality to a double urethane coating. Most urethane coated tent floors, alas, have only a single coating, and are therefore not really watertight at all. There are always pores that somehow escape being plugged by the coating and these will pass water under extreme circumstances (puddles above or wicking from within).

Seams pass far more water than accidentally unplugged pores and so floors insofar as possible should be without them. The preferred design is called a tub floor because a continuous piece of coated flooring continues anywhere from six to eighteen inches up the tent wall, forming a shallow tub of waterproof material. This avoids a wall-floor seam at ground level where it would be extremely vulnerable to ground water. The coated side of the fabric should be inside the tent where it receives more protection and reduces the slipperyness of nylon on nylon. Ideally, the only seams in the floor are in the corners where they cannot be avoided. A pieced floor or a ground level seam are marks of inferior construction.

Even tent makers acknowledge that corner seams in tent floors are liable to leakage and should be coated with a neoprene sealer (4 ounce cans cost about $1.75 in larger mountain shops). But sealant is somewhat messy and detracts from the sleek appearance that helps sell modern tents. Besides that, it has a strong smell. Nevertheless, it is a good investment for backpackers more interested in comfort than style. Even with a tub floor, a vinyl sub-floor and hand-sealed seams, a tent floor will not be one hundred percent watertight and care must be taken not to pitch it in what might become a puddle.

The roof (which in a two man tent means the walls) and the ends of an alpine tent take a good deal of strain and wear and should therefore not be lighter than 1.9 ounce ripstop nylon in a comparatively loose weave for maximum breathability. It may be treated with water repellent (standard practice at the factory) to keep out the dew but, of course, must never be coated. To shave weight and cost, some tent makers skimp on roof fabric on the theory that it is protected by its fly; they use 1.6, or 1.2 ounce nylon, and even 0.75 ounce tafetta.

corner
seams
need
sealing

In violent windstorms tents made from these lighter fabrics have a habit of literally exploding from the enormous pressures generated. Another common practice among tent makers is to make roofs from the same downproof fabrics (which they buy in volume) used in their sleeping bags. Unfortunately, the high thread count of this tightly woven material tends to inhibit the escape of moisture from within the tent, which in turn encourages condensation.

Rainflies, on the other hand, take far less strain than tightly pitched tent walls. Since they are also far easier and less expensive to replace (and since their life is limited by that of their coating), tent makers are justified in saving weight by using 1.2 ounce fabrics. For flies as for floors, the new polymer coating is probably superior to the more common urethane. Rainflies by themselves are really no different than well-pitched tarp tents. More than a few owners of nylon tents equipped with flies regularly carry the fly and poles and leave the tent at home.

There are basically two types of tent entrances, flat zippered doors and tunnels that close with ties. Doors are neat, quick and easy to operate; they comprise most of the triangular end of the tent, being opened by either a zipper down the middle or (better) two zippers, one coming up from each corner toward the peak. The latter can be partially closed against drafts and still provide considerable ventilation. The chief drawback of flat doors is their vulnerability to zipper failure (freezing, jamming, breaking). Flat doors must be vertical or lean slightly outward in a winter tent to prevent falling snow from blocking the entrance or falling inside.

Tunnel entrances are generally circular sleeves about three feet in diameter and three feet long which can be extended from the tent and suspended on the guy from the head of the 'A' pole. As entry halls, they make it possible to enter the tent during a snowstorm without bringing in a great deal of snow. They do not rely on zippers for closure which pleases mountaineers in dangerously severe weather. In heavy storms they provide additional inside storage, and they make possible the weatherproof joining of two tents for expeditionary companionship and warmth. The best alpine tents are equipped with a zippered door at one end and a tunnel at the other.

Since fierce and protracted storms often make it necessary to cook, and to store and dry equipment inside the tent, makers of alpine tents often add an alcove or vestibule—a triangular extension at one end of the tent. The best of these are floored and made of coated fabric or are carefully covered by the fly. There are a number of variations in the arrangement of doors, flaps, sills, curtains, fabrics, fly protection and vestibules, all of which need careful inspection while the tent is pitched if their suitability is to be determined. For use in snow, the vestibule should be floored, and there should be a semi-circular cookhole, opened by a coil zipper, somewhere in the tent, preferably in the vestibule, but never close to a wall and never far from ventilation. Primarily designed for use on snow, the cookhole allows a section of the floor to be peeled back so the snow beneath can be used during storms as a sink, garbage disposal, repository for unwanted snow, catchbasin for spilled food and stove fuel, and sometimes a latrine.

It is essential that even the most breathable tent be equipped with sizeable and closeable vents. These traditionally take the shape in alpine tents of six to nine inch diameter tunnels about a foot in length, the ends of which are permanently covered with netting, mounted high in the wall at both ends of the tent. One or the other of these hooded vents may temporarily have to be tied closed when facing the wind, but both are needed when the door is closed to prevent the buildup of carbon dioxide and the carbon monoxide produced in cooking.

Small hooded vents in the peaks are being replaced to some extent with doors that zip closed from the bottom up (North Face) so the ventilating area can be as much or as little as the weather allows, and by similarly shaped netting covered windows (Sierra Designs) which also permit zipper control of the ventilating area. Larger and more easily variable ventilators represent a distinct improvement in modern tents.

All doors, vents and openings of any kind must be fitted with panels of sewn-in mosquito netting, made of nylon, not cotton. Cotton netting pulls loose, punctures and deteriorates with age. Only nylon has the strength and mildew resistance to make zippered inner doors that withstand strain and remain taut. To prevent wildlife from crawling or slithering beneath it, the net door should be stitched across the bottom to the flooring, opening by zippers up the sides.

Zippers are an excellent index to tent quality, just as they are in sleeping bags and pack sacks. In tents, where a jammed or broken zipper could let in enough wind to produce disaster, they may be even more critical. Metal zippers become anywhere from difficult to unreliable in cold weather, tending to freeze, jam and break. Aluminum is even worse than brass. Nylon or plastic toothed zippers are good provided they are large (ideally no. 10), but German coil zippers which are non-jamming and self-repairing are much better.

Lap felled double-stitched seam

Nylon is unusually susceptible to unraveling and edges should be either heat fused or serged (thread wrapped). Top tent makers for the most part 'hot cut' their fabric which permanently seals the edges. All seams in tents should be lap felled and double stitched, which means the two pieces of fabric to be joined must be laid together with their edges coinciding, then folded over and secured with two lines of stitching that pass through all four layers of cloth. Simple unfolded seams made by stitching together two overlapping fabrics are faster and cheaper to construct but they are weak and always leak. It is important that lap felled seams be folded toward the ground so they shed rather than trap running water.

Stitching should be with heavy duty (size D or E) nylon or dacron thread fed through a double needle machine. Cotton, owing to its lack of strength and short life, should never be used, except in cotton tents. A tent is only as strong as the thread that holds it together. Once cotton stitching begins to give way, a tent becomes utterly worthless.

Since tent fabric is light and subject to great strain, it follows that all points of stress and all attachments should be generously reinforced. Included are peaks, corners, pole sleeves and sockets, tapes, pullouts, ties, grommets, guy line attachments, etc. For instance, guy line loops sewn directly to the fabric will quickly rip out; it is necessary to first reinforce the critical spot by sewing on one or more patches that will accept the load and spread the strain.

Pullouts on the best tents are often attached to triangular flaps or 'dog ears' sewn into lap felled seams to spread the load. Bar tacks are useful in securely fastening pole socket tapes. Peg loops should be of heavy nylon webbing, or replaceable loops of nylon cord knotted into reinforced grommets. The tent maker's goal is to discover all the points and lines of concentrated stress and strengthen them sufficiently to make every inch of the tent accept its fair share of the strain.

Tent pegs often are not included in 'the complete tent' because the particular style required depends on the type of terrain to be visited. The most common variety (and one of the lightest and cheapest) is the chrome moly stake, a 7-10-inch long skewer of 3/16 inch tempered alloy steel with the top bent into a ring; similar pegs are made from duraluminum; also common are square steel pegs that have been twisted to form screws.

A heavier, stronger aluminum stake is broadly semi-circular in cross section with a rolled lip at the top. Slightly heavier and so tough it can be driven through a wooden 2 x 4 is the comparatively new plastic peg of I-beam construction. Also new are duraluminum staples made from quarter inch rod, which offer increased adhesion in loose earth with minimum wind friction.

Since pegs weigh anywhere from one half to one and three quarters ounces each, and since some tents require as many as eighteen, the choice of peg can make a difference of better than a pound and a half. Short, light aluminum skewers are fine for tents to be pitched in forests. Sandy soil and higher winds call for broader stakes, longer pins or staples. The stoutest pegs will be required for rocky soils unsheltered by timber. Most experienced tent carriers get by with less than a full complement of pegs by managing to tie to trees, brush or rocks.

On snow or loose sand a broad aluminum angled snow peg at least 10 inches long will be required. In soft snow even watered pegs deeply sunk in stamped snow may not hold, making it necessary to use some sort of deadman. A deadman is constructed by burying stakes, staples, branches, dowels, or snow-filled fabric bags in a trench dug at right angles to the guy or pullout and filled with

tent pegs

stamped snow. They are most commonly used on tents that are to remain standing for some time. Tents erected for a single night are often pitched with the help of ice axes, skiis, poles and snowshoes.

In the 'good old days' of the pioneer, carrying tent pegs or poles would have been unthinkable. The woodsman never hesitated to fashion what he needed with saw, axe and knife. In those days trees could be felled without thought. But those days are gone and today's considerate backpacker should tremble at the thought of what the woods would look like if every camper cut down trees for pegs and poles. Saws, axes and hatchets have no place in the backpackers' kit and in my view should be outlawed in heavily-used wilderness. Fallen limbs and sticks may be utilized to peg and help rig tarps and tents, but nothing living should be damaged or cut, not even with a pocket knife. The carrying of nails to drive in trees for easy rigging of guy lines is as reprehensible a practice as cutting fir boughs for a bed.

Tents to be pitched in snow should be equipped with snow flaps—9-12 inch strips of double coated nylon fabric that extend out from the floor line at ground level on all sides of the tent. By covering these strips liberally with snow and stamping it down, considerable support can be gained. Even more important wind is prevented from getting beneath the tent, and a layer of insulation helps to hold in the heat.

Snow flaps are standard on some alpine tents and are usually available as options on the better ones. They add little weight or cost and can be folded beneath the tent when not in use. Many mountaineers feel snow flaps are just as valuable on the high barren rocky plains where the wind screams and there is no soil to accept tent pegs. Rocks piled on snow flaps are often all that prevent wind from getting under a tent and turning it into a kite.

Another specialty item for tents used regularly below ten degrees is the frost liner; essentially a set of curtains that form an inner roof, the frost liner is designed to absorb and deflect the frost that forms from condensed breath on the inside of the roof on very cold nights. When the temperature is below ten degrees water vapor freezes on contact with the colder tent roof and consequently cannot escape even through the most breathable fabrics. Without a liner, a considerable volume of frost can fall from the roof to shower the sleepers.

For maximum absorbency frost liners should be constructed of cotton or silk, not nylon. Unlike snow flaps they are detachable (snapping or tying to tapes provided for that purpose); they are also comparatively heavy and expensive. Liners that extend only part way down the walls (usually to the pullouts) will weigh at least 1½ pounds, while those that extend to the floor frequently weigh 2½.

One consolation is that if frost liners are needed, the rainfly can safely be left at home. Since they absorb as well as channel water, frost liners need to be dried out before being rolled in a pack—for the sake of weight as well as to prevent mildew. Frost liners, where they are needed, are a good investment in morale: they can make the difference between ice showers and relative comfort. Frost liner hangers are useful for rigging clothes lines and for hanging clothes to dry The latest alpine tents are now thoughtfully being fitted with extremely handy small pockets just above the floor in the corners for easy stowing of the many small articles that are always so difficult to find in a small tent.

Some of the finest expeditionary tents employ from one to three pairs of bowed fiberglass wands which slip into sleeves that run up one wall and down the other. The resulting 'gothic arch' keeps the tent bowed outward for maximum room and minimum flapping. The most unflappable tents built combine a series of wands with a catenary cut design and shock cord loops on all guys and pullouts. Shock cord must never replace or serve as a link in a guy line because of its lack of strength; instead it is used as a supplementary loop which takes up the slack that inevitably develops in the line. As such, it is more effective than conventional line tighteners which must be adjusted by hand each time lines begin to sag.

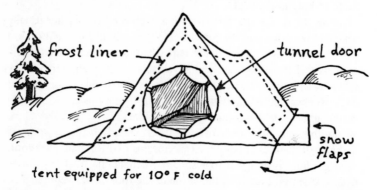

frost liner — *tunnel door* — *snow flaps*

tent equipped for 10° F cold

The finest two-man alpine tents I know are the Alpine Designs Snowline, the Gerry Himalayan, the Holubar Expedition, the North Face St. Elias and the Sierra Designs Glacier. Doubtless there are equally good tents from other makers. Although the vast majority of alpine tents are 2-3 man ridgeline models supported by double 'A' poles, a few larger tents are also available. Most of these are either McKinley-type square wall tents with a short wall and a high central peak or triple 'A' pole tents with a ridge sloping both ways from a high truncated 'A' pole assembly in the center.

Because of the larger expanse of fabric, both designs are more susceptible to wind-loading in gales and require slightly more sheltered locations than 2-man tents. They also need larger (usually eight foot square) level tents sites. Big tents, though less versatile, make happier homes for storm-bound parties. The ability to stand erect can seem the greatest of luxuries when it is patently impossible in a tiny tent. North Face makes a good hexogonal 8-foot tent supported by Triple 'A' poles, while Holubar offers an 8-foot square McKinley-style counterpart.

The construction of forest tents, some of which are floorless, is nowhere nearly as critical (or expensive) as that of alpine tents. In general, forest tents are designed for milder weather, and ruggedness is willingly sacrificed for greater room or lighter weight. There are a good many hybrids that appeal to backpackers and mountaineers alike: tents which are suitable for all but the most extreme weather and provide great comfort at a somewhat lower weight and cost.

Among these are tents made by the Ski Hut and Co-op in addition to all the makers listed above. Forest tents are often carried by summer backpackers as emergency shelter in case of storms, as dressing rooms, for insect protection, playpens, basecamp storehouses, and sometimes just for the pleasure of having along a tent. Many of the criteria for good alpine tents can and should be applied to the selection of a forest tent—but with somewhat less rigour and somewhat more tolerance.

Floors should be seamless and of tub construction, roofs should be sturdy but porous, and coated rainflies should cover entryways and always be separate rather than attached. Single zippered or tunnel doors are sufficient and the 'A' pole at the foot may be replaced by a shorter 'I' pole. ('I' poles cut pole weight in half but when used at both ends greatly reduce tent stability. And an 'I' pole at the head makes it hard to get in and out of a small tent.) Vestibules are not required but ventilation is just as important to comfort as in alpine tents, and mosquito netting must cover all openings. Reinforcing is only slightly less important and seams should still be lap felled and double stitched with nylon or dacron thread. Snow flaps, frost liners and wands can be forgotten.

Forest tents come in many more shapes and sizes than do alpine tents, and while some of them are distinctly rickety when pitched, most will survive the storms found in sheltered locations. An increasing number of tents that sleep three or four people are being offered to satisfy the growing demands of family backpacking. One of the nicest of these is a hexagonal 7-foot, 3-man tepee sold by Sierra Designs. Although the slope of the door makes it unsuitable for winter use, it is nearly ideal for all kinds of summer camping; at 8¼ pounds it can almost be justified for luxurious living for two.

Tarps designed expressly for pitching as tents can sometimes be hard to find. Styles, prices, weights and rigging points vary almost as widely as the means by which they can be pitched. The best tarps have the fewest seams and the greatest number of fastening points. Co-op offers seamed, urethane-coated tarps with eight grommets (one in each corner and the middle of each span) as follows: $11 for a 1½ pound 7 x 9 foot tarp, $16 for a 2 pound 9 x 11 footer, and $25 for a 3½ pound 12 x 14 foot tarp. There are no loops or ties on the face which limits versatility. Camp Trails sells a 2¾ pound 10 foot square tarp made of a new Zelan treated dacron-cotton fabric for $24.

Holubar offers a 7 x 10 foot urethane-coated tarp with two seams that weighs a pound and a half, costs $27 and provides 17 ties (five on the face) in addition to grommets in each corner. Ski Hut makes perhaps the finest (and most expensive) pitching tarp of all; ten and a half feet square, it weighs 2 and 2/3 pounds and offers five loops on the seamless face and twenty more spaced around the edges. Complete with stuff bag and 25 feet of nylon cord (rarely sufficient) it costs $34.

Since the new polymer coated nylon is superior to the urethane coated fabrics offered above, the backpacker interested in constructing his own pitching tarp (or building his own tent) should consider buying Co-op's 55 inch wide four ounce polymer coated nylon which costs $2 a yard. Backpackers with sewing machines and experience, who either wish to save money or construct their own designs, will find a variety of books and plans in libraries and mountaineering shops. Tarp and floorless forest tents are comparatively easy to make. Probably the best book on the subject is *Light Weight Camping Equipment* by Gerry Cunningham (founder of Gerry's Colorado Mountain Sports) and Margaret Hansson ($2).

Frostline kits offer the proficient seamstress the opportunity of constructing superior tents (and other gear) at savings in the neighborhood of 50%. Frostline's alpine tents are of advanced design, with extra heavy floors, velcro instead of zippers for more reliable closures, double, angled guy lines, etc. Frostline kits provide all materials, precut and premarked, along with clear and complete instructions, but it takes real ability and a sewing machine to turn out a quality product.

Since even 4-mil polyethylene can be pierced by hail stones, tube tents made of thinner plastic should be avoided as too flimsy. Colored models are cooler and shadier than transparent plastic, and 2-man tents with a circumference of at least ten feet are required to keep condensation below the level producing discomfort. All purchasers of plastic tube tents should be made to swear on pain of death that they will never abandon them anywhere in the wilds. To avoid contributing to the list of disposable products, Ski Hut offers a tube tent of urethane coated nylon fabric that weighs two pounds and costs $17. Unfortunately, its tapered lines and hooded ends are likely to produce an uncomfortable level of condensation inside.

When it comes to pitching flimsy-floored alpine and forest tents, careful site preparation cannot be overemphasized—if not out of kindness to the fabric, then perhaps out of consideration for the comfort of the bedsite. The ideal site is atop a gentle mound; even the slightest hollow must be scrupulously avoided to escape occupying a puddle. Duff and pine needles tend to insulate the tent from moisture while hard-pan traps water. If the site is slightly sloping and heavy rain is expected, it will be worthwhile running a shallow trench around the high side of the tent to divert runoff.

hollows can turn into puddles.

If only light winds are expected, the tent should be oriented in such a way that the prevailing wind is spilled rather than trapped by a flat side to minimize flapping. If winds are liable to be strong, an end containing a door or ventilator should face the wind so that the tent can billow quietly rather than flap. A ridge of dirt or snow protecting the floorline on the windward side will help keep wind from getting beneath a tent and carrying it away.

It goes without saying that trees and well rooted bushes are better than any tent stake for anchoring a tent in a heavy wind. The longer the guy line the less force it transmits from pole to peg. Most floored tents are easily erected by first staking out the floor taut and wrinkle free, inserting the poles and tentatively tying the two end guys, making adjustments until the poles are vertical and the ridge is tight but not straining. After staking the pullouts, it will probably be necessary to make a few adjustments in the floor stakes to remove the last wrinkles. Pitching a tent too tightly will produce as many wrinkles as pitching it too loosely.

Many tents allow the rainfly to be pitched without driving additional stakes, but if heavy weather is expected the fly should as nearly as possible be erected independently with stakes and lines of its own. If temperatures are sure to be below freezing, the fly should be left home in the interest of saving weight (there is always too much to carry on winter trips anyway). Flies are also superfluous if the tent is being carried for other than rain protection. At least half the time I carry a tent, I leave the fly at home, which explains why I disapprove of tents made by Gerry and Camp Trails in which the fly is permanently attached.

When pitching a tent in snow, the first order of business is to stamp down the platform on which it will stand. I also stamp the area around the entrance and the spots to be occupied by snowflaps and tent stakes. Pole locations generally need a little extra stamping. Trees should be sought to anchor ridgeline guys. On nights of heavy snowfall, it will be vital to strike the roof sharply from within from time to time to knock off accumulated snow and free entrances and ventilators. Snow falls so quietly that tents have been crushed and sleepers asphixiated by buried vents when the occupants had no idea that snow was even falling.

Winter campers spend a good deal of time trying to keep snow from entering the tent and then disposing of all that inevitably gets in before it can melt. To speed this work a small plastic whisk broom and a thin square of sponge are well worth carrying for winter housekeeping. If there is any likelihood of camping on soft snow, winter campers should be prepared to construct efficient deadmen to secure the tent. Fourteen inch light wooden dowels or 6-8 inch bags of coated fabric with cord drawstrings that can be filled with snow and buried are both quite efficient though the latter are more troublesome to reclaim. Water poured over a deadman buried beneath a foot of stamped down snow will effectively enlarge it into a jagged block of ice.

It is vital that fabric deadmen and snowflaps be of coated, preferably double coated, nylon; otherwise it will be impossible to extricate them from ice and snow.

Poles that stick in their sockets and frozen zippers are best thawed, except in temperatures below zero, by briefly holding them in warm hands. Although the frozen metal will initially stick to the skin, the comparatively small volume of poles and zippers causes them to thaw and release the skin within a few seconds.

Effectively pitching tarps is something of an art. Crafty veterans, calling on a wealth of often bitter experience, simultaneously consider the aerodynamics and pitching possibilities of the selected bedsite and devise a design they hope will suit their needs. Often enough, the plan will fail when flapping becomes unbearable or rainwater is neatly channeled into someone's sleeping bag; then there is nothing to do but cut the whole mess down and try to roll up in it in hopes of salvaging a little rest before dawn.

Tarps are extremely vulnerable to wind and infinitely harder to pitch than tents. In any kind of blow the odds are distinctly against

two more tarp tents:

success. Tarps, to be successful, require shelter from the wind; the sleeper in search of wind protection will do better to hunt out the natural shelter of rocks and trees than to try and rig a tarp. The best use of pitched tarps is for protection against gentle rainstorms, dew and the early morning light. Veteran tarpsters keep their creations low, allowing just enough headroom for sitting up.

Those who choose a tarp instead of a tent should do so with an understanding of their many limitations. While pitched tarps rarely pose a problem in condensation, they likewise provide no protection from insects, although in virtually windless locales a five foot strip of nylon netting sewn to the perimeter of the tarp makes it possible to construct a relatively bug-free enclosure.

Since pitched tarps contain no floors, a separate ground cloth must be carried. Since the wind blows freely beneath them, tarps are extremely vulnerable to gusts and blow down more often than any kind of tent. In a rain, tarps invariably produce puddles in the roof; if these are not emptied from time to time during the night by gently pushing up on the fabric from beneath, their weight can easily collapse the tarp and provide a bath for those below.

For those who conclude that a tarp will best suit their needs, there are almost limitless possibilities for rigging shelter. Some of the most popular are illustrated. Some tarp pitchers carry one or two sectioned aluminum poles to ensure that they can rig the type of shelter they want; a good many carry a handful of tent pegs suitable to the terrain; and the experienced carry at least a hundred feet of 550-pound test nylon line or parachute cord. A few people like the challenge of working with native materials and carry only a few feet of line. Tarp pitchers tend to be an independent lot.

But whether the choice is a Rube Goldberg rig of branches, lines and flapping tarps, or a sleek and expensive expeditionary tent, the pleasure of any trip will be enhanced by dependable shelter from the ravages of wilderness weather.

8 GETTING READY

Nothing dooms a trip like slipshod preparation. It only takes one or two little mistakes. Many a veteran backpacker has seen a trip ruined for lack of a map, knife, salt or match. Still more common is the beginner who, determined to camp in comfort, can barely stagger up the trail under a gargantuan load. The line between comfort and misery is far too thin for any backpacker to take getting ready lightly.

But preparing to go backpacking need not be drudgery. There is keen pleasure in working out a route for a fine summer trip on a dark and drizzly January night. And there is satisfaction in planning a trip into wild and distant country that delicately balances the weight of food and gear against the necessity of traveling light. The more that is accomplished beforehand at home—getting in shape, experimenting with foods, memorizing maps, breaking in boots—the smoother and more carefree the trip will be.

By systemitizing the job to reduce the work, one can make getting ready a pleasant prologue to the trip. The subject divides itself conveniently into four distinct phases: (1) Trip Planning: where, when and how to go, (2) Preparation: deciding exactly what to take, then getting it together, (3) Physical Conditioning: getting in shape before the trip, and (4) Packing up: getting to the trailhead and making up packs.

TRIP PLANNING

As backpacking becomes more popular, it becomes easier and easier for the beginner to get started. Probably the best sources of help are the big organizations like the Sierra Club, Mazamas and Mountaineers in the west, and the Adirondack, Appalachian and Green Mountain Clubs in the east. Not only are they unexcelled sources of information about their respective territories, they offer organized outings of all types on which the beginner can safely become acquainted with the country and acquire experience with equipment and technique. In addition to the big clubs with their wide ranging programs, there are innumerable local hiking clubs. These can usually be located by contacting the Federation of Western Outdoor Clubs. Route 3, P.O. Box 172, Carmel, Calif. 93921 or the Appalachian Trail Conference, 1718 N St., N.W., Washington, D.C. 20036.

If I were suddenly transplanted to some unfamiliar part of the country, the first thing I would do is join both the local and regional hiking, mountaineering or conservation organizations (found by consulting the library, phone book and mountaineering shops). From these sources I would collect all the published data on nearby wild areas. Then, based on my reading, I would purchase, in the largest scale available, the appropriate topographic maps and study the country. From the administering government agencies, I would obtain regulations and the necessary permits and licenses. From club members, lectures, slide shows and sporting goods stores, I would discover what sort of clothing, equipment and techniques were required. Depending on the nature of the country, I might make a few excursions with the mountaineering club before going off on my own.

Journeyman mountaineers and outdoorsmen will, of course, adapt themselves quickly to a change in country. Strangers to the outdoors, should probably spend more time on organized outings until they develop the necessary confidence and technique and acquire their own equipment.

Trip planning, like wilderness travel, requires the ability to read and use maps. Probably no other skill is more important to all aspects of backpacking. No one should enter wild country unsupervised without appropriate maps and the ability to use them. Of course a map is useless if directions are unknown, so a compass becomes a necessity. There is a tendency among amateurs and strangers to the outdoors to regard the compass as a toy for Boy Scouts. But in strange country where landmarks are unfamiliar, a compass is no less than indispenable. Many times I have worked out my true location or avoided a wrong turn by referring to a dollar-sized plastic compass that weighs a fraction of an ounce and cost less than a dollar.

Since there is no substitute for proficiency with map and compass, the inexperienced backpacker is well advised to invest his spare time in mastering both. The book *Be Expert with Map and Compass,* by Bjorn Kjellstrom, available from most mountaineering shops that handle books, covers the subject and offers instruction, quizzes, drills, field problems, games, sample topographic maps and related tools. Even more valuable is the chapter on navigation in The Mountaineers' *Mountaineering: The Freedom of the Hills.*

The single best map for the backpacker's purpose is the topographic (topo) map published by the U.S. Geological Survey in a variety of scales. Topo maps dependably offer more information per square mile than any other kind of map. It may be useful, however, to transfer to the topo map from more up-to-date local and Forest Service maps such useful data on 'improvements' as trails, roads, campgrounds and the like. While the very large scale 7½-minute topos provide marvelous detail, smaller scale maps that show distant landmarks will also be needed for orientation.

Though a first glance at a topo map is liable to be confusing, they are really not difficult to understand. Winter is an excellent time to study maps, plan trips and become familiar with topography. The first principle of map use is orientation—lining up the map with the country. The traveler simply spreads out his map with the compass on top so that north points directly to the top of the sheet. The map and compass are then turned as a unit until the north needle points directly to north. When the magnetic declination (difference between true and magnetic north) is set off (it is shown on all topo maps) the map will be oriented.

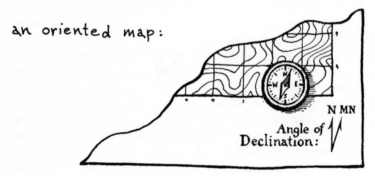

an oriented map:

N MN

Angle of
Declination:

When one's position is known and the map is oriented, it becomes easy to identify visible features of the countryside by transferring line-of-sight bearings to the map by means of a straight edge. When only one's general location is known, but several landmarks have been positively identified, it is possible to discover one's precise location by transferring line-of-sight bearings to two known landmarks onto the map. The intersecting lines reveal the compassman's exact location.

The competent woodsman or mountaineer always tries to develop some inner orientation to make him independent of his compass. To this end, my friends and I play a game on the trail—while taking a rest—that has proven both amusing and instructive. Each of us draws a line in the dirt toward what he believes is true north. Then the compass is brought out, the declination marked off, and the winner declared. The next time the game is played the previous session's winner must draw first. It is surprising how quickly this game develops a sharp sense of direction.

Reading the rise and fall of the land on a topo map is more a matter of practice than talent. The best place to begin is with solitary peaks or hills where the contour lines form concentric circles that get smaller as they go higher toward the summit circle in the center. Widely spaced lines indicate a gentle slope while lines bunched together describe a cliff. Contour lines form arrows that point upstream as they cross water courses and downhill as they decend a ridge or bluff. As one becomes adept at reading topo maps, the actual shapes of landforms begin to materialize on the map so that maps become pictures of the country.

When this happens, topo maps take on a singular fascination. They also become incredibly useful. For instance, by measuring the ups and downs of a trail one can estimate with fair accuracy the time that will be required to traverse a given section of country. This, in turn, allows the trip planner to work out logical camping spots and estimate the time needed for any itinerary. Superior map reading ability is a prime prerequisite for safely visiting the wildest of trailess country. Proficiency with map and compass has saved a great many lives.

There are various ways to travel the country. Newcomers to the outdoors may want to car camp at the trailhead for a day or two and make exploratory day trips into the wilds until they become acclimated and find an appealing campsite that seems within their reach. Families and other groups with limited range often set up a base camp within an easy walk of the car and then make daily side trips into surrounding country.

Groups with greater mobility or the urge to move may decide to shift their base camp one or more times; others make a practice of packing up and moving every other day. Inexperienced or cautious backpackers often take the shortest route to their goal, then retrace their steps going home. More practiced and imaginative hikers go to some pains to plot a route that makes some kind of circle or loop in order to see more country and avoid treading the same ground twice.

Another popular plan is the shuttle trip. Two cars drive the party to the exit· trailhead, where one car is left. Sandwiched into the second car, the party then drives to the entrance trailhead to begin a packpacking traverse between the two. There is also the rare and exotic 'double shuttle' in which two traversing parties start at opposite ends of the same route and trade car keys when they pass on the trail.

Some backpackers find a greater sense of adventure in deliberately planning no itinerary, going where and when the spirit moves them. Others, similarly motivated, spurn trails altogether in favor of cross-country travel, finding pleasure in avoiding people and the beaten path. Since true wilderness does not begin until the trail has been left behind, it should probably be the goal of most backpackers to travel cross-country, even if only for an hour's day hike from base camp.

I like to start thinking about future trips while I am still in the mountains. I find myself wondering, for instance, whether the rocky, trailess canyon I am passing could be ascended, under pack, to the lake that lies above. As I move along, I try to estimate the difficulty of reaching passes, following ridges and crossing slopes, with an eye toward future trips. I study the topo map to learn what lies on the other side of the mountain and to compare the bunching of contour lines with those on slopes I can see or have already climbed. And I often take pictures of country that interests me for reference in planning future trips.

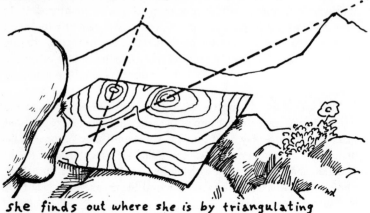

she finds out where she is by triangulating from two known landmarks.

This type of on-the-spot research becomes invaluable for plotting feasible cross-country routes in trailless country. A glance up a canyon on this year's trip may warn me against including it in next year's itinerary because the gentle slope suggested by the topo map turns out to be a series of ledges and cliffs. Or I confidently plan a route down a forbiddingly steep slope because I know it to be an easy sand and scree slide.

The question inevitably asked by strangers to the wilderness is how fast will I travel? Or, how far should I plan to go in a day? There are no answers, only generalities. On relatively level trails at moderate elevations, a lightly burdened, long legged well-conditioned man may manage 4 m.p.h. At elevations over 6000 feet in rolling country, a well-acclimated backpacker is moving extremely well if he can cover 3 m.p.h. The average backpacker, fresh from the city, with a full pack, heading up into the mountains will be lucky to average 2 m.p.h. These speeds are for hikers who keep moving and should probably be cut in half for those who want to poke along, smell the flowers, take pictures and enjoy the view.

People who are overburdened or climbing steeply or moving cross country may average only 1 m.p.h. Children, the elderly and hikers strongly affected by the altitude may manage as little as half a mile an hour. A friend of mine has devised a useful formula for predicting his speed. He plans every hour to cover two miles if the trail is flat or mildly descending. For each thousand feet of rise he adds another hour. For steeply descending trail he adds a half an hour per thousand feet, increasing that to a full hour for extremely steep downhill. By plotting a rough profile of the trail from the topo map and applying his formula, he can estimate quite accurately the time needed to walk it with a moderate—under 30 pound—load.

How far one should attempt to go in a given day is equally hard to answer. The first day out is always the hardest, especially if the hiker has gained a mile or two of altitude between home and the trailhead, carries a healthy pack and is in less than top physical condition. In these circumstances, five miles may be a full day's work. Well-conditioned backpackers who know their capabilities may cover ten or more miles the first day and not suffer unduly, but most people will be happier if they schedule considerably less. On succeeding days it becomes possible to cover more ground with less discomfort. I have covered 15 or 20 miles on the third or fourth day with greater comfort than I felt after eight miles the first day.

There is no particular virtue in covering great distances. I have received more pleasure, solitude and a sense of wilderness from backpacking less than two miles cross-country into a neglected corner than I have from following sixty miles of well-traveled trail and camping in battered, over-used campsites. I customarily spend the summer on the edge of California's Desolation Wilderness, a place of extremely heavy use, but I know any number of charming, well-watered off-trail spots within an hour or two of the trailheads where I can camp in peace on virgin ground. As backcountry use continues to increase, backpackers determined to find solitude and unspoiled country will have to invest more time dreaming over their maps to find the less obvious routes that lie between the trails.

When to go is often determined by school and business vacation schedules. In California's high Sierra, spring, summer and fall are compressed into three or four months and consequently it makes a great deal of difference whether a trip is scheduled for June or August. Often it will snow every day for a week in early June, yet the country is dusty and parched by August. The beginner should gather all the information he can about likely conditions in his area for various seasons. If there is one season to avoid, it is probably spring. Even if the weather is miraculously fair, the ground is almost certain to be wet. Indians generally avoided spring travel, preferring the middle of winter. Spring is a good time to car camp in comfort and settle for day hikes into the wilderness.

Fishing reports, water company snowmelt reports and weather forecasts are all good sources of current information on conditions. The Government Printing Office in Washington D.C. issues Climatic Survey booklets for each state which give snowfall and temperature ranges for every month for every weather station on its map. These offer a general idea of what is likely to be encountered in an average year. The Weather Bureau will tell backpackers how their forecasts relate to that mythical average year.

Climate and weather, more than anything else, determine what needs to be carried for warmth and shelter. Every year I meet people shivering in thin clothing in the snow in early season and sweating in down parkas in the middle of summer, simply because they had not sufficiently researched likely conditions. Where it is possible to schedule a trip on the basis of weather, one can simply check daily with the Weather Bureau until conditions are right and the long range forecast is clear. I never plan even a casual overnight jaunt without learning all I can about expected weather. Comfortable backpacking is hard enough without deliberately setting out into the path of an approaching storm.

PREPARATION

Once the route has been determined, the length of the trip decided and the starting date set, it becomes possible to determine what must be taken along. Actually, I like to begin my preparations before the end of the previous trip. In camp on the last leg of a trip, or perhaps at the trailhead—after exchanging my pack for an ice cold drink—I sit down with my notebook while memories are fresh, and make pertinent notes about the trip. I criticize the food, recording both the noteworthy successes and the dishes that need never be carried again. I might write down, for instance. that breakfasts were a little skimpy so the cereal allotment should be increased from three ounces per meal to four.

Triumphs and failures of clothing and equipment are duly noted. Unused food, clothing and gear are listed for future scrutiny. I write down items what were forgotten and others that would have added comfort if I had had the foresight to bring them. Breakdowns are noted; so are needed repairs and ideas for equipment modification. Everything relevant to making the next trip more comfortable goes into the notebook—while the lessons of the present trip are still vivid in my mind.

Later, in the process of dismantling my pack, my notebook is

the
trip-
planner's
friends:

kept handy for jotting down other things: the need to replenish bandaids and aspirin, a reminder to move a knot on my pack frame that rubbed my back, the need to carry a heavier grade of plastic bag for carrying garbage. When I put away my gear—after cleaning it and making repairs—I file my notebook for future reference.

By making notes before the memory fades, I accomplish three things: (1) I give myself the best possible chance to increase my enjoyment of future trips, (2) I avoid repeating mistakes for failure to remember them, and (3) by putting it all in writing, I avoid the mental drudgery of having to start planning each trip from scratch. Fifteen minutes spent making notes at the end of a trip will save two hours of preparation a month later; I cannot recommend this procedure too highly.

When I put away my gear at the end of a trip, I sort it into a series of cardboard cartons, one for containers, another for food, a third for cooking gear, and so on. These cartons are stored together, along with my notebooks, menus and checklists from previous trips, under two of the bunks in my cabin. Checklists, I believe, are as vital to comfortable backpacking as comfortable boots or a comfortable bed.

The checklist takes the place of a perfect memory, and the longer it runs the more security it provides. Every time I buy a new piece of gear, I add it to my checklist, but I rarely can bring myself to cross anything off, even the items I have not dreamed of carrying in years. Like other backpackers interested in comfort, I enjoy reading other people's lists. The abridged checklist that follows may serve as a starter for newcomers to backpacking—but only as a starter. A checklist is a highly personal thing and the beginner must eventually construct his own, updating it after every trip to make sure it contains every scrap of gear he owns.

Once a new trip has been planned, I can turn to the preparation stage with much of the work already done. Having determined where, when and for how long I am going, I get myself a pair of empty cartons, assemble my notebooks and spread out my checklist. I read my notes from the previous trip, then I make my way down the list, considering each entry in terms of my needs for the trip in question. Items with asterisks are skipped over on the first reading because they are not stored in the cartons. (My camera, fly rod, boots and socks and most of my clothing, for instance, are usually kept, or in use, in other places.) Each item selected is fished out of its storage box and put in the appropriate trip box. One box is for community gear (food, cooking paraphernalia, first aid kit, etc.), the other is for my personal gear (sleeping bag, clothing, etc.).

If I feel any uncertainty about an item, I include it. When I cannot make up my mind between a wool sweater and a down

BASIC CHECKLIST (abridged) with weights
*items not under bunks

PACKS	Pounds-Ounces
Frame and packbag	3-12
Orange daypack	9
Fanny pack	5½
Belt pack	2

CLOTHING

*Green parka shell	7½
*Felt hat	3
*Tropical cap	2
Tennis hat	2
*String shirt	7
*Moleskin green shirt	13
*Hiking shorts	10
*Bathing suit (shorts)	4½
Navy turtle-neck sweater	11
Down sweater	17
Down parka	1-8
Storm suit	1-5
*Rag socks	4
*Inner socks	1
*Wick Dry socks	3½
*Thermal socks	2½
*Light weight boots	3-4
*Medium weight boots	4-2
*Moccasins	13
*Trousers	16
*Bandana	¾
*Denim shirt	8
Watch cap	2
Dark glasses	1½
Gaiters-7"	4
*Foam lined leather gloves	3
*Wool mittens	3
*Boxer shorts	3
*Mountain parka	1-4
Balaclava	3

SHELTER

10 x 10 tarp tent	2-11
Space rescue blanket	2
2-man tube tent, cord	2-4
Poncho	1-0
Forest tent	4-8
Tent fly	1-4

BEDS

Superlight sleeping bag (stuffed)	3-5
Foam pad (54")	1-12
Foam pad (48")	1-9
Foam pad (36")	1-0
Bivouac Cover	17
5 x 8 ground sheet: 3 mil	12
5 x 8 ground cloth: 4 mil	15
3/8" Ensolite, 19" x 42"	14

COOK GEAR

Pocketknife	1½
Fork-spoon	1½
Bluet with cartridge	1-13
Extra cartridge	10
1 qt. bottle	5
1 pt. bottle	2½
Pot tongs	1½
Sigg pot, lid	9
Chore Girl	½
Emerycloth-backed sponge	½
Salt mix shaker (filled)	2
Matches (wooden)	1
Paper towels, toilet paper	2
Plastic cup	1½
Teflon frying pan	1-0
Steel frying pan	12
Primus 71L Stove (alone)	10
Primus stove box	10
1 ½pt. gas can (empty)	5½
1 liter wine skin	4
Aluminum measuring cup	¾
1 qt. plastic canteen	5
Plastic bucket-basin	3½
Soup ladle	1½
Tea kettle	3
1 gallon jug	4
Gerry tube	¾
Gerry grill	6
Camp Trails grill	4
Edelweiss cooker (1½ qt. pans)	1-8

MISCELLANEOUS

Thermometer	¾
Compass	½
map(s)	?
50' cord (550 lb. test)	3
Snakebite kit (Cutters)	1
Insect repellant (Cutters)	1
Large stuff sack	4
*Guidebook	9

*Notebook, pencil	2	Personal kit	3
*Loaded creel	9	Aerosol bug spray (fresh)	9
Mallory flashlight	3	*Konica (35mm camera)	
Birec flashlight	1¾	loaded	13
First aid kit (large)	9	*Fly rod, reel, line	7½
First aid kit (small)	6	*Paperback book	7

jacket, I put in both. Since I never actually make up my pack until I have reached the trailhead, I will have plenty of time to make a choice. When I have worked my way through the contents of the equipment boxes, I go to work on the asterisked items. Sometimes a few of these are unavailable (socks may need washing, film for the camera may have to be bought), so I put a list of missing items in the appropriate box. Having considered every item on my list at least twice, I put away the equipment boxes and start to inspect my selections.

Utinsils and containers may need washing and airing, the pack will need to have its pockets cleaned out and its rigging checked, sleeping bags, mattresses and ground sheets need to be spread out in the sun, and inspected for holes, grime, pitch and the like. First aid kits and flashlight batteries need to be checked; so do emergency supplies and personal kits. Every piece of equipment should have at least a cursory inspection to make certain that it will function as expected.

With the equipment all assembled (or at least planned and noted) I consult old menus and the comments made at the end of previous trips. After figuring the required number of breakfasts, lunches and dinners, I consider the appetites and preferences of party members, the likelihood of our catching trout and the possibility of our staying out a little longer than planned. Then I compose a tentative menu which will be discussed and probably changed before the actual shopping begins.

Once the menu is set and the food acquired, most of it needs to be repackaged. Some people go so far as to separately package every meal so they need only dig out the appropriately labeled bag. In my view, this sort of packaging is excessive for short or casual trips where measurements need not be precise and where an extra ounce of cereal for breakfast for several days will not result in starvation the last day out.

My repackaging consists of stripping away all cardboard, paper, cellophane and light plastic and replacing it with large, heavy duty polyethylene bags. I like to tie the long neck of the bag into an overhand knot rather than struggle with rubber bands, twistys, paper clips or heat sealing. Bags that will repeatedly be opened (gorp, cereal) and thus subject to more wear are usually doubled. I buy the heaviest bags I can find, rather than risk the puncture and spilling inevitable with flimsy bags that are cheap or free. After repackaging appropriately, I put fresh food (butter, meat, cheese) in the refrigerator. Everything else goes into the food box—including a boldly written reminder to collect the refrigerated food before leaving.

On the evening before departure, I assemble the clothes I expect to put on in the morning and set them beside my bed. I also gather the clothes and food and drink that I will look forward to finding in the car at the end of the trip. As a final step, I run quickly down my checklist one last time. Everything should now be ready.

CONDITIONING

Many a trip has been ruined—and I speak from experience—by the failure to get in halfway reasonable shape beforehand. I can remember trips which seemed to be one long nightmare of aching legs, bursting lungs and a desperate effort to keep up with the party. It is simply impossible to turn from sedentary city life to high altitude wilderness backpacking without a certain amount of physical strain. It is, however, possible to leave a lot of the discomfort at home.

At home, the conditioning can be as gradual as the hiker cares to make it, thus spreading and actually reducing the discomfort. It can be performed within easy reach of a hot shower, soft bed and the assurance that today's blisters can be babied tomorrow. On the trip itself, there is more than enough discomfort from hiking under load at high altitude, sleeping on the ground, wind, sweaty clothes, cold water, a noticeable lack of easy chairs and hot showers—without unnecessarily adding a lack of physical preparation.

There is no better investment of time during the several weeks prior to a demanding trip than a program of conditioning that will bridge part of the gap between city living and wilderness travel. It is far better to discover blisters while walking near home than it is at ten thousand feet in a cold, windy camp, with ten miles to cover the following day.

It is perfectly possible for a sedentary city worker in his spare time to significantly improve the capability of his legs, lungs, shoulders, feet and skin, depending on his condition, in anywhere from a week to a month. The program actually required will depend on many factors: age, experience, physical condition, time available, determination, rigorousness of the trip contemplated, etc.

The following program is suggested for a badly out of shape, no-longer-young backpacker planning an ambitious two week trip which will begin on a weekend. About three weeks ahead of time our man should, with the aid of a city map, mark out rather precise one, two and three mile courses that begin and end with his home. Traffic lights, crowded sidewalks, even stop signs should be avoided so there is no necessity to stop.

After work, instead of opening a beer, our man should go walking. Early risers may prefer to get up and walk at dawn; it is a marvelous time to be about. Since our man is in really rotten shape, he may have trouble the first time just getting around a one mile course. Nevertheless, he should time his walk in order to chart his improvement. If he is too sore after that first walk, he can take the next day off. Weight lifters and long distance runners often work out every other day, allowing the body to rest and assimilate the changes on rest days. On the third day, our man should try two miles and try not to stop. A brisk pace is actually more comfortable and less tiring than starting and stopping or an aimless saunter.

At the end of the first week, our man should be able to cover the mile courses in 20-30 minutes and the two miles in less than an hour. By the end of the second week he should be able to do three miles in an hour; the weekend before he leaves he ought to walk the three miles twice in a period of two hours. Walking regularly (at least every other day) and briskly (charting the times and always trying to improve) will strengthen the legs and provide endurance.

To develop the lungs and toughen the knees there is nothing like running. Once the body is used to walking, it is safe to go running. I find shorter distances (50 to 200 yards) of hard running to be more effective than a mile of slow jogging. The high school track is a good place to run. To increase my wind I run until I am gasping, then I run another twenty yards before slowing to a walk. When our man runs out of breath, he should walk very slowly until his breathing returns to normal and then start running again.

By the end of two weeks, he will find his wind greatly improved and he should be able to navigate the one mile course, alternately running and walking. As his lung capacity grows and begins to catch up to his leg development, he will begin to feel fatigue in his knees. The ideally conditioned backpacker on a difficult stretch should feel approximately equal discomfort in his knees and lungs.

To condition the shoulders to the pull of his pack, it is only necessary for our man—probably the second or third week—to start wearing it on his walks. Books make good ballast and ten or fifteen pounds will be enough for the first tour of his routes under load. This can be increased to twenty-five shortly before the trip. Since backpacks are not made for running, our man will want to alternate unladen run-walk tours of his routes with pack carrying tours. So far, all of his work has probably been on flat, paved sidewalk. But backpacking usually means traversing rough, steep country, so our man should hunt out the steepest, roughest terrain in the area and work out a course or two for the final week of conditioning.

Only on steep trails are the conditions in mountain wilderness closely approximated. The knees need the unique strains produced

for getting in shape, nothing beats running up hills.

by going up and down hill and the ankles need rough and rocky terrain to develop toughness and resistance to sprain. No amount of walking or running on city sidewalks can accomplish the same thing. I find the bulldozed fire trails in the steep Berkeley hills behind my home to be perfect. When I was working at a desk job and wanted to get ready for a weekend trip, I would drive to the fire trails on the preceeding Sunday, Tuesday and Thursday evenings and spend an hour or two running uphill until either my legs or lungs forced me to stop. Then I would slow to a walk until I was sufficiently recovered to run again. A great amount of conditioning can be compressed into a week in this manner—providing the body is in reasonably good shape beforehand.

In addition to run-walk tours in the hills, our man should carry a loaded pack on perhaps a total of ten miles worth of walking trips through the hills. The weight of the pack will condition the shoulders, knees, ankles and feet to the strain and jarring that rough country provides. Hiking in the hills with a pack and run-walk tours without one—this is the real conditioning. Walking and running on city sidewalks is only 'pre-conditioning' for people unaccustomed to vigorous exercise.

From the beginning of this program, the feet need to receive special consideration. On all his excursions, our man should be wearing the boots and socks he will take on his trip. This will break in the boots and mate them to the feet before the trip begins, and it will toughen the feet sufficiently to prevent chafing and blistering in the wilds. Undoubtedly, the most overlooked and easiest part of foot conditioning is cutting the toenails.

Long toenails will make boots seem too short and can be painfully crippling on downhill stretches. Cutting long toenails the night before a trip will result in pain and inflamation on the trail. Great discomfort (and worn sock toes) can be prevented by awareness of the problem. I try to keep my toenails reasonably short with frequent cutting, but I also remind myself, sometimes in writing, to cut my toenails four or five days before a trip.

I think the best way to toughen up feet is to make a practice of going barefoot. Before a trip I go barefoot around the house and I like to go for short barefoot walks. Concrete sidewalks are great tougheners and callous builders. I have the idea that sunlight and fresh air are healthy for feet, certainly a lot healthier than damp, constricting shoes. I spend enough time barefoot to sport a pretty fair tan on the tops of my feet by the end of the summer. Tanning can be extremely important to the comfort and pleasure of a trip. People who take lily white skin to high altitudes become horribly burned unless they keep themselves carefully and continuously covered.

A tan acquired in the city or at the beach will never fully protect the hiker against fierce high altitude sunlight but it will enable him to travel with only normal discretion without risk of serious burning. Nothing is worse than having to hike in the heat completely shrouded from the sun—unless it is suffering with sunburned shoulders that will have to carry a pack the next day. Trying to safely tan white skin by short periods of exposure to fierce high altitude sun is a bothersome, inconvenient process on a backpacking trip.

Our man will be well advised to start cultivating a tan by getting out in the sun (in a bathing suit if he expects to hike in shorts) on weekends from the beginning of his conditioning period—taking care to use discretion and sunburn preventatives. If there is anything more vulnerable to mountain sunshine than city skin it is sunburned city skin that has freshly peeled. Special care should be taken to avoid burning the nose to prevent starting a cycle of peeling, burning and repeeling.

Not many backpackers will need to take the full conditioning course outlined above, but most people will enjoy a more comfortable trip to the extent that they complete their conditioning at home.

PACKING UP

With trip planning, preparation and conditioning out of the way, all that remains is to pack up and go. For most people, that means taking a car to the trailhead; and sometimes that journey is the hardest trip their car ever makes. On more than a few trips, the biggest adventure, the greatest challenge and the hardest work is getting the car to the trailhead and back. I have slipped off the road, gotten stuck in the mud and hung up on rocks. I have run out of water and gas, blown out tires, smashed into rocks and killed the motor fording creeks. Trailheads have a habit of lying deserted at the ends of unmaintained rocky roads, so it behooves the backpacker to take more than a casual interest in the condition of his car.

Backpackers are often so intent on getting their gear into the car and getting away that they forget to carry the extra food, drink, clothing and money that is so welcome at the end of a trip. For purposes of acclimation and an early start, I like to drive from home to the trailhead on the eve of the trip in order to sleep at the highest elevation possible. To simplify matters, I usually take a car camping sleeping bag and mattress to insure a good rest, and no matter how late I arrive I always choose my bedsite carefully and excavate for my hips and shoulders. If I have to cook, I take along a separate stove, food and utensils rather than rummage in my backpacking gear. When possible, it is usually most convenient to eat in a restaurant.

While driving to the trailhead, I try to get a final weather forecast on the car radio. Sometimes at the last available pay phone, I call the

nearest Weather Bureau or airport or Highway Patrol office to get an extended forecast. On the basis of this information, together with weather conditions at the trailhead, I make my final selection of protective gear: tents, rain suits, ponchos, ground sheets, tarps, parkas, mittens, caps and sweaters. My usual procedure, after deciding what to carry, is to spread out an old tarp, brought along for that purpose, and empty on to it all the food and community gear.

Then, if there are two of us, one of us divides the pile on the basis of both weight and bulk into two equal stacks; the other man gets first choice. It is probably a good idea to employ a scale to be precise, but we generally just heft comparable items at arms' length and hope that compensating errors will cancel out major differences. Sometimes one man, because of his pack, will be short on space and may request less bulky items, but both hikers still split the weight evenly, unless there is a marked difference in their size. Carrying ability is usually proportional to body weight.

After combining my share of the community gear with my personal equipment, I start to make up my pack, laying it flat on the ground on the shoulder straps. First I set aside clothing that may be needed in a hurry, trail food, notebook, pencil, compass, first aid kit, camera, lip salve, sunburn cream, bandana, mosquito dope and anything else I expect to need on the trail. Then, starting at the top of the pack, I make a layer of the heaviest, densest items in such a way that the weight will lie as high and as close to my back as possible. From the remaining gear I take those items least likely to be needed and, working my way to the top, fill the remainder of the pack snugly. If I am hiking in shorts, my long trousers are packed on top for easy access, or in the lower compartment of a divided bag.

The gear set aside to be used on the trail is then systematically divided between the pack's outside pockets. To find things fast, it helps to use the same arrangement for every trip. For instance, I make a habit of sprinkling wooden kitchen matches in every pocket, but the main supply always rides in the upper right hand pocket. With the last of the small items stowed, I stuff my rolled foam mattress into (or onto) the top of the back pag and cinch down the flap over it. My sleeping bag is then strapped or snapped beneath the three quarter pack bag. Last to be attached is my two piece fly rod, broken down, but with the reel still attached. The butt ends seat in a 35 mm film can taped to the bottom right rail. A thong at the top crossbar lashes the rod to the rail.

With the pack made up and hoisted onto the hood of the car for easy mounting, I go through my pockets, reload the car, hide my wallet after extracting two or three dimes for pay phone use, and lock the car. Normally I hide the keys nearby, rather than take the chance of losing them. After making sure I know what direction I want to go, I slip into my pack and adjust the buckles so the weight is bourn equally by my shoulders and hips. With nothing further to detain me, I pop a lemondrop in my mouth and set forth up the trail.

⁹ WALKING

There is nothing much to be said about walking . . . on a sidewalk at sea level for short distances, carrying nothing. But walking long distances through high altitude wilderness, under sizeable loads, is something else. Luckily there are a few stratagems and techniques that can add considerable pleasure to walking in the wilds.

Before one starts walking it is necessary to be properly shod. For day hiking on easy terrain, moccasins or tennis shoes might suffice. For backpacking on easy trails or more rugged day hiking, ankle-high work shoes or light boots are necessary. And for backpacking in rock, cross-country or climbing, lug-soled boots made expressly for mountaineering are needed. Boots need to be well broken in and sufficiently water repellant for the conditions to be faced.

With boots snugly laced over heavy, wrinkle-free socks, the first consideration in starting down the trail is finding a comfortable pace. There is often a temptation, if one is anxious to be moving to start out too fast. Backpackers should be conscious, from the moment they shoulder packs, of the necessity for conserving energy for the journey ahead. There are two useful guides to finding a comfortable pace. The first—for maximum speed—involves increasing the pace until discomfort begins to grow, then slowing down a little. The other—for a more leisurely pace—is to travel at the fastest rate that allows for companionable conversation without difficult breathing.

There is a myth that one should find a comfortable pace and then stick to it. Nothing could be farther from the truth. The most common error among hikers is trying doggedly to maintain a set pace despite changes in the grade. Constant speed is an impossible goal. Comfortable, efficient walking depends on maintaining one's energy output—not one's speed—at a level which will not produce excessive fatigue. This simply means slowing down when the trail climbs, then speeding up when it levels off.

The length of one's stride should also be variable. When the trail suddenly grows steeper, I not only slow down, I take shorter steps. When the trail levels off, my stride automatically lengthens as I increase my speed. Walking in this manner, i.e. trying to maintain an unchanging and comfortable output of energy rather than trying to maintain a constant speed, I am never forced to stop from exhaustion, and I log more miles per day in greater comfort.

It is important to react immediately to changes in grade. Failure to cut speed instantly when the trail turns abruptly upward places a demand on the body for extra exertion. And extra exertion consumes a disproportionately large part of one's store of energy. For instance, with the energy required to run fifty yards uphill one can easily hike a quarter mile up the same grade—in far greater comfort. Large expenditures of energy—running, lunging, jumping, taking huge steps, even hiking too fast—must be avoided.

On a really steep slope, at high altitude under load, or where the footing is bad (sand, scree or loose snow), I adjust my pace even more precisely by controlling my step-to-breath ratio. I may, for instance, take two steps to the breath, inhaling as I plant my right foot and exhaling as I plant my left. If that proves hard to maintain, I may slow to a breath for every step or even two breaths per step, with a greatly shortened stride. On exceptionally difficult slopes it is better to slow to a crawl, taking six inch steps, than to make the frequent stops a faster pace would require. A dependable rule of thumb is that where the going is hard it is better to slow down and keep going than it is to make frequent stops. An unlooked for dividend of step-to-breath counting is the distraction the counting provides.

Every experienced backpacker at some time or other has experienced a sinking feeling when, coming around a bend, he sees a long, shadeless trail switchbacking endlessly upward toward a high and distant pass. When I find myself faced with a prospect of this sort, I often distract myself from the ordeal with the self-induced euphoria that comes of concentrated daydreaming. In a state of mild self-hypnosis, my daydreams so totally absorb my conscious mind that the discomfort of the grind goes mercifully dim.

As I start upward toward the pass I rummage about in my memory for some event or scene that is so thoroughly pleasant and engrossing that I recall it with consumate relish. Then I unhurriedly embelish my recollection with the endless details that enable it vividly to fill my conscious mind. At first, it may be hard to escape into the past, but as the details pile up my awareness of present time and distance almost ceases. I climb automatically, sufficiently aware of my surroundings to make the necessary adjustments, but too engrossed with my dream to feel the discomfort. It is sometimes with reluctance, when the pass has been reached, that I abandon my dream and shift my attention to the country ahead.

While I find daydreaming dependable and easily sustained, some

daydream
dis-
comfort
away.

people prefer the more companionable distraction of conversation. One of my regular walking companions, when we face a demanding stretch of trail, will say "Well, what shall we talk about?" We may very well get rid of a quarter of a mile before we settle on a suitable topic. Often we trade accounts of movies, dreams, books, trout we have caught or mountains we have climbed. Sometimes we may be driven to simple word games (especially useful with children) like Twenty Questions or Animal-Mineral-Vegetable. If we have been out in the country awhile, we may get rid of half an hour concocting menus for fantastic meals. Talking as we move upward tends to slow the pace, but that, in turn, further reduces the discomfort.

Despite my advice "to slow down and keep going," rest stops are a vital part of walking. Unless the trail is like a sidewalk, one has little opportunity for looking around; the footing requires almost undivided attention. The walking itself is usually the least memorable part of any trip. So rest stops offer a means of savoring the country as well as restoring the body. One school holds that rests ought to be ruled by the clock, i.e. so many minutes of resting followed by so many minutes of hiking. This arbitrary arrangement makes no allowance for the difficulty of the terrain or the allure of the country.

But what disturbs me most is the notion that one needs to be ruled by the clock, even in the wilderness. The tyranny of time, it seems to me, is one of the things that people go to the woods to escape. I am willing to admit the usefulness of a wristwatch in the woods for arranging a rendezvous with other watch-wearing members of the party—but I find clock time as dispensable in the wilds as doorbells, radios, telephones and cars, and I refuse to carry a watch.

If I really need to know the time my compass will give a rough approximation, provided the sun is shining. I set the compass in the sun, settle the needle on north, then set off the declination (17 degrees east in California). With the compass thus oriented, I stand a straight twig on the compass rim so that its shadow falls across the needle hub to the opposite rim. The position of the shadow on the opposite rim gives me a close approximation of sun time—by thinking of the compass as a watch with north at noon. To reconcile sun time to daylight saving time, I add an hour. To tell time early or late in the day it helps to know the hours of sunrise and sunset; and some allowance must be made for mountains that rise high to either the east or west.

I find it distinctly pleasant to wake up that first morning in the wilds, glance out of habit at my bare wrist, and realize how unimportant clock time has become. Time is still important, but it is sun time, not clock time, that counts. How long before sunset, when it starts to grow cool? How long before dark? These are the pertinent questions in the wilds.

Returning to the subject of rest stops, most walkers, provided they have a modicum of self-discipline and know how far they have to go, will find it more satisfactory to rest when they want to or need to. I like to stop, if I can manage it, beside a stream, at the top of a slope, in the first shade after a treeless stretch, where a log or rock forms a natural seat, or at any point where the view is unusually fine. I also favor mossy dells, waterfalls, brilliant patches of wildflowers, and fords where I can wash my feet or set up my rod and take a few casts.

Where the beauty of an area demands frequent stops, I sometimes sit down just along enough to bring my breathing back to normal. When it comes to a real rest, I like to imagine I have earned it. On a particularly difficult slope, for instance, I might promise myself a rest after another hundred steps. Sometimes a hundred is impossible and I have to settle for fifty or even twenty-five. But if I get to thirty-five and think I can squeeze out another fifteen—I try it. For variety, and to add to the distraction, I sometimes count my steps backwards.

When I have earned my rest I take some pains to enjoy it. I slip out of my pack (leaving it propped against a rock or tree to make it

rest stops are a vital part of walking.

easy to put back on) and sit or lie down. If my boots are the least bit uncomfortable or my feet are damp, I take off both boots and socks and set them to air in the sun or breeze. If there is water running nearby, I give my feet a soapless washing and a rub and let them dry in the sun. If I am feeling faint or tired I lie down with my feet propped high against a tree so the blood can drain from my legs back into my body.

Once my fatigue has drained away and my breathing has returned to normal, I usually have something to eat. If I am neither ravenous nor weary, I take slow acting protein and fat—nuts, bacon bar, salami or jerky; if I badly need quick energy I eat mint cake, fruit or some kind of candy. These chores out of the way, I may want to make notes, take pictures, consult the map or play the orientation game (See Chapter 7).

Sometimes the greatest benefit of a rest stop—especially if there are children along—is having some fun, doing a little exploring. I like to stroll away from the trail to have a look at country I would otherwise miss. Often enough, I discover something unsuspected—an abandoned prospect hole, a bed of mushrooms, a remarkable view, the remains of a lean-to, a tiny spring or a wild sheep horn.

A rest may last anywhere from thirty seconds to thirty minutes, but I rarely can rationalize staying more than fifteen minutes—unless the fishing is exceptional or I have made a lengthy excursion. When the time comes to move on, it is vital to start out at a moderate pace. There is a tendency, especially with children, to rocket up the trail after a refreshing rest. I have often seen eager children start off at a run, slow to a walk, then sink into a panting, dispirited trudge—all within sixty seconds.

The single most valuable (and spectacular) walking technique I know of, one which literally flushes away fatigue, is variously called the 'rest step' or 'limp step.' Though little known among backpackers, this maneuver is based on the simplest of principles. When a hiker climbs steeply or carries great weights, the strain on the muscles around the knee is excessive and these muscles quickly fill with lactic and carbonic acids, the products of fatigue. This buildup of acids in overworked muscles, in turn, produces the painful ache that makes terrific slopes or heavy loads so uncomfortable.

The rest step is designed to flush away the acids of fatigue, thus relieving the ache they create. In the course of normal walking knee muscles never quite relax. But if at some point in the step the leg is allowed to go entirely limp, even for only a fraction of a second, the excess acids are carried away and the pain miraculously disappears.

The necessary relaxation can be managed in either of two ways. The leading leg can be allowed to go limp for an instant just after the foot is placed for a new step and just before the weight is shifted to it. Or the trailing leg can be relaxed just after the weight is transferred to the lead leg and just before the trailing leg is lifted. I have gotten in the habit of relaxing the lead leg, but most people seem to find it easier to let the trailing leg go limp. The trailing leg method is also easier to learn and easier to teach. My daughter managed to learn it when she was eight.

We were day hiking up a relentlessly climbing trail that gains 1200 feet in less than a mile. When she complained that she was tired and her legs hurt, I had her stop and shift all her weight first to one leg then the other, explaining that the pain would go away from a leg allowed to go limp. After she had stopped to flush her legs in this manner several times, I suggested that she take a small step forward with the leg that was relaxed, explaining that it was less tiring to keep going, even very slowly, when you rested your legs. Before we reached the top she was able to flush the fatigue from her legs whenever she needed to, without stopping.

As few as two or three limp steps in succession will usually bring amazing relief. Of course, the acids of fatigue continue to collect as long as the knees continue to work hard, and it soon becomes necessary to flush them again. But I find that after half a dozen limp steps I can return to my normal stride for anywhere from ten to a hundred yards. Besides offering relief from aching muscles, limp-stepping also provides comic relief by causing its practitioners to look a little like staggering drunks.

A technique of somewhat narrower application is the Indian Step, a style of walking long used by cross-country skiers and European gymnasts as well as American Indians. Modern Americans tend to bob up and down, especially as they ascend a slope. The objection to this is that a certain amount of the hiker's energy is consumed in useless rising and falling. The Indian travels more efficiently.

At the end of each step he swings the hip forward as well as the leg, pivoting at the waist. And he leans forward slightly as he walks.

This forward lean and turning of the hips lengthens the stride, positions the feet directly in front of one another, and minimizes the wasteful up and down movement. The result is a more fluid, floating walk, with less wasted motion. And on easy ground the longer stride produces more speed. The chief disadvantages of the Indian Step are that it is difficult to master, requiring agility and balance; and the advantages are greatest for the unburdened walker.

I occasionally use the Indian Step if I am lightly burdened and wish to travel rapidly across level terrain that offers good footing. I also employ its principles to minimize my up and down motion on a steep climb. The easiest way to get the feel of the step is consciously to stretch the stride, thrusting the hip forward, aiming the foot for the center of the trail, swinging the shoulders counter to the hip thrust. Once the rhythm is established the shoulder swing can be reduced. Walking on narrow city curbs is a good way to practice.

Limp-stepping brings amazing relief:

Having dealt with uphill and level trail hiking, it is time to go down. It is common to feel relief when the trail starts down because it is so much easier on the lungs. But downhill travel is twice as hard on the legs as going up. When descending a steep trail I try to cushion the shock of each downward step by rolling my hip forward (not unlike the Indian Step movement) and placing my foot with the knee slightly bent. As I transfer my weight I allow my knee to flex so that it functions in much the same fashion as an automobile shock absorber, reducing the jarring that downhill travel inevitably produces.

Trails provide a measure of dependability and security. Cross-country walking is altogether different. Instead of relying on an established course, one must find his own way; instead of the improved footing of a prepared trail, there are obstacles to contend with. Carrying a pack cross-country can be serious business and requires much greater experience, strength, adventurousness and caution than does backpacking by trail.

In the California Sierra in the space of a mile, one may have to contend with brush, bog, loose sand, boulder slopes, snow, deadfalls, mud, streams and cliffs. And one of the most treacherous slopes I ever descended was covered with innocent-looking, but extremely slippery grass. Just as slippery are glacially polished slabs that are wet, mossy or invisibly dusted with sand. Footing of this sort demands caution. I often take some trouble to climb around a wet or mossy slab, and when traction is vital I test the slope for sand by listening for the telltale grating sound.

When climbing a sandy slope it is important to plant the foot as flatly as possible; the greater the surface area of boot on sand the shorter the distance one is likely to slip backward. If there are rocks or patches of grass or low brush, I think of them as stepping stones and zig-zag from one to the other. Sometimes steep sand is best treated like snow and the easiest way up is a series of switchbacking traverses or a herringbone step in which the toes are turned outward.

Spring travel in the Sierra is often over old snow; sometimes I walk all day and scarcely touch dry ground. Hard and hummocky slopes of spring snow can be extremely tiring, and nothing short of wading tests the waterproofing of boots so severely. It is virtually impossible to keep feet dry. All one can do is carry several pairs of dry socks for a single day's travel. Since wet boots are extremely slow to dry, the Indians of northern Canada carry four pairs of sturdy moccasins or mukluks instead. By the time the fourth pair is soaked through the first pair has dried. My own solution, if I am rushing the season, is to content myself with day hikes and keep dry boots waiting at the trailhead.

In the spring there is the constant danger of falling through a thin crust of snow with painful, even serious, results. There is hardly an easier way to bark shins, twist ankles and even break legs. Whenever I cross a rock-studded spring snowfield I am reminded of a trip I made with my father when I was twelve. I was walking a little in front and we were talking. When he failed to answer a question I turned around, and he was gone. There was nothing but a vast snowfield broken only by an occasional rock. As I followed his footprints back toward one of these, I heard what sounded like distant shouting. Close beside the rock, which turned out to be a boulder, I came to a hole, and ten feet below in the bottom of an ice cavern my father stood, uninjured, calling for help. It took half an hour to get him out. The cavern had been hollowed by heat from the sun transmitted through the boulder despite the fact that only a few square feet of rock actually rose above the snowfield.

The margins of spring snowfields should always be treated with suspicion. So should snow-covered logs and snow from which issues the muffled sound of gurgling water. The best strategy I know for testing suspect snow is to kick it without actually committing any weight to it. If it withstands the kicking it can probably support my weight. Sometimes a big step or jump will avoid the necessity of stepping on what looks like rotten or undermined snow.

spring snow by a rock is often undermined....

so step over such areas.

Nothing consumes energy in such big gulps as maneuvers that require extra effort, like taking a giant step up onto a rock or log. If I cannot easily make my way around such obstacles, I transfer most of the extra effort to my shoulders and arms by placing both hands on top of the knee that is making the step and pushing down hard as I step upward.

the arms can help on a long step up.

On exceptionally steep rocky slopes, it sometimes becomes necessary to step forward onto the toe of the foot instead of the heel. Toe stepping adds power and balance on steep grades, but soon tires calf muscles. I find it helps to alternate heel and toe steps to prevent the cramping the latter produce. By following ten toe steps with twenty heel steps, I spread the work over two sets of muscles. The necessity of counting helps distract me from the rigours of the climb. If this arrangement continues to produce excessive fatigue, I sheer off from the fall-line and climb in longer but easier switchbacking traverses.

When climbing cross-country it is sometimes necessary to remind oneself that the easiest route up may not be the easiest way down. Going up, I generally go out of my way to avoid sand, snow and scree; coming down I go out of my way to make use of them. Nothing is so pleasant after a hard climb up a mountain as glissading down a slanting snowfield or gliding with giant, sliding steps down slopes of sand or gravel.

The ultimate in walking is climbing up mountains. Sooner or later nearly everyone who walks in the wilderness will experience a yearning to stand on top. Most hikers climb their first peak by following a trail to the summit. The sense of achievement, the view, and the joy of standing high above the surrounding country tend to make climbing mildly addictive. A great many walkers, who certainly do not think of themselves as climbers, head for the summit whenever one is near. Sometimes a very satisfying ascent can be managed in an hour or so after a spur-of-the-moment decision. When I am resting on the trail in a mountain pass, I often succumb to the urge to leave my pack and follow the ridge to a nearby crest. Other times, a climb will be one of the principal purposes of a backpacking trip and the route and timetable will be planned accordingly.

Scrambling—climbing that requires the use of hands, but not ropes—demands agility, good balance, endurance and desire. Success may depend on the scrambler's ability to discover a feasible route by studying the slope during the approach and by consulting a large scale topographic map. The basic rules for beginning climbers include: never climb alone; never go up a pitch you cannot get down; never climb on your knees; lean out from, not in toward the slope when exposure is great; and never take chances or attempt maneuvers that are beyond your skill.

Despite the need for caution, climbing can be enjoyed by most walkers, including women and children. Both my wife and daughter have climbed a number of peaks with me; my daughter made her first ascent when she was six. It is unfortunate that so many people think climbing means inching up sheer cliffs by means of ropes, pitons and limitless willpower. There is immense satisfaction to be gained in scrambling up peaks that demand little more than determination and offer no disconcerting exposure.

Climbing can be as safe as the climber cares to make it. As I come down a mountain late in the day, I remind myself that the majority of mountaineering accidents occur after three in the afternoon, and that twice as many falls happen on the way down as on the way up. The most expert climbers force themselves to descend with caution, thinking out difficult steps in advance to keep down the chance of injury.

Rock-hopping—crossing a boulder field by stepping or jumping from rock to rock—is probably the most demanding and dangerous way to travel in the mountains, but it is often unavoidable. I mentally try to keep a step ahead of my feet so when I run out of rocks I will be able to stop. I also treat every boulder, no matter how large, as though the addition of my weight will cause it to move. To slow myself down on a dangerous slope, I sometimes think back to a cross-country backpacking descent on which a companion, when forced to leap from a rolling boulder, opened six inches of his leg to the bone. Whenever I am forced to make a sudden or awkward jump, I try to land simultaneously on both feet with knees bent, to cushion the shock and minimize the danger of injury.

With more and more people walking in the wilds, trail manners have become more important. In most states discharging firearms, even during hunting season, is illegal across or in the vicinity of a trail. Equally objectionable is the boom of gunfire which invades privacy and solitude, and shatters the wilderness experience of other travelers for miles around. Guns are not needed as protection against wildlife and they have no place in today's crowded wildlands.

Horses and pack stock, once necessary to reach remote country, are (thankfully) dwindling in use. But since stock can be unpredictable and difficult to control, it retains the right-of-way on trails. Walkers should move several yards off the trail, preferably downslope, and stand quietly while animals pass. Since walkers inevitably travel at different speeds, slower-moving parties should be considerate enough of faster walkers to let them move by. And fast hikers ought to politely ask permission to pass when the trail is narrow.

Over-riding the backpacker's concern for his comfort should be a sense of responsibility toward the country through which he passes. Increased travel in diminishing wild areas makes it necessary for all of us, consciously, to protect the environment and keep it clean. On the trail this means throwing away nothing, not even a cigarette butt, broken shoelace or match. In camp it means burning, then bagging, but never burying, garbage. Leftover edibles, not including egg shells and orange peels, can be scattered for the birds and animals. Everything else should go in heavy plastic garbage bags to be packed out. The thoughtful walker takes pride in leaving no trace of his passing.

10 CAMPING

For a majority of backpackers, a genuinely pleasant camp is essential to the enjoyment of any trip. Unfortunately, the more comfortable the camp the greater the quantity of gear that must be carried—and the harder the walk required to reach it.

The backpacker with no mattress, stove or tent travels comfortably light. He can go faster and farther than heavily laden hikers, and he is free to leave the trails and travel cross-country. But when the sun goes down he becomes increasingly vulnerable and must find comparatively ideal conditions in order to make a comfortable camp. The party carrying a floored tent equipped with mosquito netting and rainfly, stove, mattresses and all the trimmings is practically invulnerable to camping conditions, but its range and speed and traveling comfort are more limited, and it is more dependent upon trails.

The dilemma can never be completely resolved, but as a backpacker's experience, technique, and equipment improve, the cost (in pounds) of camping comfort can be considerably reduced.

The question of what to take must be reconsidered afresh for every trip. The likely weather, season and type of trip will influence the decisions regarding tents, tarps, ponchos and storm gear—so will the route, the type of outing, length of stay and familiarity with the country. There is no convenient way to avoid decisions, though some hikers persist in carrying the same gear on every trip. On a two mile trail haul to a family base camp I might seriously consider carrying the kitchen sink. On a thirty mile cross-country ridgewalk I pare my equipment to Spartan porportions.

No amount of mountaineering equipment, of course, can insure camping comfort in a steep, waterless, windy rockpile. There is simply no substitute for a wise choice of campsite. No skill is of greater value to the comfort-oriented backpacker than the ability to select the best possible spot to camp, and then to develop it for optimum comfort.

A persistent wind, damp ground, sloping bedsites, a lack of fuel or shelter, noisy neighbors, clouds of mosquitos, lack of water, etc. will rob the best equipped party of a pleasant night. There are times, of course, when bad weather, poor planning, inhospitable country or just plain bad luck make a terrible location unavoidable. The veteran backpacker will choose the least terrible site and devise the most ingenious development in order to make it yield minimal comfort.

First priority in site selection must go to bedsites since nothing is more important than a good nights' sleep. Damp and sloping ground should be avoided—so should roots and rocks that cannot be removed. Spare clothing and equipment should not be forgotten in the struggle to make a poor bedsite passable. Shelter from wind, unwelcome sun, evening downdrafts or intense cold may be essential to restful sleep. (See chapter 3 for details of bedsite selection.)

The ideal bedsite is a tiny level hollow filled with dry pine needles lying just to the west of a large, fragrant pine. If the wind is blowing and cannot be avoided I take pains to point my feet to windward, and if the night promises to be cold I build a small earth and rock windbreak at my feet. Even on a warm night a persistent wind can chill exposed limbs; the noise, the twitching of the bag and the breeze in one's face will rob even—perhaps especially—the most exhausted camper of hours of sleep. On an evening when the wind promises to blow, an extra fifteen minutes spent hunting for or constructing shelter from the wind will be time well spent.

When it comes to shelter, nothing beats a tent—so long as the shelter is from rain or bugs or cold. When it comes to wind, many experienced backpackers prefer to hunt a sheltered spot or build a rock or wood windbreak, rather than submit to the tugging, flapping, hissing or whistling of a tent or tarp. In warm weather a tent may also be a liability if ventilation is needed more than shelter. And in difficult terrain the best (or only good) bedsites often are unsuitable for erecting a tent. Not uncommonly, the camper must choose between the shelter of a tent and a comfortable bed.

The old prospector with whom I often camp in the desert considers me far too finicky about my bed. After throwing his fifty pound bedroll (including mattress) from the truck, he is guided by just one consideration: his bed must be lined up north-south—with the head in the north—to assure a refreshing sleep. He believes that the magnetic lines of force must pass through him properly (head to toe) in order to recharge him with energy for the following day.

If the bedsites in the campsite under consideration meet minimum qualifications, I next consider such criteria as proximity to water, abundance of fuel, insect population and aesthetics. Of course, all these factors are considered simultaneously. One does not hunt good bedsites in a waterless, woodless area unless one is traveling with stove and canteen in the desert.

What usually happens is that a backpacker, having chosen a generally hospitable area to camp in, needs only to discover the best of all possible campsites. I have found that the best way to find a really good spot is to take off my pack in the first place that seems to meet minimum standards and then try to find something better, unencumbered. If I search under load, I tend to settle for a lower quality site. Of course, it helps if I am neither exhausted, starving nor running out of daylight.

When camp has been chosen, especially if it is late, I find it useful to have some kind of routine in mind, to get me through the chores in the minimum time, with the minimum expenditure of energy. But before going to work, the first thing I do after taking off my pack is to treat myself to a substantial snack. Chores go quicker if the hunger pangs can first be dispersed.

My order of events might read as follows: release and flatten out my tightly rolled polyurethane foam pad so it can expand and regain its resiliency. I pull the mummy bag from its stuff sack, shake it to fluff up the down, unzip it and spread it in the sun to air. If it is early afternoon, I gather the cheese, butter and other potential spoilables or meltables (like chocolate) and stow them safely in stream, snowbank lake or shade.

Unless the afternoon is very late and dinner must be prepared, I take off my boots and wash my feet and socks and string shirt; if the lake is warm enough I take a swim, often in my hiking shorts; then I wring out the wash and hang it to dry in the sun on convenient boulders and bushes. I am careful to wash nothing that I could conceivably need before the following day.

When I have swum and basked and dozed away as much of the afternoon as I can afford to squander, I rearrange the wash—damp side out—dress to the extent I must (wearing moccasins instead of boots) and start arranging my bed. If shelter is needed and I have brought a tent, I make sure it can be positioned on my tentatively chosen bedsite before I begin development. When I have scraped and dug and sculptured the bedsite to the point where it feels comfortable lying directly on the ground, I position my ground cloth or bivouac cover and foam pad and lie down once more before zipping up my bag and slipping it—warm and fluffed— beneath the protective cover.

With a comfortable rest carefully prepared for, I sort through my pack and dig out everything I am liable to need in the night: personal kit, watch cap, bandana, flashlight, down sweater and socks for the following day. All of these are tucked in appropriate spots beside my sleeping bag inside the bivouac cover; a rock on top of my pillow assures that nothing will be dampened by the dew that will fall before I finally go to bed. The only exception is the small Birec or

Mallory flashlight, which for the time being goes in my pocket. In the process of digging through my pack, I collect everything needed for preparing dinner: packets of soup and stew, herbs, condiments, pots, cups, stove, etc.

Since even a small breeze disturbs the flame and reduces the efficiency of nearly any stove, it becomes necessary to locate the kitchen in the most sheltered, protected part of camp. The alternative, especially if preparation requires a low flame, is to build a wind screen of some sort. Sensitivity to wind is one of the largest drawbacks of stoves; unfortunately, a featherweight folding windscreen adaptable to all circumstances has yet to be developed; but a variety of stratagems have proved effective.

One morning I awoke with my family in a heavy breeze. My wife needed a cup of tea before facing the world, but the Bluet would not light in the most sheltered spot available. I pulled the four-foot foam pad from my bed, bent it into a circle around the stove and got my daughter to hold it in place while I made Sherpa tea and hot cinnamon oatmeal.

oatmeal, coming up!

Once the stove is set up, water drawn from the lake, and the soup packet emptied in the pot, I know I am no more than fifteen minutes away from enjoying the first course of dinner. If hunger and approaching darkness do not urge me to start cooking, I usually see what can be done about preparing a campfire to cheer up the evening. A good many people like to get up early in the mountains and consequently they are ready for bed soon after dinner. I carry my city habits into the wilds, rising at a comfortable hour and sitting up rather late. Without a campfire, I could not indulge myself so easily.

If my campsite has been used before, I use or rebuild the existing firepit, taking care to turn the blackened sides of the rocks inward so I do not add to their discoloring. If I am on virgin ground, I try to dig a shallow pit in sand or mineralized earth (never duff, meadow, decayed wood or vegetation) so that I can safely burn without blackening anything.

If firewood is the least bit scarce I assuage my conscience by burning rotten wood which another winter will render unburnable, chunks of bark, smashed pine cones and other wood which others might reject. And I keep my fire comparatively small. Since heaps of chunk charcoal are unsightly in the wilderness, I try to burn all that I find in a campsite, as well as all the fuel I use, down to an ash which will blow away and convert quickly to soil.

When I have scavenged enough wood for the evening fire, I build a tepee of light, dry twigs over a few loosely crumpled squares of toilet paper or paper towel on which I have first balanced a handfull of tinder dry pine needles or dead grass. Since tinder and paper is quickly dampened by the dew that begins falling in the high mountains the moment the sun disappears, I am careful not to wait long past sunset to light my fires—especially if the day has been cloudy or it has recently rained.

At sunset or thereabouts, I light the stove beneath my soup, put on warm clothes for the evening, zip extra food securely into my pack, take in the wash and stow it also in the pack, stir the soup to make sure it is not sticking, adding whatever butter, milk or bacon bar I can spare, then light and nurse my campfire past the critical stage. The best single rule I know for successful firebuilding is for the fire builder to be supplied with twice the tinder, matches, twigs, paper, etc. that should be needed.

A great many fires die while the builder is out looking frantically for more of something that burns well. Other common mistakes are packing the paper too tightly and smothering it with tinder: any kind of fuel needs plenty of oxygen to burn properly. At the other extreme, spreading the fuel so loosely that it fails to concentrate its heat is a familiar cause of failure.

Before the soup is ready, I arrange all the components of dinner —opened packet of freeze-dried food, sumptuous supplements and condiments and water so that as soon as the last of the soup has been poured the main course can be started. In parties of three or more, this usually means that the stove need not be shut down in order to conserve fuel—extremely desirable in gasoline and kerosene stove cooking—and the pot neither cools down nor scorches. Simplicity of meal preparation, of course, is essential to such exquisite timing.

Before the main course is ready, I lay out the makings for tea, and the stewed fruit or pudding that will very likely be eaten in the dark. If my craving for sweets and liquids promises to be hard to satisfy, I may also select a packet of lemonade or perhaps freeze-dry ice cream or gorp or trail candy. Since I tend to spend a good deal of time beside the fire in the evening, it is often worthwhile to drag or roll a boulder or log before the fire to serve alternately as a seat or back rest—providing, of course, that the dislocation does not disfigure the immediate landscape.

It is generally advisable to schedule dinner so that the meal is over—except for desert, snacks and drinks—well before dark. I like to go fishing or walking between dinner and dark. These excursions, I have discovered, often turn out to provide the most pleasant experiences of the trip. After a long day it is easy to lie in camp, feeling comfortably tired, and often I do exactly that.

But the wildness I have come to see does not really begin until camp and trail are left behind. Campsites and paths are simply extensions, however faint, of civilization. To experience wildness one must wander away from all travelers' routes to see what lies in the country beyond. It never seems hard, even if I know the immediate area quite well, to find someplace intriguing to go walking after dinner. Since my jaunts have a way of running longer than planned, I always carry matches, pocketknife, jacket and flashlight.

Unless I am leaving early in the morning, I give the soup-stew pot only a brisk, brief cleaning after dinner, planning to wait for better light to finish the job. But quick attention after dinner—even before the pan cools (and food congeals)—will save work in the long run. I scrape the pot with a big spoon to loosen all excess food and empty the contents in thick brush, for the nourishment of small animals, well away from camp and water. (There is nothing quite so grim as stepping down to the shore of a pretty pool, only to see the remains of someone's spaghetti dinner strewn across the bottom.) Then I add a little water (hot if the tea kettle has been on the fire), scrub briefly with a Chore Girl or abrasive pad and empty the scourings in the brush again. The pot, filled with water, is easily cleaned later.

When the campfire is really burning and the coals are hot, I toss in not only the paper and plastic refuse, but foil packages and Tea Kettle aluminum pans as well. If the fire is hot enough these are largely consumed; at the very least they are cleaned and much reduced in volume for the trip home. I usually drink tea in the evening, keeping the teapot warm in the fire even though the water is usually heated on the stove. In the city, I like only a little sugar in my tea, but camp tea often suffers from boiling, debris, weakness or bitterness and I find I prefer it in the English manner well laced with milk powder and sugar.

Since on short trips in small parties I usually do not carry pails, jugs or buckets for carrying water, it is often necessary to refill my plastic bottle. The great advantage of both the Mallory and Birec flashlights over those requiring conventional sized batteries is that by holding the light in one's mouth both hands are left free for cooking, washing dishes, gathering wood or drawing water. It is even possible, with practice, to carry on a conversation.

When the time approaches to go to bed, I customarily brush my teeth in my last cup of tea and stir up the fire to coax as complete combustion as possible; partially burned sticks make unrewarding scenery. If the night is cold I put on a Navy surplus wool watch cap to ward off the cold (heat is rapidly lost from the head). If I am putting on pajamas or long johns or other clothes to sleep in I warm them first over the fire and change quickly. I tend the fire until it has burned down to a safe bed of ash and coals. If there is a breeze or danger of traveling sparks, I spread the ashes to reduce heat and cover with sand or water.

There are easier jobs than getting undressed in the cold and dark and wriggling into a dew-soaked mummy bag without getting cold or wet. I generally sit on my pillow, take off my shoes and turn them upside down; then I take off my socks and trousers and slip into bed in a sitting position in my shoulder hole. From this point it is comparatively easy to peel off the rest of my clothes and tuck them under the tarp or bivouac cover before sliding the rest of the way into bed. After pulling the drawstring that converts the top of my bag into a hood, and locking it, I zip up the bag, leaving my flashlight by the top of the zipper.

In the morning the first thing I do—after rising and getting on my clothes—is to dismantle my bed and set it to dry. Even if the dew seems already to have dried, there is liable to be ground dampness and condensation from my body. Weather has a way of changing fast in the wilderness, and it is nice to have one's bed bone dry and securely packed; the same goes for tents and tarps; anyone who has had to pack and carry a wet tent will go to some lengths to avoid repeating the experience. I spread my foam pad, bivouac cover and sleeping bag out flat on sunny rocks or breezy bushes until they are warm and absolutely dry, then I turn them over. When the outsides are nicely toasted, I turn them inside out and repeat the process. In the dry air of a high Sierra the whole process rarely takes more than half an hour, even after a heavy dew or drizzle.

relaxing after breakfast

Since I am more likely to wake up feeling sticky than hungry I usually wash, or possibly swim, before thinking of food. On most summer days my breakfast consists of cold cereal and fruit, along with Sherpa tea, so I am not obliged to clean the stew pot before eating. But if the morning is cold and blustery, and cold breakfast is unappealing, I clean the pot sufficiently (often by merely wiping it out carefully with a paper towel) to avoid unduly flavoring the hot spicy applesauce I customarily make; if the morning is really foul, I empty in my Birchermuesli too.

After a bad night, a very hard yesterday, or just for fun if there is no great hurry—I like to lie down and take a rest after breakfast on my foam pad. I sometimes read, make notes, study the map and make plans for the day, while lying comfortably on my back. Often I just examine the treetops, and sometimes I accidentally fall asleep.

When it comes time to relieve myself I play a kind of game; I pretend to be a trapper who is traveling in the country of the sharp-eyed, sharp-nosed Sioux, and I hunt for a concealed spot unlikely to be visited by scouting parties—under a deadfall, in a thicket of brush, behind a boulder. I roll away a rock or kick a hole in loose soil, and slip the rubber band from the toilet paper roll around my wrist. When I have made my contribution, I cover it deeply and jump on it once or twice to pack down the soil; then I roll back the rock, kick back a covering of leaves, duff or pine needles and branches, artfully landscaping the site until an Indian scout would never give it a second look.

I am careful to avoid any place that might serve as a campsite or trail. Running water, dry streambeds, empty snowmelt pools and any location within a hundred feet of a camp are also shunned. There is nothing more discouraging than finding that the second best campsite in an area has been used as a latrine by the people from the number one camp—unless it is streamers of used toilet paper fluttering in the trees.

In recent years I have increasingly become interested in cleaning up the country. Restoring a quality of wildness to the wilds by erasing the blighting marks of man has become one of my chief pleasures in the areas I travel. It seems the least I can do to repay the joy that wilderness has given me—and the one thing I can do to help make it last a little while longer.

Like many backpackers, I used to try to leave a camp as clean as I found it; it did not occur to me to try to leave it any cleaner, much less to go looking for other people's trash. I shook my head sadly at badly littered camps and passed them by in hopes of finding something cleaner. Then two years ago I spent several days on a cleanup party into Desolation Wilderness behind my cabin on Echo Lake. Carrying burlap sacks, we systematically scoured the trails, circled the lakes and worked our way through commonly visited areas, picking up litter, tearing down fireplaces, filling latrines, restoring battered campsites hiding blackened rocks, scattering firewood, and so forth. By the end of the trip I found myself hooked on cleaning up the country.

When I say cleaning up other peoples' trash can become addictive, I expect to raise a few eyebrows. How can picking old toilet paper out of the trees or broken glass from the ashes in a ruined fireplace possibly be fun? My answer is that the pleasure comes from the sense of accomplishment, from the restoration of an ugly site to its previous condition of natural beauty. For instance, a handsome little alpine lake may be marred by a sheet of glittering aluminum foil lying on the bottom. The act of fishing out the foil, crumpling it up and packing it into a corner of the knapsack restores, actually recreates, the beauty and naturalness of the setting. Simple acts of this sort, surprisingly enough, can provide immense satisfaction. I highly recommend cleaning up wild country, not only for the good of the country but also for the happiness it is capable of bringing the cleaner.

dismantling a poorly-located fireplace.

On day hikes, when my pack is light, I carry a good sized paper bag (because the mouth conveniently stays open) in which to put gum and candy wrappers, film boxes, cigarette butts, pop tops, bandaid wrappers, Kleenex, and all the odd (but usually small and light) litter that thoughtless people commonly drop on the trail. I also carry heavy duty plastic garbage bags, to which I transfer my treasures before putting them in my pack. And I always carry matches so I can burn any large accumulation of paper and plastics. When I go fishing or climbing, I am similarly equipped. The shorelines of popular lakes, especially those used by campers, often yield more than can be carried away.

Sometimes I carry a burlap sack or plastic garbage can liner with me on these excursions. If I gather more than I can carry, I leave the partially filled bag on the edge of a prominent trailside campsite, then on my return I mention its location to the Forest Service ranger or packer who works that area. It is remarkable the effect that a clean campsite and a half filled bag of rubbish can have upon succeeding campers. Almost invariably they carry on the job, filling the sack and stacking the overflow neatly beside it. Often the volume has grown two or three fold by the time the packer comes to haul it away.

When I am backpacking, my procedure is slightly different. It is no longer possible to bend over and pick litter from the trail while wearing a full pack. And there is a limit, of course, to what I am willing to add to my load. My scavenging activities are necessarily limited to forays from wherever I am camped. When I find such large or heavy items as cast iron skillets, ruined life rafts, abandoned sleeping bags, air mattresses, ensolite and canvas or plastic tarps, disposal becomes something of a problem.

If the area is near a pack stock trail, I consolidate the trash, bag it if I can, and notify the authorities of its specific location, estimating the number of sacks and pack animals that will be needed. If the area is remote and cannot be reached by stock, and if carrying everything out is simply beyond feasibility, I set about trying to hide my collection so well that the likelihood of its being found again is exceptionally small. In an area of boulders and talus, for instance, quite large objects can often be stuffed out of sight into cracks and then covered by a minor avalanche of loose rock, hopefully never to be seen again by anything larger than a Cony.

Both the weight and the volume of trash I collect must be greatly reduced for optimum carrying purposes. Raw garbage or spoiled food left in a campsite can often be scattered well back in the brush where animals, ants and decay can dispose of it. Egg shells and other indigestibles must be treated like foil, unless they will burn. Orange peels, plastic and discarded clothing can usually be burned, along with waste paper, if the fire is sufficiently hot. I save the more difficult items for the evening campfire, and I am careful not to breathe the often poisonous fumes of burning plastics.

I shake or rinse the dirt from ancient rusty tin cans before crushing them flat beneath the heel of my boot. Foil and new tin

cans can be cleaned and partially consumed in a hot fire, before being crushed. Bottles can be shattered for reduction in bulk, but only if a suitable (heavy) container is available for safe breaking. Broken glass is best collected in an uncrushed tin can which should then be packed upright in its own plastic bag.

Often enough I have circled a small remote lake, visiting all the campsites, cleaning up several messes, collecting an empty six pack of beer, hiding blackened rocks after carefully dismantling inferior camps—all in less than an hour. And I have left, with less than two pounds of junk in my pack, well satisfied at having largely restored the area to a natural and inviting condition.

A friend of mine carries cleaning up one step farther. He carries with him a spray can of powerful oven cleaner with which to remove the names and comments of that strange breed of traveler who goes hiking with a spray can of paint. Oven cleaner also removes the soot from unfortunately blackened prominent slabs and boulders. By getting rid of the black and rearranging the rocks it is possible to discourage future use of an inappropriate spot.

The fact that 'trash begets trash' is as true in the wilds as it is in the city. Let litter accumulate and travelers will feel free to help swell the accumulation. But when a public place has been freshly cleaned people become reluctant to scatter their trash. And if containers are provided most people will use them. After the cleanup trips in Desolation Wilderness it was found that extra burlap sacks left behind in popular campsites were generally filled by the parties that followed.

Enthusiasm for cleaning up the country is not peculiar to me; it is shared by nearly all of my friends who have tried it. I have found that people who endlessly procrastinate about cleaning out their cellars will conscientiously clean up other people's campsites. And children whose rooms at home stand knee deep in litter will patiently pick the broken glass from someone else's fireplace. The annual cleanup trips in Desolation Wilderness have become so popular they simply cannot accommodate all the people who want to go; veterans take care to make their reservations early. The companionship, sense of accomplishment and the beautiful country combine to make these trips highly memorable.

Every hiking club, summer community or group of backpacking friends owes it to itself—and to the country it enjoys—to try a cleanup trip. The Forest Service stands ready to encourage serious groups by providing empty sacks and hauling collected debris from agreed upon locations.

Before leaving camp on short excursions—cleanup, fishing, an after dinner stroll—I always take a look around to make sure it is secure against the incursions of small animals, near neighbors and fire. Brazen chipmunks, mice, bluejays and squirrels have more than once escaped with significant portions of my larder without even waiting for me to walk away from camp. Enticing food should always be stowed in a pack, preferably in a zippered compartmen* which can be tightly closed, before leaving camp, and the pack should be hung from a tree or rope—depending on the type and voracity of predators.

One spring, I followed the snowplow into the mountains and made camp with a friend in an alpine meadow—after a long and heavy winter. Either the wildlife in the region was starving, or our food had unusual appeal. The first night, despite a fire that burned continuously, we spent half the night yelling and throwing pine cones at a bear who refused to leave us alone. We moved our camp the next day and that night we built a bigger fire, but the snuffling and stomping of the pacing animals that circled us all night gave us little rest. In the morning we found a profusion of tracks of bear, coyote and deer just beyond the firelight. After two sleepless nights fending off the wildlife, we gave up and returned home.

There was a time not many years ago when one could leave money lying around camp in perfect safety—provided one was beyond the range of day hikers. Nowadays, it is a good idea not to leave wallets or cameras in camp at all, unless they are carefully hidden. Merely tucking them in a sleeping bag or pack is insufficiently safe. A camp that will be seen by a large number of day hikers is far too vulnerable to leave. More than one group of hikers in recent summers has come back from a hike to find their camp entirely vanished. And backpackers in roadhead camps have awakened to find that everything but the bags they were sleeping in was gone. Packs, boots, down bags, parkas and the like have significant resale value and are easily fenced, so it pays to protect expensive gear—and to camp well away from the boulevards whenever possible.

It should be a matter of common sense never to leave camp for even a few minutes if a fire is burning. A gust of wind can carry flaming embers into the woodpile, dry pine needles or a hundred dollar sleeping bag and cause substantial damage in a matter of moments. The fire should be absolutely stone-cold dead whenever camp is left untended. Every summer I pass empty camps in which a fire still burns or smoulders. The incidence of man-made fires is climbing every year.

Long excursions from camp require more precautions than short ones because weather must also be taken into account. There is nothing so discouraging as returning to camp in the rain to find all the gear uncovered and wet. Consider my recent experience. We had left our high Sierra camp close under a mountain on a clear summer day, without any thought of a possible storm. Our mistake was in forgetting that camped where we were we really had no idea of weather conditions on the other side of the mountain.

By the time we reached the ridge the storm that had been hidden was almost upon us. By the time we returned to camp, late that afternoon, it had been raining steadily for several hours. Fortunately, our clothes and food were safe in our packs and our sleeping bags, though damp in places, were under tarps. The Bluet stove was soaked and would not light, but with difficulty we lighted a big fire and stood before it in the wind and rain for another long hour

he wasn't ready for rain.

before the sun came out a few minutes before sunset. There was just barely time to dry out our beds and get them back under tarps before a drenching dew began to fall. By dinnertime we were warm and dry once more. Even without seeing the sky behind the mountain I should have been suspicious because the breeze, though faint, was blowing from the south. Although we carried no tent the wind should have alerted me to the danger of a storm and I should have taken the trouble to pitch my tarp as a lean-to over my bag. Wind blowing from the south, east or northeast is liable to bring a storm. Wind from the north, northwest or southwest generally heralds fair weather; the major exceptions are mountain thunderstorms which often come from the west.

Clouds offer the backpacker another aid to weather forecasting. Big fluffy cumulus clouds are harbingers of fair weather—so long as they do not join together and begin to billow upward. When they cease to exist as individual clouds and the bottoms darken and the tops form columns and flattened anvil heads—a thunder storm is not far away. High, thin cirrus clouds are generally filled with ice particles; when they whiten the sky or their mare's tails reach upward, a storm can generally be expected within twenty-four hours.

Stratus clouds, as the name implies, come in waves or layers or bands; when they are smooth and regular and rolling the weather should be fair, but probably cool; when the stratus clouds are mottled or fragmented into a buttermilk sky, a storm is usually on the way.

The astute wilderness traveler learns to recognize a number of signs of impending weather change. Sun dogs or halos around the sun forecast rain or snow; so does a ring around the moon. A red sky at dawn or an early morning rainbow, or the absence of dew on the grass—all of these should warn the traveler that bad weather is brewing. So should yellow sunsets and still, ominously quiet moist air.

Sensitivity to the signs should influence the backpacker's choice of camps and trip itinerary. If the signs are bad, he should erect the tent, lay in a good supply of firewood beneath a tarp and schedule close-to-home amusement rather than exposed activities like climbing. On the other hand, a careful reading of the weather may enable him to set out on a climb, confident of good weather, even before the rain has stopped.

Thunderstorms, those exciting, dramatic, generally shortlived phenomena, are nevertheless frightening to a good many people. I have seen tall trees virtually explode when struck by a bolt of lightning, sending huge limbs flying in every direction. Lightning kills several hundred people each year. But the danger is negligible for anyone willing to take the necessary precaution—leaving vulnerable locations before the storm begins. The places to avoid are high, open exposed slopes, hills, ridges and peaks, isolated or unusually tall trees, lakes, meadows or open flats. The safest places are in caves, canyon bottoms and a part of the forest where the trees are comparatively short.

lightning strikes prominent exposed places.

The hiker or climber anxious about lightning usually has considerable warning. When cumulus clouds have darkened and fused and still air has been replaced by sudden eratic winds, the storm is about to break and backpackers should already be snugly sheltered. Lightning usually appears to be striking closer than it is, especially at night. The distance can be accurately gauged by counting the seconds between flash and boom. Every five seconds in time means a mile in distance. Thirteen seconds between flash and boom means the lightning is striking two and a half miles away. No matter how fierce the storm may seem, summer afternoon thunderstorms characteristically are short, and the chances are good that the sun will be out before sunset. If my camp is battened down and I can watch in some comfort, I enjoy the noisy melodrama of an afternoon storm.

When the time comes to pack up and move camp, I like to see how wild I can make my campsite look. If I have camped on virgin ground, I take pains to restore it to its natural condition so that a passerby would not guess it had ever been used. There are far too many campsites already in existence; my aim is to decrease, not increase the number. After collecting all the unburned foil and metal from the ashes and packing it in a garbage bag, I bury charcoal, ashes and partially burned twigs or scatter them well back in thick brush.

The firepit is filled in, blackened rocks are hidden and turned black side down in the brush, and the hip and shoulder hole from my bed are filled in and smoothed over. Pine needles, sand, soil, duff, pine cones and branches are scattered naturally about and if the area still faintly resembles a camp I sometimes roll in a few rocks and large limbs or small logs to fill up the bare spots. After firewood is scattered, all that remains are a few footprints. Once rain has fallen it would be difficult to tell that the area ever had been disturbed.

When my camp is an old one all signs of habitation simply cannot be erased. I can, however, remove extraneous fireplaces, leaving one that is neat and modest, dispose of all garbage and litter, and restore badly located bedsites to a natural state with rocks, twigs, branches, etc. Except for the fireplace, I make the site look as unused as I can.

The extra effort I would invest in disguising a virgin camp, I am likely to spend destroying surplus or inappropriate camps in the neighborhood. Campers who arrive late at night or on crowded holidays often camp in gullies, or boggy meadow and even in the middle of the trail. These camps, which are rarely used a second time, can often be entirely obliterated with a little work, greatly improving the wilderness character of the area.

Even a day hike no longer seems to me complete unless I have dismantled a few fireplaces, disguised a few old camps, and stuffed a little debris in my pack. The blackening on granite from a single evening's fire will withstand erasure by the elements for as long as fifty years. Though I cannot hasten the process I can at least enjoy hiding some of the evidence.

11 FIRST AID & SURVIVAL

"Keep it short and simple," warned the backpacking surgeon who counseled me on this chapter, "and hope that people will read it. People get confused by complicated procedures—besides it's not good first aid. There are only half a dozen important things to remember. The best medicine of all is prevention."

The greatest danger in wild country is traveling alone. Trail hiking is bad enough, but cross-country travel is infinitely worse, and climbing alone is idiotic. Unfortunately, some of the joys of wilderness travel are only to be discovered by traveling alone. Every step in the wilderness can mean life or death when there is no one to witness an accident, offer first aid or go for help. A good many people have perished when help was quite near because they were alone. The hiker traversing an icy slab and the swimmer far out in an icy lake are in considerable danger when there is no one to come to the rescue. I frequently hike by myself but, recognizing the danger, I try to minimize it by taking all possible precautions.

Protection comes from a combination of what gets carried and what gets left behind. What should be left behind is a knowledge of one's plans. I tell someone responsible—usually another member of the party or my wife, where I am going, what route I plan to follow both directions, when I expect to be back and the latest time (the time to begin worrying) that I could possibly be back. If the trip will take several days, I usually draw the route on an old map and make an 'X' where I expect to spend the nights. Lastly, I indicate in a general way my preparation for emergencies (tent, first aid kit, extra food and clothes), so the urgency of my situation can be judged if I fail to return.

First aid kits on the market are so far from suitable that I make my own from scratch. Since it is little more trouble to make two than one, I constructed one for picnics, day hikes and easy trips, and a second for climbing, cross-country, family and more extensive trips. My 'little' kit consists of a dozen Bandaids in two sizes, four individually wrapped gauze pads in two sizes (2 x 2 and 3 x 3 inches) a roll of three inch Johnson & Johnson 'Kling' gauze, a roll of one inch old-fashioned adhesive tape, a small bar of soap, a sheet of Molefoam or a lump of foam rubber, a small pair of scissors, a needle, a backed razor blade, a selection of pills, a clean washcloth and half a dozen matches.

I used to carry my first aid kit in three containers: a Bandaid can for bandages, a soap box for soap and a pill bottle for pills, but I never could find the right container when I needed it, and sometimes I left the vital one home. Now I carry everything together. The above kit fits snugly in a screw-topped plastic ice-box jar three inches deep and four inches in diameter, which is marked top and bottom with big red crosses to distinguish it from the sugar jar.

Plastic tape is all right on Bandaids, but it does not have the necessary strength for use on large bandages. Unfortunately, the adhesive on old-fashioned tape deteriorates; it should therefore be checked every season and replaced when necessary. Carrying soap is a problem. For awhile I cleverly made one bar do triple duty: dish-washing, personal washing and first aid. I carried it, wet or dry in a perpetually sticky plastic bag. Unfortunately, it was always back at camp when needed on the trail—usually covered with grime.

I solved the problem, finally, by carving a chunk of soap to fit snugly in a waterproof aluminum 35mm film can (marked with an 'S'); it is just the right size when used only for first aid. In a second film can (marked 'P'), I carry the following pills: six 500 mg vitamin C tablets to ward off colds, four 12-hour antihistamine spansules for cold symptoms or hay fever, half a dozen milk of magnesia laxative tablets, half a dozen aspirins and several aspirin with codene tablets for severe pain. All pills are checked the beginning of each summer. I often wedge in half a roll of anti-acid tablets and a yard of folded toilet paper, along with the small washcloth. The needle and razor-blade are taped to the inside of the lid. My 'little' kit weighs six ounces and resides permanently in my daypack.

My 'big' kit, which fits in a five inch deep, four inch diameter jar and weighs nine ounces, contains the same ingredients as the little kit, but the number of Bandaids and individual gauze pads is doubled, a good pair of tweezers for splinters is included, and so is a three inch Ace bandage for sprains. There are several extra needles and half a dozen safety pins.

My surgeon friend advises against first aid creams, antiseptics, inhalants and tourniquets. "Soap and plenty of water are better than antiseptics," he says. "First aid creams seal in more dirt and bacteria than does a dry, clean wound. Tourniquets are dangerous and rarely necessary since pressure and elevation will stop all but the most serious bleeding. Amateurs should not attempt to set broken bones, but splinting for protection is part of first aid. Either the patient should be moved to a doctor, or a doctor be brought to the patient."

My big kit—and the little one, too—is modified or enlarged for different country. For instance, in rattlesnake country (the foothill and lower elevations in the west side Sierra) I carry a Cutters Snakebite Kit (1 ounce, $3). and in Poison Oak country I carry extra soap, washrag and towel. In the dessert or where water loss or perspiration is likely to be great, I carry salt pills. Other preparations that might be considered are Tetracycline for fever-producing infections, Pryidium for bladder infections and Tridol for nausea.

In addition to my first aid kits, which are only opened to give first aid, I also carry a personal (toilet) kit which contains items I expect to use every day. Included are vaseline, athletes foot powder, sunburn ointment, glacier cream, dental floss, toothbrush, and any special medicines. If the water is suspect, it would include Halazone water purification tablets. I usually carry salve for my lips in a pocket.

Thus armed, I am in position to give first aid treatment to myself or others for a variety of ailments and accidents. The ability to treat common injuries is one of the prerequisites of the experienced backpacker. Techniques are so simple (and potentially important) that no wilderness traveler can afford not to learn them.

Shock is a state produced by injury or fright. The victim feels cold and clammy and weak. The treatment is to lay the patient down on level ground and make him as comfortable as possible, usually by loosening constricting clothing and covering him if it is cold, until a feeling of well-being returns.

In case of a small or slightly bleeding wound, bleeding usually will soon stop if the wound is elevated so it lies higher than the heart; and pressure is applied with a gauze pad. (For a cut foot or leg, the patient lies down and props his leg against a tree; a cut hand should he held above the head.) A large or heavily bleeding wound may have to be closed by hand pressure. A puncture can be firmly blocked by the palm or a finger. On a slice or cut it may be necessary to draw the edges together with the fingers before applying pressure. Closing the wound to stop the bleeding is vital. Once bleeding has been controlled, the wound should be kept elevated to reduce the blood supply and aid clotting. One should never attempt to substitute a tourniquet for these procedures.

As soon as bleeding is under control, the wound should be washed with soap and water, or irrigated with water, to carry away bacteria and dirt. It may be necessary during the washing to keep the wound elevated to lessen bleeding. Once cleaned, it may be gently blotted dry with a clean cloth or towel (not to mention toilet paper or clean socks). The clean, dry wound can then be bandaged. On heavily bleeding wounds that do not respond sufficiently to elevation, it may be necessary to tape the edges of the wound together with a butterfly bandage in order to stop bleeding. In the majority of cases, however, a combination of pressure and elevation will be sufficient to control bleeding.

elevation and pressure usually control bleeding.

Minor cuts and scratches, especially on protected parts of the body, are better left un-bandaged. Protected but uncovered wounds are more easily kept clean and dry; healing is faster and the chances of infection are lower. Antiseptics (mercurichrome, iodine, merthiolate and the like) should not be applied; they tend to do more harm than good—inhibiting scab formation and traping bacteria which cause infection. Small wounds need only bandaids. Larger ones will require a gauze pad held in place by narrow strips of adhesive tape. The largest may require wrapping the limb or body with roll gauze. Gauze and adhesive bandages should be applied directly on top of a wound held closed by a butterfly bandage.

The greatest enemy of wounds is dampness. A wet bandage inhibits healing by providing a favorable environment for the growth of bacteria. Once a bandage has become wet, whether from serum, perspiration or water, it is a menace to health and should be replaced. No bandage at all is far superior to a wet one. The drier the wound the less the chance of infection.

My backpacking doctor is a strong believer in foot care. "At the first hint of discomfort," he says, "stop, take off the boot and have a look. Wash and dry a place that is getting red, then tape a thin sheet of foam rubber over the spot." I had always relied on moleskin for covering blisters and inflamed places on my feet. Moleskin's disadvantage, the doctor points out, is that once it is stuck directly to the injured or tender area it cannot safely be removed (without removing the skin) until the end of the trip. In the meantime, of course, the moleskin is certain to get damp and dirty, encouraging bacteria growth. I have switched to either Molefoam or foam rubber and find both perfectly satisfactory. If I run out I can steal a fragment from a corner of my mattress. Scissors make the job neat and fast and are worth their weight for foot care alone.

Often as important as bandaging an inflamed foot, is attacking the cause of the inflamation. On occasion I have had to hammer down a nail with a piece of granite or whittle away a protruding ridge of leather. More often the problem is solved by kneading new boots that pinch, removing a pebble, loosening laces, removing the wrinkle from a sock, adding an extra pair of socks, or changing to a dry pair.

Dry socks are vital to happy feet. Wet, clean socks are far harder on feet than dirty, dry ones. Experienced hikers tend to do far more sock washing and sock changing than beginners, and they take off their boots and air (or wash) their feet at every opportunity. People unaccustomed to walking are likely to suffer from tender feet. Foot powders and alcohol rubs may help, but are no substitute for adequate conditioning (see Chapter 8).

A good case can be made for carrying camp boots on the basis of sensible foot care. Many people like old tennis shoes, but feet tend to sweat in canvas and rubber shoes. I prefer leather moccasins, and Zoris (also known as thongs and go-aheads) are extremely light and air the feet although they offer very little protection. I have developed the habit, once the day's hiking is done, of immediately taking off my boots (before the sweat dries), washing and rubbing my feet, washing my socks and hanging them in a tree, then slipping on dry socks and moccasins.

Nothing is more common among backpackers accustomed to doing their walking on sidewalks than turned or sprained ankles. Severity varies greatly. Some sprains amount to nothing more than a momentary twinge. Others require the victim to be immobilized immediately. Often the wisest course for the person who has suffered a bad sprain (the ankle immediately turning black and blue) is to apply a tape cast and head for the car before the ankle can swell and stiffen.

Moderate sprains should immediately be treated with cold to constrict blood flow and prevent swelling. Putting the foot in an icy rill or applying cold compresses made by filling plastic bags with snow or ice water are fast and effective. Elevating the ankle also helps greatly to reduce the swelling. If sources of cold are not handy or it is inconvenient to stop, an elasticized ankle brace or three inch Ace bandage may be applied.

sprained ankles can be chilled in icy streams or with snow-filled plastic bags

Braces are likely to be carried only by people with weak ankles who have come to rely on them. Ace bandages have the advantage of being usable on other parts of the body. In either case, it may be necessary to remove all (or at least the outer) socks to make room for the bandage in the boots. And people (like myself) who have sensitive Achilles tendons may find it impossible to wear an elastic bandage very long. Bandages need only be worn while walking. They should be removed at night and at any other time that the ankle can be elevated.

All of the swelling that is going to take place will happen on the day of the sprain or the day that follows. On the third day, with the swelling stopped, the treatment changes from the application of cold to the application of heat. The intent now is to stimulate blood flow through the injured area in order to reduce swelling. Hot compresses made from bandanas, towels, diapers, or washrags dipped in heated water are excellent, or the ankle can be baked before an open fire. Hot water bottles can sometimes be fashioned from large plastic bags, but care must be taken not to burn the patient. The exception to heat treatment is the ankle which is immediately encased in a cast of tape. Such casts should be left undisturbed for two or three days and heat applied only after removal.

While rattlesnake bites are uncommon, a snakebite kit ought to be carried in snake country. First prerequisites in prevention are caution and the ability to recognize poisonous snakes and the sort of terrain they like. I have spent a good deal of time in heavily infested areas and have encountered a great many rattlers. But by never extending any part of my body into a concealed place that could contain a snake, I have avoided being bitten. Although the Cutters kit offers more elaborate and valuable instructions, the treatment can be summarized in three works "Cut, Suck, Tie" (the order is important). Avoid the tendency to cut too deep (¼ inch is sufficient) and tie too tight (just dent the skin). Since suction cups are useless on any but flat, fleshy, hairless skin, mouth suction will often be required. Once first aid is given, the patient should be taken to a hospital.

Salt pills (5 grain) are not required by most people unless the perspiration is literally pouring off the body. The usual dosage in such cases is one pill every 4-8 hours. Poison oak, like rattlesnakes, is a hazard that can usually be avoided by caution and the ability to recognize the danger. Poison oak in the west (and poison ivy in the east) have oily-looking distinctive three-lobed leaves that are easily remembered once they have been identified. Tolerance to the oil, which remains potent for some time on clothes and on the fur of pets, varies widely. Persons exposed have a second chance to avoid the itching, easily-spread rash, by washing thoroughly with soap and hot water on the same day. Skin irritation generally begins four to five hours after exposure. In the west, poison oak rarely grows above 6000 feet.

Sunburn is a constant threat, especially at higher altitudes, to city dwellers who are not deeply tanned. At 6000 feet the skin burns twice as fast as at sea level, and the liability continues to increase with altitude. Sunburn often ruins a trip when a pale backpacker walks all day in shorts with no hat or shirt in hopes of getting a fast tan. Precautions should be taken to cover—or at least shade—all parts of the body for most of the day. Few people ever acquire a deep enough tan to expose themselves all day at high altitude without burning.

Glacier Cream is an excellent sunburn preventive: the red tube stops both burning and tanning, while the green tube allows some tanning. Sea & Ski greatly reduces burning, while its companion, Snooty, prevents burning but allows some tanning. The lips are extremely liable to sunburn and should be frequently coated with preventatives or Chapstick. The best treatment for sunburned skin, says the doctor, is to keep it clean and dry, but I prefer, after washing gently in the evening, to lightly rub in petroleum jelly, wiping off the excess. For the inevitable burns from fire or stove, I also rely on petroleum jelly rather than carry a burn ointment.

As altitude increases the oxygen content of the air decreases. In order to adjust, the body strives to process more air by means of faster and deeper breaths, to better extract and utilize oxygen from the air. Adjustment begins at only slight elevation, but shortness of breath and dizziness do not usually appear until about 7000 feet. Individual tolerance to altitude varies widely. The more gradual the change in altitude, the easier the acclimitization (physiological adjustment). The well-rested, vigorous, healthy individual usually acclimitizes easily. Smoking, drinking and heavy eating before or during a climb make acclimitization difficult.

butter-fly bandage

Failure of the body to adjust to reduced oxygen intake results in mountain sickness. Mild symptoms include headache, lassitude, shortness of breath and a vague feeling of illness—all of which usually disappear after a day of rest. Acute mountain sickness is marked by severe headache, nausea, vomiting, insomnia, irritability and muddled thinking. The victim must descend to a lower elevation. Mountain sickness can be avoided by beginning a trip in good condition, spending a night at the trailhead before starting out and choosing modest goals for the first day's walk. Most acclimitization occurs in the first two or three days.

People who acclimitize poorly, when they reach elevations in excess of 10,000 feet, are susceptible to high altitude pulmonary edema (fluid accumulation in the lungs). The first symptoms include a dry, persistent, irritating cough, anxiety, an ache beneath the breast bone and shortness of breath. If the victim is not evacuated promptly to lower elevation or given oxygen, breathing may become rapid, noisy and difficult, the skin often takes on a bluish tinge, and death may occur quickly.

This section on first aid has been necessarily brief. All backpackers are advised to buy (for only $1) and carry a pocket-sized pamphlet entitled *Mountaineering Medicine* by Dr. Fred T. Darvill, Jr. Designed expressly to be carried by mountaineers, it deals precisely with the difficulties most common in the wilds. *Mountaineering: The Freedom of the Hills* offers an excellent section on first aid, principally for climbers. Also published by The Mountaineers is *Medicine for Mountaineering,* the last word on the subject.

SURVIVAL

Survival should not be a problem for the backpacker—unless he is hurt or lost. A first aid kit and the ability to use it should enable him to cope with all but the worst accidents and health failures. His equipment, experience and trip preparation should enable him to survive whatever bad weather or minor mishaps befall him with no more than extreme discomfort.

Getting lost—or thoroughly confused—is not uncommon in the wilds and rarely leads to tragedy if sensible procedures are followed. I have been unsure of my location a good many times without suffering unduly. The lost backpacker's ability to regain his sense of direction and rediscover his location (or make himself easy to find) depends largely on his ability to control panic and fear so that reason can prevail.

The best insurance I know against getting lost in new country is to study the country as I move along. I consult the map and reorient myself with each new turning of the trail. I identify and study the configuration of new landmarks as they appear. I frequently look backward over the country just traversed to see how it looks going the other direction. If I am traveling cross-country or on an unmapped trail, I stop several times each mile to draw the route on my map. And at critical points (stream crossings, trail branchings, confusing turns), I make appropriate entries in my notebook.

A compass is the easiest means of orientation, but the sun, the stars and the time can also be used to determine direction—and to act as a check on the compass. More than a few disasters result when lost travelers refuse to accept what their compasses tell them. Unaware that they are lost and convinced they have their bearings, they assume the compass has somehow failed or is being unnaturally influenced by a nearby deposit of iron.

A roughly accurate watch will function as a compass on any day that the sun is out. If one turns the watch so that the hour hand points toward the sun, true south will lie halfway between the hour hand and the number twelve. An allowance must be made if the watch is set on Daylight Saving time, which is generally an hour earlier than standard (or sun) time.

If the time is known generally, even if only within two hours, a rough but very useful idea of direction can be obtained simply by knowing that (in western America) the summer sun rises a little north of due east, stands due south at noon (standard time), and sets a little north of due west. In the winter the sun's path lies considerably to the south, rising south of east and setting south of west. Early and late in the day, one can easily determine directions with sufficient accuracy for most purposes.

If the night is reasonably clear (in the northern hemisphere), it is relatively easy to find the North Star (Polaris) which is never more than one degree from true north. Its location is determined from the Big Dipper (or Big Bear), a bright and easily identifiable constellation nearly always visible in the northern sky. A line drawn upward from the outermost stars at the bottom and lip of the cup will point to Polaris (see drawing). In the southern hemisphere, the long axis of the Southern Cross points toward a starless region that lies due south. The prominent constellation Orion lies in a nearly north-south plane, and the uppermost of the three stars in the belt rises due east and sets due west—from any point on the face of the earth.

There are so many variables in every situation that it is difficult to advise the backpacker who has managed to get lost. However, a few general rules nearly always apply. The novice hiker has a tendency to plunge on through country that has gradually grown unfamiliar in hopes of reaching a familiar landmark. The veteran backpacker will resist this impulse, stop, admit to himself that he is at least temporarily lost, and sit down to review the situation. When he has overcome the anxiety that often accompanies such an admission, he will rationally review the situation, carefully considering all the information available.

day-pack survival kit

After studying the map and thinking carefully, he may find a landmark he can identify that will reveal his approximate position. Or thinking back over the country he has traversed he may feel that by retracing his steps he can return to a known point in a comparatively short time. After all the evidence has been sifted, the important decision is whether to try and return to a known point, whether to stay put and await rescue, or whether to head hopefully toward civilization. Only full consideration of the situation in a rational, panic-free manner will reveal the best course of action. The subject is too broad for further treatment here. I recommend *The Survival Book,* published by Funk & Wagnalls, and *Mountaineering: The Freedom of the Hills,* published by The Mountaineers.

Survival kits, like survival books are increasingly available in mountaineering catalogs and shops—largely because there is excitement and adventure in preparing for survival. The backpacker well equipped for recreational travel in the particular country he is entering is generally well equipped for survival. Backpackers willing to carry an extra half pound as insurance against emergency will probably do best by carrying extra food. Dayhikers are not so well provisioned and ought to carry, in addition to a good first aid kit, something that might be called a survival kit.

The one I carry in my creel or daypack whenever I go out (in addition to the small first aid kit) consists of an ancient tin cup, which can be used for cooking, a dozen kitchen matches, a yard and a half of toilet paper, about fifty feet of 550 lb. test nylon cord, a tiny one-bladed knife, two heavy-duty plastic bags, a quarter of a rum fudge bar broken into squares, three tea bags, three bouillon cubes and the stub of a pencil. All these items pack in the cup which in turn is packed in one of the plastic bags. Total weight is only six ounces.

There are many more items that might be worth carrying, but one must draw the line somewhere. A small waterproof match box with built-in compass and whistle might be worthwhile. So might the three ounce, 56" x 84" Rescue Blanket which is strong and a good reflector. In harsher seasons, when accidents can prove more dangerous, considerably more survival (and backpacking) gear can be justified. Fire starters, for instance, are part of my basic equipment when traveling in country that is cold, wet or otherwise unfriendly.

In mild summer weather, if adversity fails to strike, I can always use my survival kit to brew a cup of tea beneath the shelter of a tree while I wait for an afternoon thunderstorm to pass.

¹² FAMILY TRIPS

All parents who love the outdoors would doubtless like to develop the same feeling in their children. But many parents who badly want their children to enjoy the wilderness either cram it down their throats or fail to make sure those first trips are enjoyable. The world is full of people whose first experience in the wilds was unpleasant—and who therefore have never been back.

If a child's first experiences in the outdoors are reasonably comfortable and pleasant, chances are great that he or she will come to enjoy it. It follows, then, that considerable effort should be invested in seeing that those first experiences are happy ones. This doesn't mean dragging children along on a short adult trip. It means carefully planning an easy trip into pretty, familiar country and tailoring all aspects to maximize the enjoyment of the children. The same principle applies to anyone who is a stranger to the mountains, whether girl friends, children, parents, new brides, or even fit and eager young friends.

In my view, there are a great many parents who are not ready to take children into the wilderness—and a great many children who are not ready to go. Every summer I see miserable families struggling up the trail or bickering in camp. The parents are bitterly disappointed because the children are spoiling their trip, and the children are tired of being nagged, picked on and yelled at. The parents vow never to take those "ungrateful brats" again, and the children are equally determined not to go.

Generally speaking, I feel parents should not take their children backpacking until: (1) they themselves can travel in the wilds with some degree of comfort and competence; (2) the children have been taken on a number of successful day hikes; (3) parents are willing to tailor an overnight trip to country they know, expressly for the pleasure of their children; (4) the children want (or are at least willing) to go; and (5) the parents genuinely want them along. Families able to meet these criteria have a fighting chance for a pleasant trip.

The most common cause of disastrous family trips, it seems to me, is the failure of parents to see the trip through their children's eyes. Any child will ask 'If it isn't fun, why do it?' He does not insist every minute be fun, but he will expect that, taken as a whole, the trip should be pleasant. After all, what good is a vacation if it isn't fun? The honest adult will find no satisfactory objection to this reasoning. If parents are not willing and able to make the trip fun—for themselves as well as for the children—there is little point in going.

Parents with little experience in backpacking generally have difficulty enough without the added burden of children. People who cannot go into the woods with confidence are not likely to have the patience or the skill to provide children a happy time. There is rarely a good reason why children cannot be taken on a considerable number of day hikes before taking them overnight. I first took my daughter backpacking when she was eight. Because she had made many day trips with me, had climbed a few peaks and had slept overnight in the forest by our cabin—she took the trip in stride. Very little was strange to her, she required very little persuasion, and she apparently enjoyed herself.

That first trip was simple and short. With another family, we walked no more than a mile and a half from our cabin. Though we traveled cross-country rather than on a trail, and climbed perhaps eight hundred feet, walking conditions were good and I knew every inch of the way. The campsite I had chosen offered a spring, a marvelous view, a cozy dell for sleeping, wildflowers and small caves. The children were allowed to arrange their beds together, apart from the adults, before gathering wood and water for dinner. There were songs and marshmallows by the campfire before bed. Everything was planned with the children in mind. We were home before lunchtime the following day.

Once it has been decided to take children backpacking, the trip should be planned with the weakest, most timid member in mind. Backpacking parents might normally scorn camping at the first lake or stream on the trail, but if the children are young (under ten) that may be the wisest plan. Chances are that the country will be wild enough to excite them. Being relatively close to civilization (telephone, campground, motel, grocery) has its advantages. If the weather turns bad, the children get sick, the mosquitos are unbearable, or something else goes wrong—the car is only a short dash away. And the shortness of the trail may seem a blessing to parents who find themselves carrying twice their normal loads.

I do not believe children should be taken backpacking for the first time to an area that has not been thoroughly reconnoitered by their parents. The campsite should be known in advance and selected on the basis of its appeal to a child. Adults often arrange their itinerary for the photography, fly fishing and rock climbing afforded, but a small child will be interested in none of these. Trips should be planned for the warmest weather and fewest bugs. In the Sierra, that means August. The fact that the traffic is heavy, the wildflowers past their prime and the fishing slow will not bother children in the least. For a child's first trip, one or two nights will be long enough. If camp is to be moved it should be moved in the morning, with lunch and a leisurely afternoon planned in the new campsite.

As on any backpacking trip, there is a limit to what can be carried. But parents should not expect children to be voluntarily Spartan—or even to be impressed with the size of dad's pack. Emphasizing sacrifice only makes it harder for them to understand where the fun comes in. Clothes must be carried to protect children from extremes of heat and cold. Sunburn must be guarded against with long-sleeved shirts, long trousers—and, if possible, hats. Extra quantities of sunburn cream should be provided so that children can carry individual tubes. The same goes for lip salve.

Extra aerosol cans of mosquito repellent (kept away from small children) are important, and nylon netting and head nets may be required if the bugs are likely to be fierce. Too much protection is better than too little—even though it swells the pack. Rattlesnake country should be avoided if possible.

The first aid kit should be enlarged by the addition of extra bandaids and spare soap, and wash cloths and towels are certain to be needed. Petroleum jelly will be invaluable to ease chafing. Since children have an unfailing affinity for water, three pairs of extra socks will be needed, the heavier the better. Wool and synthetics are best because cotton tends to stretch and sag, producing first wrinkles then blisters.

In recent years, a great many cheap, small knapsacks and packs have appeared on the market, many of which are suitable for children. Flimsy plastic knapsacks that roll up into their own pockets cost as little as $2. Of course, canvas or nylon packs are preferable. For older children who can carry larger loads, a small aluminum pack frame (available from surplus stores, Jansport and Camp Trails) will be a better investment.

My daughter likes to carry a fanny pack (ski belt), which gives her greater freedom of movement than any shoulder pack. She often wears it with a knapsack which will just hold her sleeping bag. All but the youngest children should be encouraged to carry at least a token pack—of course, if the trail is too long or the load too large it may end up being carried by dad.

The number of children's sleeping bags is constantly increasing.

North Face makes a beautiful little down bag for less than $50, and the Co-op offers 52 and 63 inch dacron bags for $10 and $16. Coleman's new backpacking bags and the growing availability of Japanese imports (copied from American models) provide still more inexpensive bags that are light enough to carry. Children's bags, hopefully, will soon be found in rental equipment inventories.

Extra sleeping bags tend to make dad's pack unwieldy, so children should carry their own bags, if possible. Since even an adult sleeping bag should not weigh more than five and a half pounds, most children old enough to backpack should be able to carry their own. If suitable bags are not available, an adequate cocoon can usually be fashioned from cotton sheet blankets and old wool blankets or a quilted comforter fastened together with large safety pins.

For small children, a tube tent can be important, even if there seems no chance of rain. The small cozy space tends to be reassuring. Tents are extremely useful for afternoon napping and changing clothes out of the wind. And children fearful of the dark may insist on sleeping inside no matter what the weather. Children are usually intrigued by tents, and parents can often generate enthusiasm for camping by pitching one on the lawn at home before a trip, putting in sleeping bags and serving a picnic lunch. A tarp tent, though more difficult to pitch, is also a good low-cost family shelter where insects and wind are not great problems. In addition to the tent, a sizeable extra tarp can serve as picnic blanket and dining table. When children are along, there is generally a need for something on which gear can be spread out.

Kids love tube tents

Food that meets the adult backpacker's demands will usually do equally well for children, but special emphasis should be put on snack foods and liquids. To maintain energy and prevent dehydration, children will need plenty of both. To encourage the between meal eating so necessary in the wilds, considerable candy must be carried, but cheese, salami, nuts and dried fruit should be equally available. Children should be urged to drink small amounts of water often, and quantities of lemonade, Koolaid, Fizzies and reconstituted milk should be periodically provided. Since kids will immediately notice that camp milk tastes 'funny,' powdered flavorings should be carried to transform it into chocolate milk, cocoa and milkshakes.

Young children will probably want to take along toys from home and since these will promote security and supply entertainment, parents ought to indulge at least one, so long as it is light and appropriate. Generous parents can sometimes be recognized on the trail by the teddybears and Raggedy Anns riding on top of their packs.

family camping means carrying a little more.

When the trailhead has been reached and the loads handed out, the real work begins. Getting children up the trail and into camp demands patience, a strong back and considerable psychology. Parents unwilling or unable to keep the children amused and moving —without losing their sense of humor—will wish they had left them home. And so will the children. Without supervision, children tend to start out fast, which means they will soon want to rest. It is hard to curb the enthusiasm and effervescence that eats up their energy without curtailing the fun of the trip; it is also hard to keep them going when they feel tired and want to rest: and children fatigue quickly.

It is unreasonable to expect children to have the self-discipline necessary to conserve energy for the climb ahead. Instead, one has to supply incentives, goals and just plain entertainment—with the minimum necessary discipline mixed in.

The rest of this chapter comes from notebooks carried on a number of trips with my daughter, other people's children and other families. Since, like children, it seems to defy organization, I offer it more or less verbatim.

Call the trip a 'walk,' 'walking' is fun but 'hiking' is work. Making the trip a lark for the kids means getting into the spirit of their adventure rather than fretting about the slowness of the pace. Keep children moving but don't try to make them hurry; it will only slow them down and rob them of their cheerfulness. Make sure they get away from the trail occasionally. Let them put down their packs and go investigate something they've discovered.

Take them off the trail to see mossy glens, snowbanks, waterfalls, a tree that looks like a witch. If they've been trudging along wearily for awhile, don't wait for them to ask for a rest or simply sit down. Stop voluntarily and show them something interesting. Keep in mind the fact that the long range goal is not just to get them to camp before lunch—it's to make the trip so much fun that they'll want to come again.

It's always a good idea to keep watch on childrens' feet. By putting a stop to chafing in the early stages you may avoid having to carry a child to the car! I have more than once discovered my daughter hiking happily along despite the fact that one sock had worked so far down her foot that it had disappeared entirely into her boot. Fortunately, children's feet take the abuse of rough country much better than their parents' and do not easily blister.

I find it important on the trail to talk to children a good part of the time. I give them progress reports "We're more than halfway . . . It's only fifteen minutes until lunch . . . There's a spring where we can get a drink behind that big tree . . . It's all downhill to camp." Whenever I can, I praise their achievements. I try to distract them from the drudgery of the trail, and in doing so I find I have distracted myself.

When they grow weary of such temporal phenomena as birds' nests, rills and rock rabbits, I try to stir their imagination by pointing out a cloud formation that looks like a ship, a leaning tree that resembles a poised runner or a patch of lichen that looks like a lion. Finding strange likenesses can be made into a contest in which children point out their own discoveries. The reward for the most imaginative can be a specially prized piece of candy.

I carry a considerable stock of sweets in wide variety, and I keep them concealed to add mystery and anticipation. It's important that kids eat well—if they're not too tired—at mealtime, but sometimes it is more important to feed them snacks between meals to keep their energy and spirits up. I pass out candy with the smallest provocation and often with none at all. Sometimes I substitute cheese or nuts.

It's always important to keep the kids happy, but there's still the problem of getting them up the trail. A minimal amount of discipline, and self-discipline, is indispensable. So is a certain amount of desire on the child's part to please his parents and do his part. I explain at the outset that while we're going to stop and rest, play games, explore and generally have fun, we still have to make it to camp before lunch, so we'll have time to set up camp and spend the afternoon without our packs. And that means we have to keep moving. As we move along, I show kids easier ways to get around obstacles, help foot draggers, readjust packs, show how the indians walk, and if the trail grows steep, I demonstrate the rest step, which I represent variously as the "polar bear shuffle," "kangaro limp," "dromedary drag," etc.

If there are several children, I work most with the slowest ones. Sometimes the slowest becomes the fastest if you put them in the lead, explaining that they now have the responsibility for keeping the group on the trail, showing them how to recognize blazes and ducks and the footworn groove. It is usually best to bring up the rear when hiking with children, so you can help the ones who fall behind and so you'll know if a child quietly sits down on a rock or wanders off while the rest of the party marches by.

The hardest part of handling a group of kids is keeping them together and controlling the rest stops. Energetic older boys will want to keep going while younger girls will frequently want to rest. It's not difficult to spread your party all over the mountain. I urge the stoppers to keep going, and as a last resort I take their packs. If other kids get too far ahead, I saddle them with the unwanted packs. When we stop for a rest I encourage the energetic ones to explore the immediate area while the tired ones sit and puff.

When the weariest seem to be somewhat restored, I simultaneously announce we must be off and pass out lemondrops all around. It is important after a rest not to let children dash up the trail with recharged enthusiasm or they'll burn themselves out after only a few yards and plead for another rest. If they fail to restrain themselves, after you've explained the reason for starting off slowly, there is nothing to do but nag. Chronic fast starters are best reminded at the end of the rest instead of after they take off.

Even with all these strategems, the trail can become monotonous, and when the group becomes dull or dispirited I call an early rest. Everyone takes off his pack and we make a little side trip to some interesting spot out of sight of the trail—usually a waterfall or a cool glade or a lookout point, and we have a drink of lemonade (powder and plastic bottle must be handy) or lie in the cool grass, or throw snowballs off the cliff. This side trip is likely to refresh the group and the .ime spent seems a worthwhile investment. Progress, in this fashion will be anywhere from a quarter mile to one mile per hour.

When camp is reached (and by now it should be evident why it needs to be close and the trail well known) some kids will want to flop down and rest, others will want to explore; almost no one will want to unpack, lay out beds or gather wood. The best strategy is to let everyone squander half an hour in whatever way seems appropriate, before assigning chores. Everyone should have something useful to do; if the tasks are thoughtfully assigned and described, children will go to work with enthusiasm.

Kids are good at gathering firewood...

Limit the amount that thirsty children drink, but allow them—in fact invite them—to drink frequently from unpolluted streams and rills and your water bottle or canteen. Snowball fights and singing make good diversions. So do yodeling and echoing. Give kids the sense of helping you and finding the way. Don't communicate anxiety about reaching camp, snakes, storms, or mosquitos. You

don't panic
at every danger

must be relaxed and at home in the woods if you want your children to feel the same way. Don't panic if they step near the edge of a cliff; their natural caution should protect them. Don't yell at them. Be alert for excessive fatigue, dizziness, blisters, chafing clothes, sunburn and chapped lips.

Explain in advance that you want to keep them comfortable and therefore they must let you know what's bothering them. They'll tell you all right! When you come to sand on slab or wet slippery surfaces, calmly warn them and demonstrate how to cross safely. Celebrate all achievement; be liberal with praise and rewards. Teach your kids not to litter and get them to help you pick up gum wrappers and trash—if the going is not too difficult —to be deposited in one of your spare plastic bags. This activity is best persued in camp.

The only material it is permissible to leave in the wilderness is toilet paper but impress upon children that it must be carefully hidden. Going to the bathroom must not be left to chance. Every child should carry perhaps three feet of toilet paper folded flat in a back pocket. Explain the necessity of finding a place where no one is likely to go, away from trails, campsites, lakes and streams. A hole should be kicked in lose earth and the used toilet paper covered by a layer of dirt, sand or gravel and then by a good sized rock. Make it a point of pride with kids to leave no sign of their passing. Unless you provide instruction there are sure to be toilet paper streamers deco·rating the trees, and the responsibility will be yours.

It's a poor idea to plan to take children cross-country in rough terrain unless they are large, strong, proven hikers. Being closer to the ground, children see relatively small objects as real obstacles. A rock that's just a knee-high step to you will be a waist-high road-block to a six-year-old; a good scramble for you may be a nightmare for them. Forget boulder-hopping altogether. Be wary of fussy eaters. Explain before the trip that the food—in order to give everyone more energy—will be a little different. Then serve them sample dishes or meals at home, making the change of diet an adventure.

In camp, find them rocks to climb, rills to dam, a snowpatch to slide on; define the bathroom area boundaries, explain camp rules regarding fire, food, muddy feet in the tent and the sanctity of the kitchen during meal preparation. Alert them to the continuing need for wood and water. Explain that, like indians, you plan to leave this camp so no one will know you've been there.

Taking children into the wilderness can be demanding, even maddening, but by allowing yourself to see the trip through their eyes you can share their wonder, joy and adventure. You can remember what it feels like to be a kid in the woods when every-thing is new and mysterious and exciting. And when the trip is over and you're homeward bound there is satisfaction in hearing your youngest ask "Daddy, when can we go again?"

¹³ TROUT FISHING

It has always seemed to me that many more people would enjoy catching and eating trout . . . . if only they knew how to go about it. Of course, catching trout is not the only measure of fishing success. The pursuit of trout, even when unsuccessful, is the best way I know to become intimately acquainted with the watery side of the wilderness. Whether following the rocky shore of a mountain tarn, watching trout feeding in a crystal pool or making my way cautiously along the bank of a brook, angling has shown me many more wonders than all the trails I have ever traveled.

The hunt for solitude and challenging country often leads the backpacker past trout waters that would fill a fisherman with envy. More than once I have caught so many trout (and put them back unharmed) that the feathers were totally stripped from my fly. Of course, I also have been skunked on water with a reputation for fine sport. I do not consider myself first of all a fisherman. I sometimes pass good trout water without setting up my rod. Sometimes I even fail to take a rod along. But I am fond of eating freshly-caught, wild trout. And I rely upon trout fishing and cross-country climbing to get me off the trails and into corners of the country that I otherwise never would see.

Some writers suggest that it is enough for the backpacker to carry a few yards of line, a few feet of leader and a couple of hooks. The idea is to cut a willow rod, catch grasshoppers or grubs for bait and then go blithely forth to catch fish with this clumsy rig. An expert might catch unsophisticated trout, and a hard working angler might land starved fish, but this kind of outfit is utterly worthless for the beginner who would like the best possible chance of eating trout for supper.

Trout fishing gear, happily, is neither prohibitively expensive nor immoderately heavy. Basic outfits (rod, reel and line) for both fly casting and spinning are commonly offered for as little as $8. Neither pleasure nor fish-taking ability are much sacrificed in modestly priced gear. Of course, high quality backpacking outfits can

"natural" fishing rods mean frustration —not fish.

easily cost $75. The fly fishing equipment I generally take backpacking weighs anywhere from 11 to 24 ounces. Of course, the cheapest equipment will weigh a little more, but the beginner should not have to carry more than a pound and a half for fly fishing or two and a half pounds for spinning.

Trout fishing tackle, like backpacking gear, is designed for maximum lightness, because the lighter the gear the more sensitive it will be to the antics of the trout. Fighting an eight inch rainbow on a three ounce fly rod is three times as exciting as playing the same fish on a five ounce rod. A first rate outfit for taking trout will often weigh less and cost less than a pair of binoculars or a camera.

Trout fishing gear sharply divides itself into two different types: fly casting and spin fishing. In traditional fly casting, it is the weight of the comparatively heavy line that carries the nearly weightless fly out across the water. The angler must lift the line into the air and keep it suspended there with alternate forward and backward casts until he is ready to place the fly on the water. Most people find fly casting harder to learn and more demanding than spinning. But it provides more challenge, satisfaction, sport—and fish—with less equipment and fuss for anglers who have gained a reasonable proficiency.

In spin fishing, the comparatively heavy weight of the lure propels the almost weightless line out over the water. There is no back cast and no necessity to keep the line suspended in the air. Spin fishing is applicable to a broader range of fishing situations and enables the angler to cover more water. It is also easier to learn and physically less demanding. While the fly fisherman is largely restricted to flies the spin fisherman can cast spinners, plugs and bait, as well as flies. Though spinning does not provide intimate contact with the trout—largely because the equipment is heavier and less sensitive—it generally produces more fish for the beginner.

Of course, the angler who has mastered both types of fishing and is prepared to use whichever seems most likely to be effective, will double his chances of catching trout. He need not carry two complete outfits since a fly-spin combination rod will suffice for both techniques. In recognition of the backpacking boom, tackle manufacturers are designing more and more gear for lightness, durability and easy carrying. Today's equipment is better than ever before. Some of it, thanks largely to quality imports from Germany and Japan, is even growing more reasonable.

For more than a hundred years fly rods were traditionally constructed of split bamboo: narrow triangular strips carefully laminated and glued together to form slender, strong, limber sections. But the last twenty years have seen the development of fiberglass rods that match the action of split bamboo but are lighter, less brittle and less expensive to make. The emergence of fiberglass has been a major breakthrough for all anglers. For years I carried a three-piece, split-bamboo, eight-foot rod weighing 5½ ounces and fastened together with metal furrules. And I held my breath every time the fragile tip caught on a branch.

Today, I carry a virtually unbreakable, 2-piece Fenwick seven foot rod weighing 3 and 1/8 ounces, fastened together with hollow slip joints instead of furrules. Fenwick makes half a dozen rods that are admirably suited to backpacking. They range in length from seven to eight and a half feet; all weigh less than 4 ounces, and several break down into four pieces for easy carrying inside a pack. A seven foot combination spin-fly rod weighs 3 and 7/8 ounces, breaks down into four sections and offers remarkably good action for both types of fishing. All rods come in both cloth and aluminum tubes and are priced rather expensively at $40-45.

There are less expensive, slightly heavier glass rods, some of which break down into four sections. Sporting goods shops and discount houses offer a variety in the $5-15 range. And there are split bamboo rods ranging from an amazingly cheap $5 to more than two hundred. Over the years, the optimum length for fly rods has steadily shrunk from the once standard nine feet to approximately seven and a half, and I would not hesitate to choose a well balanced rod of only six and a half feet for Sierra backpacking.

Single action fly reels of extremely light and simple construction may be purchased for less than two dollars. The best and most expensive reels are made by Hardy, Orvis and Phlueger. Four models of Phluegar Medalists cost from $12 to 18. Nearly identical Japanese copies cost $10 less, but reel spools are not interchangeable and parts are not readily obtainable. Automatic reels are heavy and ought to be avoided. All good rods are balanced for a reel of a certain weight, and proper mating between the two is required if the combination is to perform well. Line capacity of the reel is seldom a problem because few fly fisherman need more than fifty yards of line.

Traditional fly lines of braided Japanese silk, which required periodic dressing with oil or wax, have been replaced by lines of braided nylon and dacron encased in smooth plastic coatings that never need dressing. Fly lines are classified as either floating or sinking. Sinking lines are heavy and highly specialized for expert use on deep lakes or swift rivers and should never be purchased by beginners. Even confirmed wet fly fisherman use floating lines (with sinking leaders) to fish their flies anywhere from an inch to six feet below the surface.

Fly line is classified as either 'level' or 'tapered.' The tapering in a tapered line takes place in the last few yards at the end (tippet). The taper avoids an abrupt change in diameter between the line and the leader while retaining the line weight necessary for casting. Efficiency of casting and smoothness and naturalness of fly presentation are greatly increased by the use of a tapered line—especially for the novice.

spliced loop

Conventional tapered lines are tapered at both ends ('double tapers'), so when one tippet wears out the line can be taken off the reel and reversed to make use of the other taper. Double tapered lines (by Courtland, Sunset and Gladding, for instance) cost about $15 for 25-35 yards, but cheaper makes are available in the $4-8 range. Level fly lines, though less than half the price of tapered, are not worthwhile investments for anglers interested in assembling competent fly casting outfits.

Depending on the water to be fished and the angler's experience, it may be necessary to back the tapered fly line with a length of level line. The junction of the two should be spliced and whip-finished, rather than simply knotted. The fly line tippet should have a whip-finished, spliced loop for easy knot-free attachment of the leader. A knot both catches the air to obstruct smooth casting and catches the water to disturb shy trout. A nail knot coated with Duco cement will substitute for a spliced loop.

ordinary knot

Leaders are also either tapered or level, and the tapered leader is much to be preferred. The reasoning is similar to that for tapered lines, except that the difference in weight is negligible and the difference in breaking strength important. The stiffer butt section—usually three quarters the diameter of the line it joins—helps transmit the thrust of the line while the delicate tippet allows the fly to settle lightly on the water after the leader has straightened out. The biggest benefit for the beginner—especially in brush- is that when the fly is caught on an obstruction the tapered leader always breaks at the weakest point—next to the fly, so the leader is rarely lost.

The rule of thumb for leader length is slightly less than the length of the rod, which avoids the necessity of drawing the leader-line junction through the guides. In murky water, spring fishing under cut banks, or lowering a fly through brush, as little as two feet of leader may suffice, while nine to twelve feet may be needed when casting in the fall over clear, glassy pools. Tapered leaders are rated according to tippet diameter (1X for heavy bass bugs down to 6X for the smallest flies on the clearest water) and also by breaking strength (from perhaps 5 pounds down to half a pound). I like Berkley 7½ foot knotless tapered leaders with tippet tests of 1 and 3/4 pounds (about 4X). Individually packaged in cellophane, they cost only 35¢ each. Level leader, in rolls, is less expensive.

Trout flies come in three basic types: dry, wet and streamer, but wet flies are scarce since they can only be fished wet, while dry flies can be fished either wet or dry. Dry flies are designed to resemble flying insects; streamer flies and bucktails imitate minnows and large bugs; and a fourth category, nymphs, are tied to look like grubs, worms, caterpillers, larvae and other fish foods.

One school of thought insists that flies must closely resemble the insects on which trout are feeding in order to be effective. But a majority of fisherman find that trout are more sensitive to size than shape or color. Rarely will they make any noticeable distinction between patterns, so the angler can choose the flies he likes best—as long as they are comparable in size to those on which trout are feeding. Even size is less important, some experts say, than the manner in which the fly is presented and fished. The most common mistake is to fish flies that are too large. For mountain trout, sizes 14 to 16 are more appropriate than the 10s and 12s that are most often available. It is only a myth that "it takes big hooks to catch big trout."

A beginning fly fisherman on a three day trip should have at least a dozen flies, divided into three or four patterns. For variety I would choose a Royal Coachman because its white wings make it easy to follow, a grey hackle peacock with a thick body, and a mosquito, because these are among the commonest of summer insects. Flies cost anywhere from five cents to a dollar apiece. The cheapest flies, imported from Japan, often are not glued securely to the hook, have clogged eyes and tend to break easily, but I have used dozens of them and most were satisfactory. For most anglers, the disadvantages will not offset the cost advantage, especially if the purchaser inspects and sorts carefully. More than anything else, the price of a fly reflects the quality of its hook.

Another source of reasonable flies—in the long run—is fly tying, a common hobby among fly fishermen. Kits cost anywhere from $10-25. There is real satisfaction in devising and tying flies—and then taking trout on them. Since I pay nearly as much for fly tying hooks as I do for Japanese flies, dollar savings tend to be negligible.

Far and away the best fly box for backpacking is made by Perrine and sells for $2-3. This little marvel, the size of a package of cigarettes, easily holds a hundred flies in six spring loaded slips. Mine weighs 2½ ounces, loaded.

A creel is a considerable luxury for a backpacker, and the traditional woven willow basket is out of the question. On easy trips I sometimes carry an Abercrombie & Fitch two piece creel (6 ounces, $6), which doubles as a day pack. It consists of a nylon net creel for use while fishing, and a waterproof nylon bag for carrying cleaned trout back to camp. The two zip together. Often I leave the waterproof bag home, substituting a heavy plastic bag. An excellent and inexpensive creel can be made from nylon mosquito netting, but most backpacking anglers are content to cut a V-shaped willow stringer or use a short length of nylon cord tied around a stick. Either can easily be threaded through the trout's gills and mouth for easy carrying.

Since it is necessary to be able to control the floating or sinking of the leader and fly, I often carry a small tin of Mucilin with Silicone and a plastic vial of Orvis Leader Sink, although combined they add two ounces. When it is vital to keep a fly floating on choppy water, Mucilin is invaluable. Of course, a fly can also be dried by vigorous false casting. A film of mud, mosquito repellant or sunburn cream rubbed on the leader will cause it to sink, but Leader Sink is more convenient. Such small amounts of these chemicals are needed that they probably could be repackaged at a fifty percent saving in weight. In the swiftest water, split shot clamped directly on the hook can be used to sink a fly—but casting becomes difficult.

trout
on
willow
stringer

A necessity in any angler's kit is a sharp knife, with a sharp point, but this the backpacker already has.

Spinning equipment is not so light, neat or compact as fly casting tackle, but it, too, has been developed during the past few years with the backpacker in mind. In addition to the 3 and 7/8 ounce, 7-foot spin-fly combination rod, Fenwick makes two admirable spinning rods. The lightest is a 2-piece, 2 and 3/8 ounces tubular glass rod with hollow slip joints which is 5½ feet long and sells for $35-40. The other is a 5-piece, 7½ foot glass rod that weighs 4 and 1/8 ounces and sells for $40-45. Though intended for spinning, the latter will take a fly reel and offers better than average fly casting action. There are other casting rods of split bamboo and tubular glass that break down or telescope for backpacking, but most have ferrules or solid slip joints and are significantly heavier. A great many five to six foot spinning rods are available in the $5-10 range.

Conventional spinning reels tend to be heavy, and folding back-packing models are significantly lighter. Probably the best in the field is the Quick Microlight No. 110 made in Germany and selling for $25-30. It weighs only nine ounces, folds to form a compact package, and is adjustable for either two or four pound monofila-ment and either left or right handed anglers.

There are a number of lightweight Japanese reels available, but most of them are inferior: castings break, gears are easily stripped and parts are unavailable. An exception is the Fiord which is well made, lightweight and a bargain at less than $10, despite a lack of replacement parts. The seven ounce Zebco, an American reel of comparable quality (but with available parts) costs more than twice as much at $20-25. Unlike cheap fly reels, cheap spinning reels tend to be big, heavy, angular and lacking in durability—especially closed face plastic reels. Of course, since spinning outfits (rod, reel, line) are generally available for $5-10, the beginner can afford to try spinning very reasonably before making a larger investment.

Backpacking spin fisherman commonly use either two or four pound test monofilament which serves as both line and leader. The lighter the line the lighter the lure it will cast. Backpackers need only 100-150 yards of line, which costs little more than a dollar per 100 yards if bought in bulk and wound on the spool at a sporting goods store. Hundred yard spools of four pound Berkley Trilene cost about $2 each. Several spare loaded spools should be carried.

The principal use of spinning gear is to cast hardware: metal spinners, spoons and other lures. These commonly weigh from 1/16 to 3/8 ounces and cost 50¢ to $1 each. Most of the price of the more expensive lures pays for fine quality treble hooks. Lures are subject to changes in fashion. The Super Duper Craze was preceded by the Daredevil fad and succeeded by first the Mepps and then the Panther Martin. There is evidence that trout in heavily fished waters may actually grow wary of familiar looking lures, while accepting new ones with a different action. But most veteran anglers believe that the lure or fly which the fisherman uses with the greatest persistence and confidence will catch him the most fish.

Beginners are advised to buy as great a variety of lures as possible —probably half a dozen to start—in the smallest sizes available. Considering the advice of the salesman is a good way to begin, provided he knows the type of water to be fished. Most accom-plished spin fishermen use tiny swivels to reduce line twisting. Perrine makes a good aluminum lure box for about $3, but a number of much lighter plastic boxes are available for less than $1.

To make light lures cast farther and sink deeper, the spin fisherman should carry a small selection of various sized split shot or sinker putty, which can be clamped onto or next to the lure. Even more useful are plastic bubbles which can be filled with shot and fastened to the leader to make lures run deep. The same bubbles, partly filled with water, serve as floats and provide the necessary weight for spin-casting flies. Many bubbles accept water but not shot, so the angler must shop carefully to assure versatility. Bubbles are inexpensive (15-40¢) and almost weightless, so three or four can easily be carried. To minimize chances of scaring trout and tangling line, bubbles should be fastened two feet from the fly for beginners and three feet for more experienced casters.

The most popular bait for trout is the salmon egg. Small bottles of identical looking pink eggs may range in price from 50¢ to $3. The difference lies in the quality (firmness, toughness) of the egg and the appeal of the ingredients used to treat it. Trout rely principally on the smell of an egg rather than its appearance. Eggs are soaked in chemicals which toughen the skin and impart a flavor to the milk within. When the egg is punctured by the hook, the milk oozes out to flavor the surrounding water and attract the trout.

Pautzke's Balls O' Fire stay together, stay on the hook and do a good job of attracting trout. Despite their $3 a bottle price, they are the choice of regular egg fisherman. Salmon eggs are the most popular bait because they are neat, easy to use and do not wiggle. But they are generally much less effective than such natural baits as worms, grubs, helgramites and grasshoppers; and heavily fished trout often learn to ignore them. Size No. 14 egg hooks, either snelled or unsnelled, are required to completely hide the hook.

The most successful bait fishermen go prepared to catch whatever the trout are feeding upon. They roll rocks to collect ants and beetles. They dig in rotten logs for grubs. They catch grasshoppers with their hats in the early morning before insects become active. And they prowl the margins of a stream or lakeshore for whatever

stalking grasshoppers gets harder once they're warm & awake.

insect life is plentiful, digging in the mud beneath hovering dragonflies to capture their larvae and turning over rocks to uncover helgramites.

Serious bait fishermen work in pairs, one holding a sheet of nylon mosquito netting in the water while his partner turns over rocks just upstream. The same netting will produce a variety of wildlife when spread beneath violently shaken shrubbery. Most natural bait must be impaled—preferably alive—on long shank hooks, although ladybugs will require the smallest salmon egg hooks. Worms, which should be brought from home to save digging up the meadow, require worm hooks which have two or three barbs on the back of the shank.

All trout are not the same, and the angler needs to know which kind(s) inhabit the water in question to know how most effectively to fish. Probably the most common trout is the rainbow with its pink lateral stripe and black speckled silvery body. The rainbow likes fast water, lying in the swiftest current in streams. It feeds near the surface, even when surface water turns warm, feeds readily on insects, follows the lakeshore in search of food and tries to throw the hook by repeatedly leaping from the water.

Rainbows fight energetically, attack all manner of food and lures and are the most easily caught species of trout. As a consequence, they are the most widely planted trout, both as fingerlings dropped from the air in wilderness lakes and as catchables delivered by truck to easily accessible trout waters. Rainbows spawn in the spring the later the spring the later the spawning—but in order to reproduce they must have access to a free flowing, gravel bottomed stream.

Second in popularity to the rainbow is the brook trout, an olive and black-bodied fish with light and dark spots on the sides and varying amounts of yellow, white and orange-red on the underside and fins. The brookie rises readily to the fly, but seldom jumps when hooked. It prefers quieter water in streams and tends to shift its feeding to deeper water when the surface begins to warm in mid-season. Brook trout do poorly below 4,000 feet, but reproduce very well at higher elevations, tending to survive better than rainbows above 8,000 feet. Since it does not require running water for its fall spawning—being able to reproduce in spring-fed lakes—it is the most frequently planted fish in small high elevation tarns.

The most sought after trout, at least in the west, is the brightly colored golden with its vivid red lateral stripe, spotted olive-green back and yellow and orange underside. The vertical grey parr marks beneath the red stripe are also seen on young rainbows. Native to California's 11-12,000 foot Cottonwood Lakes Basin, the golden has been extensively planted, but principally in remote high country waters, because it neither competes well with other species nor withstands heavy angler pressure. The golden breeds readily with other trout, particularly the rainbow, and pure goldens are found only where no other species are present.

Contrary to myth, goldens will thrive at sub alpine elevations. I regularly catch them in a 7,800 foot lake. Goldens tend to be small and their mouths are porportionally smaller then those of other trout. Though they feed readily on flies they tend to suck them in daintily from below, barely dimpling the surface. Since they do not strike in the abandoned manner of the rainbow and brookie, they rarely hook themselves. This, coupled with their ability to instantly spit out unappetizing objects—like hooks—makes them extremely difficult to catch, especially by inexperienced anglers.

The other commonly found trout is the brown, which includes both the Loch Leven and the German Brown. As the name implies, this trout is predominantly varying shades of brown. The charcoal black shades to a golden brown on the sides and a yellow tan on the underside. There is considerable variation in spotting, but no other breed boasts both red and black spots.

Brown trout tolerate comparatively warm waters, but customarily lie deep where they grow very large. In cold streams and in the spring and fall when lake surfaces are cold, browns will take a fly readily, although they do not fight with great energy or jump. More intelligent and circumspect than the rainbow or brookie, the brown is difficult to catch and is therefore not much planted although brown trout waters are seldom fished out.

There are other well known species of trout—cutthroat, Dolly Varden and Mackinaw, for instance—but the four discussed here are easily the most common.

Trout, for the most part, are not very smart, i.e. they learn very little from experience or association. But their instincts and senses are often acute and serve to protect them. Trout see well underwater, but distinguish only movement, not shapes, above the surface. And their field of vision does not extend to the area behind their eyes—which is why knowledgeable fisherman work their way upstream in order to approach the fish from behind. (Trout generally face the current in moving water.) Trout have demonstrated a preference for red, but probably distinguish other colors as well.

Trout do not actually hear, but are extremely sensitive to vibrations. They will often be frightened by the tread of a heavy-footed angler they do not see. As demonstrated by the makers of various salmon egg sauces, trout have a well developed sense of smell. This tends to explain why natural live bait is successful while exact rubber imitations are not. Taste is closely related to smell and since trout are able to discriminate between food and non-food, a good bait must satisfy both the trout's taste and smell. Fly fishermen, while little concerned with either, must be prepared to set the hook before the trout can reject the indigestible fly and spit it out.

It is popularly believed that trout feed principally at dawn or dusk. The principal basis for this contention is that poor light early and late conceals the angler and the artificiality of this offerings, and trout are apt to venture farther from shelter to feed when protected by shadow. It is true that trout tend to feed on the surface, especially in lakes, more at dawn and dusk than during the brighter part of the day, but the very early fishing usually does not justify very early rising.

Trout seem to have several spurts of appetite during the day, and if the angler happens to hit one, the fishing is likely to be unusually good. Another saying of some substance is that fishing will be better in the dark of the moon. It is generally true that the brighter the moonlight the better the fish can see to feed at night—and the less avidly it will feed during the day. If I am making a trip primarily to fish, the phase of the moon will be a factor in scheduling the trip.

More important than the time of day or the phase of the moon is the angler's technique, and passable technique comes most readily from practice. The scarcity of fly fisherman stems from the fact that it takes a little time and patience to learn—and instructors are not easily found. An expert fisherman and tournament fly-caster friend suggests the following for beginners.

Using a seven to eight foot fly rod, matched reel, tapered line and leader and a fly from which the barb has been filed, the student should measure his fly line and wind it with different colored strips of tape at 25, 30 and 35 feet. On a stretch of lawn with plenty of back casting room, he should lay out a sheet of newspaper for a target. Fly casting demands a relatively stiff wrist and the student will benefit by fastening his wrist to the rod handle with a big rubber band to remind him to use his elbow instead. A book held in the armpit will discourage excess movement of the shoulder and promote good form.

Starting with about fifteen feet of line stretched out on the grass in front of him, the student, holding the rod in one hand and the line in the other, should lift the rod tip quickly from the 10 o'clock position—as viewed in profile against a giant imaginary clock—stopping at the 1 o'clock position. The motion's suddenness must lift the line into the air and into the backcast. The student must wait until the line is stretched out tight behind him before bringing the rod forward with enough force to carry the line out straight in front of him when the rod is returned to the 10 o'clock position.

False casting should be continued until the student can keep the line suspended in the air with a minimum of effort without exceeding the 10-1 o'clock range with the rod. To make the cast, it is only necessary to aim the forward cast to a point three feet above the newspaper and then drop the rod tip to 9 o'clock and allow the fly to quietly settle.

The student should become adept at dropping the fly accurately with 15-20 feet of line before trying longer casts. It will be helpful to use a highly visible white winged fly and to watch the path of fly, line and rod continuously at first to become acquainted with the paths they travel and to discover the necessary rhythm. When the fly can be placed gently on the newspaper every time at a distance of thirty feet the caster will be ready to catch fish.

The beginner, to avoid frustration, should never try to handle more than 35 feet of line. Long casts are not essential to catching trout. The uncle who taught me to fly cast regularly outfished me on a stream with casts no longer than twenty feet. The most important factor in his success, it seems to me, was his knowledge of where trout lie. Nearly as important was his ability to present the fly in a natural manner without frightening the fish. Learning the places that fish like comes with time, but it may be helpful to remember that trout will choose protected feeding places during the day and will not venture more than a few inches away from that protection to take fly, lure or bait. Random casts into open water will only serve to scare them.

Placing the fly so that it floats on the current without drag past the likely lie, or casting quickly to a rise in a lake comes with experience. But approaching carefully so as not to spook the fish is largely a matter of patience and self discipline. The difference between scared trout and a full creel is often the angler's willingness to crawl slowly to the protection of a tree and then carefully cast from behind it. Concealment is far more important to the fly caster than to the spin fisherman because he is operating at closer range with trout on or near the surface, and will often be within the trout's field of view or vibrations.

Two other essentials for fly casting success are keeping a tight line

stealth & concealment are
important in fly fishing

and setting the hook. Only a small percentage of trout will hook
themselves—even rainbows—and nearly all trout, if given the chance,
will reject artificial flies and try to spit them out. It is up to the
angler to strike back when a trout takes the fly, before it can throw
the hook. The angler's strike—lifting the rod tip with a snap—must
be an instantaneous reaction, a reflexive response, or the fish will
escape. With a slack line, obviously, it will be virtually impossible to
strike back in time. So the angler must balance the need to let the
fly float naturally without drag, against the need to keep the line
tight enough for setting the hook with a single jerk.

Since excessive casting tends to spook the fish, the fly caster must
exercise restraint and emphasize accuracy. Whether in a lake or
stream the closest lies should be explored first before working out
toward the casting limit. Various retrieves can be tried to intrigue
trout: leaving the fly motionless, twitching it, skittering it, or dunk-
ing it—until a strike is forthcoming. If fishing it dry fails, it should be
allowed to sink below the surface. For wet fly fishing, only a single
backcast should be used. If rising fish ignore the fly, either: (1) it is
too large (2) it is being presented unconvincingly, or (3) the fish are
too small.

It is nearly always worthwhile to immediately examine the food
in the mouth, throat and stomach of the first fish caught for a hint
in the choice or modification of flies. For instance, finding a
stomach full of small beetles, I might trim the hackles very short to
make my fly more beetle-like.

Once a stretch of water has been well prospected, even if unsuc-
cessfully, it is a good idea to move on. If I get a good strike, but miss
the fish, and several further casts bring no response, I immediately
move away to rest the water, making a mental note to return later.
When the water is still and well lighted it is next to impossible to
catch trout on flies and casting will only frighten the fish. But the
turbulence of current, the shadows of trees or clouds, the swirl of

rising fish, or a wind ruffled surface will hide the angler, disguise his offering and give the trout an illusion of protection, which will allow him to feed uninhibited.

Fly rod fishing, though more limited in variety than spinning, offers several variations. When the trout are numerous and receptive, but not overly large, and casting room is ample, I often attach a dropper fly to the middle of my leader by means of an eight inch length of monofilament. It more than doubles the chance of a strike and provides wild action when two fish are hooked. Early in the

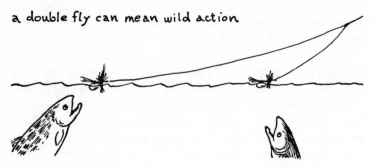

a double fly can mean wild action

year, I sometimes crimp a split shot to the curve of the hook and, fishing off a ledge, jig for bottom feeding trout. And in desperation, I have even stripped the fly off my hook to impale an ant or ladybug or grub when there seemed no other way to catch my dinner.

Spin fishing is a good deal easier to learn for the beginning angler. Spinning covers more water, offers less risk of frightening fish and permits a greater variety of lures and baits, especially in lakes. The elements of spin casting can be learned in fifteen minutes. All that is required is the synchronization of the release of the line with the forward thrust of the rod. Backcasting room is not required; neither is false casting, nor the stealthful approach. The greater the weight of the lure or lead or water-filled bubble, the greater the range of the caster. The beginner is not limited to short casts; in fact he will easily cast farther than the experienced fly caster. Of course spinning's advantage lies in fishing big water: lakes and big rivers. In small or brushy creeks, spinning is virtually impossible.

Spin fishing divides neatly into three categories: lures, bait and flies. Lure casting, being easier, is naturally the most popular. It also produces the most fish. The beginner should purchase as many different types of lures as he can afford to buy and carry: spinners with both wide and thin blades, wobbling spoons that are thick, thin, heavy and light. Several sizes of split shot will also be needed. The angler's imagination will suggest various combinations of lures and lead, fished with various kinds of retrieves at varying depths. There is no end to the possibilities. I have taken trout by skittering an unweighted spinner-fly rapidly across the surface—and by bouncing a weighted spoon along a gravel bottom. Most fish, of course, are caught somewhere in between. The angler needs to be conscious of the depth at which a trout strikes in order to determine where fish are feeding.

The great advantage of spinning is the increased water that can be covered by longer casts which can be retrieved at any depth, but the advantage demands that the spin fisherman keep moving and experimenting in order to show his wares to a maximum number of fish. When trout follow a lure peacefully at a respectful distance they are only mildly curious, or well fed, and a change in lures is indicated. If trout follow closely or dart around the lure in an agitated manner they can sometimes be induced to strike by changing the action, or the depth, or the size of the lure, or perhaps by baiting the hook to add appeal. Lures should be connected to the monofilament by a swivel to prevent excessive twisting. Lure casting in streams or shallow water or weedy areas can be a very expensive sport!

Bait fishing looks deceptively simple. Unfortunately, it requires considerable art to make bait impaled on a hook attached to a line behave in a convincingly natural manner. There are two types of bait fishing: still fishing for the lazy and casting for the ambitious. The still fisherman hopes he has a likely spot, hopes the fish are feeding on the bottom and hopes the fish will hook himself. The bait caster at a lake generally attempts slow deep retrieves, tumbling his bait along the bottom, but also experiments with different depths. In some cases he is a still fisherman who occasionally moves.

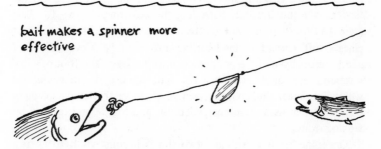

bait makes a spinner more effective

In streams and rivers, the bait fisherman who can drift a bait along the bottom through likely lies with a tight enough line to feel a strike, but without tell-tale drag is an artist who will never lack for fish. The beginner who wishes to use bait will do better using a bubble for a bobber, attaching it at a point what will allow the lightly weighted bait to bob a few inches above the bottom.

Spin fishing with flies is much the same. A partially water-filled bubble is fastened two and a half or three feet from the fly and cast. Flies can be fished either wet or dry. Despite the splash of the bubble and its wake during the retreive, the fish are not much bothered by relatively long casts on a wind ruffled lake.

There are certain techniques applicable to both spinning and fly casting. The most important is to keep moving. Ninety percent of the water contains no fish. The angler's objective is to eliminate much of it on the basis of experience, knowledge and inspection and to prospect the rest with diligence and imagination. The greater the area effectively fished the greater the chances of filling the creel. Beginners are apt to cast endlessly to water that has yielded a fish or a strike or a rise. The veteran angler will generally move after playing a fish, knowing the water is too disturbed to produce.

Trout lie facing upstream in running water and will generally hold in the same positions all day unless badly frightened. Under cover of dusk or darkness, however, they will move out into shallow or still or unprotected water to feed on morsels they would not have dared to pursue during the bright part of the day. The water that can be safely eliminated without a second glance during the day often yields the most fish in the evening. (Trout fishing is commonly permitted for an hour after sunset.)

Though difficult to reach and maddening to fish, the most productive water—even in heavily fished areas—will often be in brushy, swampy, heavily wooded country. Fishermen endowed with great patience—and some skill—often seek out just such hard-to-fish spots when they are determined to catch fish. The backpacker should not scorn accessible water because it is regularly fished, any more than he should depend on remote water to produce sensational results.

Trout are a roaming species in lakes and they tend to follow the shores near the bottom, patrolling the area they know. The best place to find them is where a stream feeds the lake. The second best place is off a point of land jutting into the lake. Coves are often good, especially if there is drainage into the lake. The foot of a dry watercourse is often attractive to trout, as are undercut banks and willow and alder thickets that overhang the water. Boulders, ledges, blankets of moss and submerged brush and logs all are favored by feeding trout.

Once the trout is hooked, two things become vital: to keep a tight line, and to keep him from reaching underwater obstructions. Slack in the line helps the fish throw the hook and invites knots and snags. Brook and brown trout instinctively bore for the bottom when hooked and must be turned before they can rub the hook free or cut the leader. Rainbow and golden usually jump in hopes of throwing the hook and relatively little pressure is required to keep the line tight.

Beginning anglers tend to drag in their fish in great haste, often jerking them so violently from the water that the fish sails over the fisherman's head. This technique not only risks breaking the leader and pulling out the hook, it eliminates the pleasure of playing the fish.

For the backpacker—who cannot afford the weight of a landing net—playing the trout to exhaustion is more than just sport. Exhaustion greatly reduces the chance of escape. The trout should be maneuvered to the terrain most closely resembling a beach. The critical moment comes when the leader is grasped a few inches from the no-longer-flooping trout and it is smoothly lifted from the water, deposited several yards inland, and pounced upon before it can flop back into the water. Careless landing technique may cost the beginner one trout in two. The seasoned angler rarely loses a fish.

violent landing technique leads to trouble

BLOINK

YIKES!

Of course, small trout—under seven inches—or fish not needed for food should not be landed at all. The exhausted fish should be grasped gently but firmly underwater with one hand while the barb is backed out with the other. If the maneuver cannot be managed underwater, the hand grasping the fish should first be wetted to prevent it injuring the skin or ripping off the scales. Injured trout of any size should never be released. Nearly all trout taken on flies may be released unharmed, while nearly all fish taken on bait are injured by the removal of the hook.

Once a trout has been landed, it should promptly be killed. Putting my index finger in the mouth, I quickly bend the head all the way back until it touches the back, breaking the neck and killing the fish instantly. After rinsing off the dirt, I usually lie the trout on a rock in the shade to let the breeze dry first one side then the other before putting it in my creel or on my stringer.

A creel should be well filled with grass or leaves to assure ventilation. Trout that are allowed to grow warm or stay wet or go uncleaned will lose texture and flavor in a matter of hours and will begin to spoil soon after. But by proper care and handling, I have often kept trout without refrigeration for three and four days in camp with no loss of freshness or flavor. By getting the trout dry to the touch almost immediately, and not allowing the sun to warm it, I can carry it in my creel for three or four hours before cleaning without risk.

Cleaning trout is simple enough. I insert a sharp pointed knife blade in the vent and with a short, rapid sawing strokes slit open the body cavity all the way to the base of the jaw. After cutting across from one gill opening to the other, I break the colon loose from the vent, and pull the viscera and gills loose. Then, running my thumb-nail down the inside of the backbone, I remove the last blackness of the kidney and the job is done. After thoroughly rinsing the fish inside and out, and promptly drying all surfaces, it is ready for cooking, refrigeration or several days storage in a dry, cool place.

There are innumerable recipes for preparing trout, but fresh trout fried in butter is hard to beat. For years I have carried a plastic bag containing varying portions of corn meal, corn starch, salt, pepper, garlic and onion salt and other spices. After dampening the fish and putting it in the bag for a quick shaking, it is ready for the buttered skillet. Crumbling a little left over bacon bar over the frying fish enhances the flavor—so does a squirt of lemon joice. I am fond of smoked trout, but the process is not suited to most backpacking trips. Trout wrapped in aluminum foil and baked in ashes, on the other hand, is easy and saves the weight of skillet. So does trout toasted on a stick.

When it comes to catching trout, there is no substitute for persistence. Almost anyone, equipped with reasonably efficient tack-le and situated on reasonably stocked trout water, should eventually catch trout if the necessary effort is put forth. As one of my old fishing partners used to remind me: "You can't catch fish unless your line's in the water." He fished with great determination—and considerable imagination—and always caught fish.

The innocent angler should beware of guidebooks that promise marvelous fishing. Wild trout simply cannot be promised. The excel-lence of the fishing varies with the skill of the angler, recent fishing pressure, feeding activity, phase of the moon, available food, time of day, weather, season—and, of course, that great imponderable luck.

Angling for trout has many alures. The chance of a great catch is endlessly exciting. The vision of a succulent dinner is intriguing. But the opportunity to explore predictably fine country is what makes angling for trout most delightful to me.

14 a SaMPLe TRIP

To bring together the material on equipment and technique, I have set down in detail an account of a trip a friend and I made during the writing of this book. Events and equipment are actual, rather than ideal, and not meant to represent perfection. The trip began at my cabin in Echo Lake on the edge of Desolation Wilderness in the California Sierra. I wanted to revisit a lake I had camped at briefly the year before, and to visit two nearby lakes I had never seen. Although I planned to approach from a new direction over a trail I had not previously walked, knowing precisely where we would camp was of great help in planning a comfortable trip. It suggested what food and equipment we should take and determined the time of year we should go.

I knew the three lakes would be thawed by early May, that insect activity would start the trout feeding on flies by mid-June, and that the nearby Boy Scout Camp did not open until immediately after the fourth of July weekend. To avoid the holiday campers, yet find the water warm enough for swimming, it seemed clear that the last week in June was the time to go. It would be the dark of the moon, which meant poor nighttime visibility, but probably better fishing. The only possible drawback was that mosquitos were likely to be active; since the country was open and well-drained, and since we meant to be prepared for insects, this was a negligible factor. (There are places, of course, where the mosquito menace is the *most* important factor in determining when to go.)

We decided to allow ourselves three days and two nights. Trip length was determined after considering several alternatives. The hike would be comparatively short, the country we wanted to see quite small; and there was a limit to what we could do to amuse ourselves (neither of us cared to spend a whole day swimming or fishing, and there were no convenient peaks to climb). On the other hand, there would be several hours of driving each way and possibly an hour of canoeing. Alloting only two days and one night would mean going in one day and coming out the next; that would be too rushed. Four days and three nights was likely to lead to boredom. So we settled on three days—sometime during the last week of June.

Normally, the next step is to work out a menu, buy the food and assemble the necessary clothing and equipment. But, since food, clothes and gear were already at the cabin in preparation for this and other trips, we postponed deciding what to take and turned to the decision of when precisely to go. The problem was weather. Few backpackers can afford to wait for perfect weather. Vacation schedules often dictate departure dates, and trips must be planned well in advance. But far too many backpackers see their trips spoiled for lack of knowledge about likely weather.

On the twenty-sixth of June at Echo, the sky was threatening all day, the wind was from the southeast and the barometer was low and steady. The forecast on the portable radio was for 'thunderstorms afternoon and evening' over the central Sierra. Weather in the Carson Valley to the east and the Sacramento Valley to the west was cool and unsettled. It rained a little in the afternoon and that night it snowed. The outlook for a happy trip was distinctly unfavorable.

On the twenty-seventh, the forecasts for the Sacramento and Carson Valleys were for 'fair and warmer,' and the temperature climbed a little at Echo. The morning of the twenty-eighth the barometer was beginning to rise, and although scattered thunderstorms were still forecast afternoon and evening, these represented only the tattered remnants of the passing storm and would probably be weak and brief. Since the fourth of July weekend was almost upon us, we decided to leave the next day.

Most of my equipment is packed in cartons under a pair of built-in bunks flanking the fireplace in my cabin. The first step in preparing for a trip is to prop open the bunk lids and fish out the notebook containing my latest checklist. It may be possible to remember everything needed on short notice without such a list, but before I made lists I nearly always left something vital home.

I like to postpone final choices and making up my pack until the last possible minute at the trailhead, so I begin by finding two empty cartons: one for food and community gear (box No. 1) and the other for personal equipment (box No. 2). Items on my list in general use, and therefore not stored beneath the bunks (like hiking boots and fly rod), are marked with an asterisk, and these I usually skip over the first time down the list.

Because I expect mild temperatures, even if it rains, I choose my lightest down mummy bag, a 3-pound North Face Superlight, pull it from its stuff bag, turn it inside out and lay it out doors in the sunshine to evaporate any moisture condensed inside. The one pound North Face bivouac cover which serves as ground cloth, clothes bag and sleeping bag cover, is also stretched inside-out in the sun. I unroll an egg-crate 54-inch Sierra Designs foam mattress, covered like the bivouac cover with coated nylon below and uncoated nylon (for breathability) above, and spread it, too, in the sun.

On this trip, I am field testing a hybrid rucksac-packframe made by North Face called the Ruthsac, and I try it on, make some preliminary adjustments of the straps, and divide a handful of kitchen matches between its two side pockets. While my mummy bag will fit inside, my full length foam pad will not, so I attach two, 2-foot lengths of woven parachute cord through leather eyelets at the top, sealing the easily unraveled ends in the flame of a match.

Although I hope to leave all three at the trailhead, I pack into box No. 1 a two and a third pound, 2-man plastic tube tent, a one and a quarter pound plastic storm suit from Japan and a coated nylon poncho with hood. The tube tent has brought me a lot of luck. I have carried it more than a hundred miles and never been forced to pitch it. The line required to rig it is not included with the tent, so I toss in the box a 25-foot hank of 550-pound test nylon cord, which would go along in any case.

Cooking gear is the next consideration and I inspect and put in box No. 1 the Bluet stove which, with windscreen and fresh cartridge of butane, weighs less than two pounds. One cartridge should suffice and luckily there is none in the stove (cartridges cannot be removed until empty). In box No. 2 I put a large, single-bladed

deciding what to take

jacknife (the blade is sufficiently pointed to clean trout, yet broad enough to spread butter) and my folding aluminum spoon-fork. With that goes my large plastic cup marked with lines at every quarter cup. Since weight is not vital, I add an almost weightless aluminum measuring cup as well.

Although our menu is still to be determined, I know we will want a big pot for soups and stews and a smaller one for other dishes. The single burner of the Bluet limits the possibilities (thereby simplifying menu planning). I put in box No. 1 a two and a quarter quart Sigg kettle, the lid of which has been fitted with a small knob so that it can be lifted with aluminum hot pot tongs. A one quart pot embraced by two spun aluminum plates (one of which doubles as a frying pan) and packed in a heavy plastic bag also go in the box, along with the pot tongs, to complete the cooking equipment.

For carrying water to camp and making fruit drinks, I choose a wide-mouthed polyethylene quart bottle. For this weekend-sized trip my half empty shaker containing a mix of various salts and pepper does not require refilling. One quart of milk will be ample so I open a quart packet of powdered Milkman and empty the contents into my plastic milk squirter bottle (originally a mustard dispenser). After carefully plugging the spout from within with a matchstick, this, too, goes in box No. 1.

powdered milk in a plugged mustard dispenser

I know my partner, Don, prefers tea to coffee and will bring along his own saccharine (convenient enough, but without sugar's energy), so I throw eight tea bags in the box (powdered tea may be simpler in the city, but bags are still best in the woods). A rigid plastic, screw-topped, wide-mouthed pint 'ice box jar' that holds about two cups is selected and filled with a cup and a half of sugar. Sugar requirements vary considerably, depending on the menu and individual tastes. For instance, we carry pre-sweetened Wyler's drinks, and I package sugar with applesauce in advance, so sugar is principally needed for morning cereal and tea. Sugar is the food I consistently take too much of and have to bring home. Years ago, I ran out two days early on a one week trip; since then I find I carry an ounce or two more than I need.

From my container box comes a Gerry plastic squeeze tube that was boiled clean after the last trip. I make sure the cap is screwed on tight, and fill it approximately half full of apricot-pineapple preserves through the open bottom. After cleaning the opening with a wet cloth I fold it over, leaving plenty of room in the bottom, and force on the plastic clip. I give the tube a good squeeze to make sure it will not open in my pack (it never has), then I wipe off the remaining stickiness and toss the tube in the food box.

It cannot be denied that margarine keeps better than butter, but I much prefer butter, and with minimal precautions it will always stay fresh for the three to five days I am usually out. Butter and margerine are heavy and many think of them as luxuries, but they are high in food energy and probably the most palatable source of badly needed fat. I find it possible to consume an almost unlimited quantity: in soups, stews, on crackers and frying trout, and even, like the Himalayan Sherpas, in my tea. So I select a large, wide-mouthed aluminum can with a plastic liner and take three quarter-pound cubes of fresh butter out of the refrigerator and set them on the kitchen table to warm to a workable consistency.

A slightly smaller aluminum can with liner is chosen for cheese, and into it I fit wedge-shaped chunks of the four varieties I find in the refrigerator. Hard orange cheeses like cheddar are more melt-resistant than, say, Monterey Jack. After screwing the lid down tight, I put the can of cheese back in the refrigerator.

In my supply boxes beneath the bunks, I keep a variety of heavy duty plastic bags—containers that have become indispensable to backpacking. I choose six large ones (two of which are for bringing home trout) and two smaller ones, and stuff them all into the bottom of my pack. A Chore Girl, a Flip pad (an emery cloth-backed sponge) and a half-empty one ounce tube of Paket bio-degradable hand and dish soap go into a small plastic bag which is closed with a twisty. I find half a roll of toilet paper secured with a rubber band, and since that looks like plenty I throw it in the box. Paper towels are more easily used in a wind, and they also serve as dish towels and hot pads, but I could not find a partial roll and a full roll is much too bulky for three days.

Next comes my small (six ounce) first aid kit packed in a screw-top plastic icebox jar, like the sugar, but marked with conspicuous red crosses. It contains a dozen assorted plastic Bandaids, a pair each of 2 x 2 and 3 x 3 inch gauze pads, a one-inch roll of adhesive (not plastic) tape, a roll of three inch Kling gauze and a clean washcloth. There are a few lumps of foam, a sheet of Mole foam and a pair of nail scissors to cut them. Taped to the lid is a needle and a backed razor blade. Scattered about are matches.

One aluminum film can contains a dozen aspirin, half a dozen 500 mg vitamin C tablets for fighting colds, a sprinkling of anti-acid and milk of magnesia tablets, and several long-lasting anti-histamine spansules. A second can contains a lump of soap. I test the backing on the adhesive tape (which deteriorates after a year) and replace the short-lived vitamin C and crumbling milk of magnesia tablets.

The next item is my personal kit, packed in a plastic zippered pouch. There was a time when I painstakingly gathered the contents for every trip, but it soon became evident that it would be easier to keep a kit permanently assembled. Mine contains a toothbrush, a tiny flat plastic container of dental floss, a spare tube of chapstick, one ounce tubes of Sea & Ski suntan lotion and Desenex athlete's foot ointment, half a roll of anti-acid tablets, a stub of pencil and the remains of a tube of glacier cream. The little packet weighs three ounces, and I put it directly into an outside pocket of the pack.

Mosquitos in the area are likely to be active, so I put in the box a nearly full aerosol can of Off repellent. Though it weighs seven ounces it will provide instant relief when, wearing only shorts, we come suddenly into a cloud of hungry mosquitos. An equally efficient piece of equipment is the Mallory flashlight, which with two long-lasting manganese batteries, weighs only three ounces and will throw a 250-foot beam. I switch it on and though the batteries are a

year old the light is still strong so I tape the switch in the 'off'
position to make sure it cannot turn on in the pack and put it in the
box. A single flashlight will be ample for the two of us, since we do
not expect to be roaming at night. A spare bulb is carried in the first
aid kit.

The best existing map of the area we are visiting is the seven and a
half minute USGS topographical map. I have an old, but still
serviceable copy that shows not only the area we will visit but also
the surrounding territory, so we can identify the peaks we will use as
landmarks. To orient the map, we will need to know directions, so I
dig out a liquid-filled plastic-cased compass that weighs only half an
ounce and put it in box No. 2.

mallory
flashlight
with
switch
taped
shut.

Also in box No. 2 goes a four by six inch Spiral notebook with a
section of pencil pushed snugly through the spiral binding. Every
serious backpacker who hopes to refine his equipment and improve
his comfort will find it useful to make notes during the trip. Pencil
and paper also make it possible to leave notes for other party
members in camp or on the trail. And my notebook pages have
served as emergency toilet paper, started fires in rainstorms and
supplied mountaintop registers. My notebook and pencil weigh two
ounces.

Except for food, that takes care of the equipment kept under the
bunks. To make sure nothing has been overlooked, I quickly sort
through the remaining boxes of gear. My search turns up a film can
containing a tiny G.I. can opener and I toss it in the box in case we
take along a can of apricots or peaches. It is difficult to open a can
of fruit packed in heavy syrup on a mountaintop with nothing but a
sharp rock!

With the bunk lids closed, I turn to the selection of clothes. First
comes a long-sleeved, permanent press shirt of heavy green cotton. It
is just about impossible to do without a long-sleeved shirt where
there are going to be bugs. The two large buttondown breast pockets
are very useful. Over the shirt in the evening (or in the wind) goes an
unlined pullover nylon shell parka with a drawstring on the hood,
elastic at the wrists, a drawstring at the bottom (over the hips) and a
front zippered pouch into which both hands can be stuffed. The
parka weighs only 7½ ounces and is rarely left home.

Beneath the cotton shirt goes a short-sleeved string shirt which is
superior to a t-shirt or undershirt in almost every way; it is cooler
and dryer in hot weather, warmer and dryer in cold weather, lighter
and more easily washed and dried enroute. I also prefer it as a
pajama top. I expect that these three garments will be sufficient for
the trip, but to protect against the possibility of really cold weather,
I also put in the box a Navy surplus wool sweater that fits snugly,
but not tightly, and has a high turtleneck. Purchased inexpensively

more than ten years ago, this sweater still competes successfully with my down sweater in some situations.

Since I expect to hike in shorts and also swim, I decide on an old boxer-style bathing suit of heavy cotton in which I probably have logged at least two hundred miles. When shopping for hiking shorts, I test their roominess by putting one foot onto the seat of a chair. If the shorts bind or pull on the top of the leg, there will eventually be painful chafing on the tender flesh inside the thighs. My test finds a majority of bermudas, bathing suits and even hiking shorts unsuitable for hiking.

For the same reason that I carry a long-sleeved shirt (evening wear and bug protection), I always take a pair of long trousers. I have yet to find the perfect pair, which would be beltless in consideration of the need to wear a hipbelt. I finally decide on a pair of tough Rough Rider cotton tans which are snug enough not to need a belt. My spiral notebook just fits into one of the front patch pockets. While my trousers are before me, I fold a yard-long strip of toilet paper and button it into a back pocket. Into a deep front pocket goes a clean bandana handkerchief, which also will function as a wash rag, pot holder, towel, etc.

This takes care of all but the extremities. I have tried a good many different hats. In the warm and friendly summer Sierra I am concerned with sun protection and maximum ventilation, not rain protection. Summer days are long and the high altitude sun beats down relentlessly, so that a hat brim that partially shades the nose and neck and ears can make the difference between developing a protective layer of tan or a painful sunburn. For the country we will visit I choose an old, shapeless once-white cotton tennis hat that weighs two ounces. The underside of the two and a quarter inch brim is dark green for reduced glare, and fully a third of the crown is nylon netting that provides good ventilation. Since I never wear dark glasses, I always take a hat when I go out overnight.

The hiking will be more trail than cross-country, so I choose light boots, a three and a quarter pound pair of Vasque (formerly Voyageur) Yosemites resoled during the winter. Despite some hundreds of miles of wear they remain very useable. Since it is still springtime in this part of the Sierra, there will be a good deal of water, and boots need to be waterproof. Mine were liberally rubbed with hot Sno-Seal only two weeks before and need no further treatment. I give the leather laces a jerk to make sure they have not rotted and put the boots in box No. 2.

From my dresser come two pairs of thick outer stretch socks and two of thin inner socks. One pair of outer socks are year-old, but still good Thermals, the other are nearly new Wick Drys; both are part wool, part synthetic with bulky, moisture-trapping interior loops. The inner socks are both of all-synthetic fabric that passes moisture to the outer sock.

Whenever space and weight allow, I like the luxury of camp boots to change into at the end of the day, so I set aside an old but intact pair of 14 ounce leather moccasins with crepe rubber soles.

Many walkers will take a change of shorts and an extra T-shirt on a three day trip, but I expect to be able to wash and dry both my trunks and my string shirt without inconvenience, as well as a pair of socks. Having selected clothing to cover all contingencies, I make a neat pile of what I expect to wear the next morning—which is everything except the boots, spare socks, nylon shell and wool sweater—and put the pile on my bed, where it cannot be missed.

The fly rod I plan to take is a 2-piece, 7-foot, three and a quarter ounce Fenwick of furruleless fiberglass. The attached Phlueger Medalist reel is loaded with fifty feet of level backing, an HDH tapered fly line, and a seven and a half foot leader tapered to a one and a half pound tippet. I reel the No. 12 mosquito dry fly to the tip of the rod, disjoint the two sections and fasten them side by side—the tip protected by the butt—with stout rubber bands at each end. Though reduced to 3½ feet the rod will still stick a foot above my pack, but I am accustomed to making the necessary allowances, and this arrangement leaves me ready to cast within thirty seconds of stopping. Because the rod does not fit well in a box, and because leaned against the wall it is easily forgotten, I set it inside the open pack.

I take my six ounce, two compartment Abercrombie and Fitch creel off the peg behind the door and unzip the waterpoof pocket to check the contents. Inside are a Perrine fly box the size of a cigarette package which comfortably holds a hundred flies. Fastened to it with a stout rubber band are three extra cellophane-enclosed rolled, tapered leaders. The top one contains my fishing license. There is nothing else in the creel but a small tin of Muselin for dressing my line and fly. On this trip fishing is a principal purpose and I expect the creel to function as a knapsack on walks away from camp.

My Konica camera is advertised as the 'world's smallest, lightest, rangefinder 35' and that might be true. Its automatic exposure control makes it excellent for fast shooting. It weighs 13 ounces loaded with a 36 exposure roll of Kodachrome-X (without case, which is the way I carry it). I find the camera empty and have no spare film, so I write myself a note to buy a roll on the way to the trailhead. The camera goes in box No. 2 while the note stays on the kitchen table. I fill a small plastic bottle with about four ounces of brandy and put it in an outside pocket of the pack.

Late in the afternoon my partner, Don, arrives carrying a small, well-blackened European-style teapot which he praises highly and which we decide to take. (If weight were critical we would leave the smaller kettle home.) I carry several boxes of backpacking food out to the back porch, and, while Don picks through the collection to see what looks good, I get the notebook and pencil from box No. 2 and note that we will need provisions for three lunches, two dinners and two breakfasts. We discuss our preferences (within the scope of our food supply) and decide on the following: for breakfast both mornings there will be the Birchermuesli Familia with milk and sugar, and Sherpa tea; one morning we will have left-over apricot slices, the other, left-over applesauce. Since Familia will constitute the bulk of the meal we will need four ounce servings. A fresh 13 ounce package and a third of another are emptied into a doubled plastic bag, which is then knotted at the top.

For dinner we decide on a Richmoor Beef Stroganoff (rated to serve four) for one night and beef stew, which I have offered to concoct that evening, for the other. Both meals will start with soup and we select foil packets of Maggi ham and pea, and mushroom, each of which will yield four full cups. A Richmoor package of sliced apricots with sugar, serving four, is set aside for one dinner-breakfast. For the other, I empty about four servings of bulk dehydrated apples into a plastic bag and add a heaping teaspoon of cinnamon, half a teaspoon of nutmeg and four heaping teaspoons of sugar before knotting the top. Desert one night will be Richmoor Banana Cream Pudding; the other night we will splurge, since weight is not crucial, and take a can of Del Monte sliced peaches in heavy syrup.

Lunch always seems the most complicated meal. To the cheese, butter and jam already packed we add half a package (four ounces) of salted wheat crackers, two Wilson's Bacon bars, half a pound each of mixed candy and Kendall Mint cake, a half pound mixture of raisins, chocolate drops and salted almonds (gorp), half a dozen sticks of jerky and small bags of date bits and banana flakes, left over from a previous trip, that have captured Don's fancy.

GORP
is good
any ol'
time.

Provisions are completed by adding five packages of Wyler's Lemonade and Orange—one for each lunch and dinner—and a three ounce plastic bag of 'trout dip,' a mixture of corn starch, corn meal, salt, pepper, onion and garlic salt and probably other now forgotten ingredients. Having suffered in the past from taking too little or leaving home something vital, I spread all the food on the table grouped by meals, and we give it a hard look. The lunch, which must supply three meals, and snacks as well, looks a little skimpy, so I get half a salami from the kitchen while Don adds a handful of dried apricots to the fruit mix and puts in the other half box of crackers. Satisfied now, we dump everything in the food box and turn on the portable radio for the hourly weather report.

Scattered afternoon and evening thunderstorms are still forecast locally, with fair weather both to the east and west. The late afternoon sky, though more than half filled with billowing, black-hearted thunderheads, is not particularly threatening, and the barometer has continued to rise. We plan to meet at 9 a.m. the next morning at my pier.

After Don leaves I inspect the mattress, bivouac cover and sleeping bag that have been airing in the sun. Both bag and cover have several pitch spots and these I wipe off with gasoline, taking care to immediately wash away the gasoline with soap and water. The bottom of the pad cover has a thumb-sized area of punctures and abrasions, so I remove the backing from a two inch section of ripstop tape, trim off the corners and press it in place. By the time I have re-rolled the mattress, the bag and cover are dry and I can stuff them into the small, waterproof stuff bag. Both mattress and stuff bag are then put into the pack.

Back in the kitchen, I find the butter has softened and after removing the wrapping I have little difficulty pressing all three cubes into the plastic liner inside the aluminum provision can. After screwing the lid down tight I put the can in the refrigerator, along with the cheese. Then before I can forget, I write boldly on a large sheet of paper "Butter and cheese in icebox" and put this reminder on top of everything else in the food box.

That evening, I spread out on the kitchen table the various ingredients for my stew. In order to make some record of my creation, I decide to make two identical dinners, combining ingredients in a double plastic bag for the one we take, and keeping them separate in individual small bags for the one I leave behind. That way, if the stew is successful or needs obvious modifications, I am in a position to measure portions and make adjustments.

The ingredients I choose are: dehydrated potatoe cubes and mixed carrots and peas, a bouillon cube, half a package of instant gravy, dehydrated mushrooms, half a quart package of Milkman dehydrated milk, three ounces of freeze dried ground beef, salt,

making the stew from scratch

pepper, and onion and garlic salt. It is my intention to cook this in the uncleaned soup pot for added flavor, and to add half a cube of butter—if we can spare it—and any bacon bar left over from lunch. I knot the top of the doubled bag and toss it in the food box. Everything, now, is ready to go.

The following morning dawns cloudy and threatening and the weather forecast is unchanged, but the barometer has continued to rise. When Don arrives, my pack, fishing rod, and the two boxes—including the butter and cheese from the refrigerator—are stowed in the outboard motor boat at my dock. We have decided, both to add variety to the trip and to save three and a half miles of hiking, to canoe a mile and a half across the lake from the end of the road. So we tow the canoe from my dock down lower Echo Lake to the resort, where I buy a roll of film. With the canoe lashed on top of the station wagon, we load up and start off.

Our principal concern is still the weather, which remains murky as we drive west and then north along the western slope of the range, listening for a change in the forecast. At the end of the gravel road on the shore of a large mountain lake, we unload the car under an overcast sky, launch the canoe, and spread the food, cooking equipment and all other community gear (the contents of box No. 1) on a shelf of granite. I ask Don if he wants to divide the gear; he says no, but he would prefer weight to bulk since this pack is small. By now it is nearly noon and we decide to eat lunch here rather than pack it away and start out hungry.

We sit on a glacially polished slab, looking out across the lake to the mountains in the east as we make all kinds of sandwich combinations from the bacon bar, four kinds of cheese, jam and salami and buttered crackers. After eating our fill of fruit and nuts and candy, and finishing a quart of lemonade, we close the plastic bags, stuff candy in our pockets and pack all the lunch food in a large heavy-duty plastic garbage bag. Hefting an item of community gear (or food) in each hand, I quickly divide everything into two piles of roughly equal weight, taking the bulkier pile for myself.

By this time, we are happy to note, a band of blue sky has appeared in the west, and is steadily growing larger as the gloomy cloud mass moves slowly to the east. I decide against taking my poncho, storm suit and wool sweater, but, since the trip will be easy and short, we agree to carry the two and a quarter pound two-man tube tent as insurance against rain. Don puts it in his pack after giving me back about a pound of his gear.

I stuff my sleeping bag into the bottom of the full length Ruthsac, then lay the pack flat so that I can easily make a layer of the heaviest items (food, pots, stove, etc.) against the back of the packsack (closest to my back). Since the day is warming steadily, I take off my moccasins and trousers and make a second layer of clothing and lighter items, zipping the pack closed as I fill it. Starting at the bottom and working toward the top, I pack the two deep side pockets with brandy, personal kit, flashlight, extra plastic bags and the first aid kit. On top go my camera on one side and an aerosol can of Off repellent on the other.

At the top of my pack are my trousers and shell parka in easy reach in case of insect attack, or a sudden change in the weather. I rub a little Sea and Ski on my face and the back of my neck, put on my boots, and carry my pack, mattress and fishing rod down to the canoe. Don loads the canoe while I return to lock up the car. After pocketing a couple of dimes because I know there are pay phones at nearby trailheads, I lock my wallet in the car, then hide my keys under a nearby rock, thus saving pocket room, a few ounces and the possibility of losing either valuable. As I climb into the canoe I tell Don where the keys are to protect against emergency, then I settle myself in the stern, and as we paddle slowly out into the lake the last of the preparations can finally be forgotten. The trip, itself, has begun.

The small, heavily-laden canoe moves slowly through the light chop, but the wind is with us and we cross the lake in less than an hour—an estimate, since Don shares my unwillingness to wear a watch in the woods. We drag the canoe some distance up the bank and hide it, well separated from its paddles, in some brush to discourage borrowers. I lash my fly rod to the pack by means of two nylon cords attached to the right side, and lash my full length foam mattress to the top of the pack by two more loops of cord.

Canoeing across the lake saves many miles of walking.

We put on our packs and move up through the brush for a hundred yards before finding the well-marked trail which follows the lakeshore. By now the western half of the sky is blue and clear and I know it will be hot in the bright sunlight, so I take off my shirt and stuff it in the top of my pack. For awhile the trail climbs gently away from the lake, but when it turns to the east toward a pass and grows steeper, I tell Don to go ahead. From past experience I know his comfortable pace uphill is faster than mine, and there is no need for either of us to travel at an uncomfortable speed. I know he will be waiting at the pass when I arrive.

As he takes off, I stop to adjust my shoulder straps to make the pack ride more comfortably and to prevent my shoulders from growing sore. A hundred yards farther I stop again, and this time I get it nearly right, although I have come to the conclusion that the pack is a little too large for me, causing the hipbelt to ride too low. As the pitch steepens, I automatically shorten my stride and cut my speed to maintain an unchanged energy output. After a little while my hips begin to ache, reminding me to loosen my hipbelt and tighten my shoulder straps to put a larger portion of the weight on my shoulders. On the steepest stretch my knees start to hurt, but after three limp steps the discomfort goes away.

When I reach the pass, Don is waiting in the shade, sitting on a rock, looking out over the lake-dotted granite basin to the east. I take off my pack and join him. Both of us are better acquainted with the basin as viewed from the opposite direction, so we try to identify all the visible lakes and peaks before bringing out the map and compass. I need to be sure I am properly oriented because the route from this point to the lake is mostly cross-country. After a snack of mint bar we put on our packs and start off.

When we reach the turnoff point, I confirm its location by finding a small, unobtrusive duck that I built beside a tree the previous year. The cross-country trip is unusually easy, passing up a broad grassy draw and dropping over a little rise to the small, sparkling lake. Tucked in a shallow depression in the rolling granite woodland, the lake is flanked by a thicket of willow on one shore and a small, glacially polished dome on the other. We take off our packs in a choice campsite on a little peninsula between two bays. Apparently, we are the first visitors of the year, and there are only a few mosquitos—both excellent signs. The little peninsula has no fringe of marsh to harbor insects, and the parklike stand of pines upon it serves to break the wind, but let through enough air for good ventilation.

I show Don a tilting slab that forms a beach on the more sheltered bay and, after testing the temperature of the water, we immediately take off our boots and dive in, wearing our shorts and socks and shirts. After an exhilarating swim we peel off our wet clothes, rinse them, wring them out, and stretch them to dry on a flat topped boulder. We lie on the hot slab, talking and dozing and watching the clouds for perhaps an hour before putting on our dry shorts and returning barefoot to set up camp.

I unload the main cavity of my pack onto a convenient ledge, and unroll my foam mattress to give the cells a few hours to refill with

air. My mummy bag is pulled from its stuff bag, given a shaking to
fluff up the down, and laid on the spread-out bivouac cover in the
sun. We gather all the food which might be of interest to birds or
mice or squirrels and zip it into my pack. Don assembles the Bluet

the mummy bag gets a fluffing while the foam pad expands.

stove and selects a little bench to serve as a kitchen while I take the
butter and cheese cans and our quart water bottle down to the lake.
The tins I partially submerge and secure with rocks; the bottle I rinse
and fill with water.

My inner socks and string shirt are now dry and I put them in my
pack and hang the thick damp outer socks in a tree. My feet are fully
restored by a swim and an hour going barefoot in the sun, so I put on
my spare pair of heavy socks and my moccasins. Next, I set about
making my bed. I want a level spot well-shaded in the east from the
morning sun, where the ground is soft enough to be shaped to the
necessary contours. I find an ideal patch of granite sand in the lee of
a boulder and go to work scooping a shallow depression about two
and a half feet long and a foot and a half wide with tapering sides
and a relatively flat bottom, placing the excavated material in a
mound on the end I propose for my head. To test the result, I lie
down on my back, make mental notes for repairs, then roll over on
one side to check the fit again.

After a little more scratching, I test it again and find it satisfactory. I know that if the bare earth feels comfortable I am sure to rest
well with the addition of two inches of foam, a down bag and my
bivouac cover. I now assemble my bed by sliding the mattress inside
the cover and positioning it over the hip and shoulder hole. After
lying on it once more to make sure it is aligned, I refluff my sleeping
bag with a few seconds violent shaking and lay it inside the cover on
top of the mattress. From the pockets of my pack I take my string
shirt and personal kit and clean inner socks and tuck them inside the
bivouac cover, making sure that everything is covered from what will
likely be a heavy fall of dew. Now I can forget my bed until time to
crawl inside.

My experience the previous year was that the fly fishing was good after the sun went down, but not before. Since the lake surface is still, with no sign of feeding fish, we decide to eat early and fish until dusk. While Don drags in some old logs and rearranges already blackened rocks into a campfire circle, I tear open the foil package of ham and pea soup, empty it in the large Sigg pot, along with the quart of water from the bottle, and set the covered pot on the stove. I light the stove, taking care to hold the lighted match to the burner *before* turning on the gas, then turn down the flame until none of it is wastefully rising above the windscreen.

I take Don's teapot and the water bottle down to the lake and fill them, coming back with the butter can. While the soup is cooking, I get the salt and paper shaker, sugar, pot tongs, forks and spoons, applesauce and stroganoff and spread them on the ledge near the stove. Then I empty the dried applesauce (with sugar, cinnamon and nutmeg previously added) in the smaller one quart pan and add enough water so that, after stirring, all the apple bits are wet and rehydrating. I put the lid on, leaving it to soak, then lift the lid of the big pot with the tongs to give the soup a vigorous stir, using the opportunity to add about a third of a cube of butter.

Moments later the soup comes to a boil and I turn down the flame until the boiling subsides to a slow bubble. The recipe calls for five minutes of simmering, but at a mile and a half above sea level I let it go more than twice that long before calling Don. Using the aluminum pot tongs as a handle, I pour it in our plastic cups. By now it has cooked to a thick consistency that makes a spoon helpful, but we still get nearly two delicious cups apiece.

The moment the last cup is poured, I measure four and a half cups of water into the pot, which is covered and set back on the stove at the highest efficient flame. Between courses we go to work on the applesauce. After stirring in a little more water to improve the consistency, I hold open a spare plastic bag while Don empties in about half the contents of the pot. The bag is knotted and gently tucked into a protected corner of Don's pack for tomorrow's breakfast. The other half we divide into the frying pan and the other aluminum plate, so we can eat it with the stroganoff instead of having to finish it off beforehand.

The package of Richmoor Beef Stroganoff is now opened and the small packet of seasoning is taken out and emptied into half a cup of water in our spare (measuring) cup and stirred until smooth. Before the water in the big pot gets hot, I scrape the soup remains loose so they cannot burn. When the water boils, I pour in the noodles and dehydrated beef and stir, and as soon as it boils again I add the seasoning, rinsing out the measuring cup with a deft dip in the boiling water.

I turn the flame down to a low simmer, and for the next twenty minutes (only 10-12 at sea level), I take off the top a couple of times a minute to stir and scrape the bottom to prevent scorching or sticking. Between stirs, I open the sour cream packet, empty it in the rinsed measuring cup, add half a cup of water, and stir until smooth. When taste as well as estimated cooking time tell me the stroganoff if ready, I call Don, who has been rigging his fly rod, and stir in the sour cream.

The moment I remove the Stroganoff from the stove I set Don's teapot, containing about half a quart of water, on to heat. The stroganoff, though heavier, more expensive and more difficult to prepare than some of the Tea Kettle casseroles I usually carry, is extremely good. We eat and eat, and by the time we are full and the teapot is boiling, there is still a little stroganoff left for later in the evening. I turn off the stove now and drop a tea bag in the teapot. While the tea is steeping, Don takes the three cups to the lake, fills them with water, loosens the clinging food with a spoon and tosses the resulting garbage into the bushes well back from the lake. In the meantime, I am similarly cleaning our two plates. The big pot will not be needed until dinnertime tomorrow, so there is no hurry to empty and clean it.

Though I am too full of stroganoff to think of eating, I know something sweet will taste good after we come in from fishing, so I empty the Banana Creme Pudding mix into the still wet quart pan and add two cups of water. After stirring briskly for a minute or so, I cover the pot and put it aside to thicken. Unlike jellos which need an icy rill or a snowbank to help them set, puddings need only a little time. I put good sized rocks on both pot lids as insurance against disturbance, and, after a cup of hot tea apiece, we are ready to go fishing.

Since fly casting at dusk around the shore of a Sierra lake can present difficult footing, I change back into my boots, put on long trousers over my shorts and a long sleeved shirt over the string T-shirt. And since my skin has an unusual attraction for insects of all kinds, I shut my eyes and give myself a shot in the face with the aerosol can of mosquito repellant. Then I briefly squirt not only all exposed skin, but also places where my clothing may be pulled tight against it—like shoulders and thighs. (I have been severely bitten, on occasion, through Levis and heavy denim shirts.) It takes me less than half a minute to assemble my rod since reel, line, leader and fly were never removed. Carrying my canvas creel which now contains my nylon shell and flashlight in addition to fly box, leaders, license and muselin, I make my first casts in the little bay where we draw our water. Don begins in the bay where we swam, planning to fish in the opposite direction.

The sun has now set, but only just, and it is still light and warm.

There are only a few clouds to be seen in the east and the breeze is hardly sufficient to ruffle the darkening water. There are only a fe rises and these suggest small trout. I cast to several avidly feeding fish, but the rises merely move away from the fly, confirming my suspicion. The year before there were fair numbers of fat eleven inch brook trout. Could they have frozen out during the previous winter? Or have their tastes turned from flies to the fingerlings which evidently had been air planted since my last visit?

Out of the corner of my eye, I see the widening circle of a stronger rise. I turn back into the woods and circle fifty feet to the nearest part of the shore, making my way to the water's edge behind a good-sized tree. On my third cast to the area of the rise there is a strong underwater strike and I set the hook. The fish runs for deep water, taking line, then surges toward the shore and I am alarmed to feel it rooting on the shallow rocky bottom, trying to tear the hook from its mouth. I lean out over the water and lift with all the weight I think the leader will safely stand. The fish comes to the surface, beginning to tire, and within another minute I have safely beached a deep bodied brook trout of over thirteen inches.

In less than an hour we hook and play nearly a dozen good trout between us, keeping four of the best and returning the rest unharmed. By now it is nearly dark, but Don volunteers to clean the catch if I will hold the flashlight. The entrails he puts well out of the way in thick brush, where they probably will be enjoyed by a garter snake, and the washed trout are hung from a willow stringer threaded through gill and mouth, which in turn is hung from a limb on the west side of a small pine so the fish will not catch the morning sun.

The night air has grown chilly and our wet hands are cold, but Don's campfire blossoms quickly and after a sip or two of brandy we are soon warm and relaxed by the fire. Don finishes off the Stro-

cleaning up the lakeshore can be satisfying.

ganoff in front of the fire, and since both of us are thirsty, I make up a quart of Wyler's orange drink, which is promptly consumed. Hiking in the dry air of the summer Sierra often results in a daily water loss through perspiration of several quarts. By evening, even after frequent drinks during the day, the hiker craves liquids and sweets. We therefore plan on drinking a quart or two apiece every evening to maintain body fluids. Menus, of course, must be planned accordingly.

It is my habit—and Don's, too—to sit up late beside the campfire until I am so drowsy that I go to sleep promptly and stay asleep until the morning sun has warmed the air. Don, who has studied astrophysics, talks entertainingly about the brilliant sky full of stars spread above us, and we polish off the pudding and a fresh quart of water before our fire burns low. When Don computes by the stars that midnight is approaching we find our way to our beds, which are as wet from condensation as though it had rained. A corner of Don's sleeping bag, not covered by his tarp, is soaked, I wriggle carefully into my bag, roll my trousers in my shirt and stuff them into my sleeping bag stuff bag to enlarge my pillow (which goes under my mattress to smooth out the lumps), and fall asleep almost at once.

In the two days that follow, we spend our time swimming in the little bay, dozing in the sun on the slab beside the water, and hiking cross-country to fish and swim in two nearby lakes. The storm has vanished entirely and the humidity quickly drops so there is far less dew on the second evening. In the other lakes we have good luck, finding a few large brook trout in one and a dense population of smaller cutthroat, brook and rainbow in the other. Between the lakes, we climb a high dome that yields an excellent view of the surrounding country.

For dinner the second night we try my stew, which Don kindly rates as equal to the Stroganoff; at least it is easier to prepare: we simply add water and boil, then simmer. After dinner, tired of fishing, we scale a second dome and find an abandoned trail on the far side, marked by ducks which we follow until darkness forces us back to camp.

On the third day, the eve of the fourth of July weekend, we pack up, and before leaving camp try to obliterate all sign of our passing, except for a little charcoal inside a ring of already blackened rocks. Carrying a dozen good trout in the cool middle of our packs, we return to the trail and make good time back to the canoe on the shore of the big lake. Then we paddle upwind for an hour against a brisk chop to the opposite shore and the car. Driving home through the mountains to the cabin, my reluctance at leaving the wilderness is nicely balanced by my anticipation of a hot shower and a trout dinner with my family.

GOING BACK

When I get back
to the high bright world
of the windblown sun
and the meadowed rock
things will be all right.

When I return
to the mountain wild
on a turning trail
through a summer rain
my rhythm will return.

When I can escape
to a land left wild
on a still starred night
drowned deep in peace
my life will turn around.

When I get back
to the wilds again
and the easy peace
of a dreaming fire
I'll be content again.

LIST OF SUPPLIERS

Alpine Designs
P.O. Box 3561
Boulder, Colorado 80303

Dri-Lite Foods
11333 Atlantic Avenue
Lynwood, California 90262

Blacks (Thomas & Sons)
930 Ford Street
Ogdensburg, New York 13669

Eastern Mountain Sports
1041 Commonwealth Avenue
Boston, Massachusetts 02215

Bugaboo Mountaineering
689 Lighthouse Avenue
Monterey, California 93940

Eiger Mountain Sports
P.O. Box 4037
San Fernando, California 91342

Camp & Trail
21 Park Place
New York City, New York 10007

Frostline
P.O. Box 2190
Boulder, Colorado 80302

Camp Trails
P.O. Box 14500
Phoenix, Arizona 85031

Food Storage Products
(Oregon Freeze Dry, Richmoor, Trail Chef)
P.O. Box 6128
Albany, California 94706

Gerry
5450 North Valley Highway
Denver, Colorado 80216

Ocaté Corp.
P.O. Box 2368
Santa Fe, New Mexico 87501

Holubar
Box 7
Boulder, Colorado

Recreational Equip. (Co-Op)
1525 Eleventh Avenue
Seattle, Washington 98122

Kelty
1801 Victory Blvd.
Glendale, California 91201

Sierra Design
Fourth & Addison Streets
Berkeley, California 94710

L. L. Bean
Freeport, Maine 04032

Smilie Co.
575 Howard Street
San Francisco, California 94105

Mountain Master (Denali)
1947 West Dayton Avenue
Fresno, California 93705

Trail Tech
108-02 Otis Avenue
Corona, Queens, New York 11368

Mountain Traders
1711 Grove Street
Berkeley, California 94709

Trailwise (Ski Hut)
1615 University Avenue
Berkeley, California 94703

North Face
P.O. Box 2399, Station A
Berkeley, California 94702

Universal Field Equip.
Bldg. 811-A Mira Loma Space Center
California 91752

INDEX

Long a tinkerer with backpacking equipment and a searcher after comfort in the wilds, Robert S. Wood has been walking and climbing for twenty-five years in the Sierra Nevada, the Cascades, Mexico and Europe. He has written and edited for a number of magazines, including *Time, Life, Sports Illustrated, Sierra Club Bulletin* and *Wilderness Camping.*

A forestry graduate from the University of California, he is the author of the trail guide *Desolation Wilderness.* Although a native and resident of Berkeley, he lives with his wife, daughter and St. Bernard during the summer at a cabin on Upper Echo Lake near the edge of Desolation Wilderness at 7400 feet in the California Sierra.